The Return of Polyandry

THE RETURN OF POLYANDRY

Kinship and Marriage in Central Tibet

Heidi E. Fjeld

berghahn
NEW YORK · OXFORD
www.berghahnbooks.com

First published in 2022 by
Berghahn Books
www.berghahnbooks.com

© 2022, 2025 Heidi E. Fjeld
First paperback edition published in 2025

All rights reserved. Except for the quotation of short passages
for the purposes of criticism and review, no part of this book
may be reproduced in any form or by any means, electronic or
mechanical, including photocopying, recording, or any information
storage and retrieval system now known or to be invented,
without written permission of the publisher.

Library of Congress Cataloging-in-Publication Data
Names: Fjeld, Heidi, author.
Title: The return of polyandry : kinship and marriage in central Tibet / Heidi E. Fjeld.
Description: New York : Berghahn Books, 2022. | Includes bibliographical references and index.
Identifiers: LCCN 2022019393 (print) | LCCN 2022019394 (ebook) | ISBN 9781800736078 (hardback) | ISBN 9781800738645 (open access ebook)
Subjects: LCSH: Marriage customs and rites--China--Tibet Autonomous Region. | Tibetans--Marriage customs and rites. | Polyandry--China--Tibet Autonomous Region. | Kinship--China--Tibet Autonomous Region.
Classification: LCC GT2783.A3 F54 2022 (print) | LCC GT2783.A3 (ebook) | DDC 392.50951/5--dc23/eng/20220606
LC record available at https://lccn.loc.gov/2022019393
LC ebook record available at https://lccn.loc.gov/2022019394

British Library Cataloguing in Publication Data
A catalogue record for this book is available from the British Library

ISBN 978-1-80073-607-8 hardback
ISBN 978-1-80539-719-9 paperback
ISBN 978-1-80073-608-5 epub
ISBN 978-1-80073-864-5 web pdf

https://doi.org/10.3167/9781800736078

The electronic open access publication of *The Return of Polyandry* has been made possible through the generous financial support of the University of Oslo.

This work is published subject to a Creative Commons Attribution Noncommercial No Derivatives 4.0 License. The terms of the license can be found at https://creativecommons.org/licenses/by-nc-nd/4.0/. For uses beyond those covered in the license contact Berghahn Books.

For friends and colleagues in Tibet

Contents

List of Figures — viii
Preface — xvi
Acknowledgements — xviii
Notes on Tibetan Terms — xxi

Introduction — 1

Chapter 1. The Return of Polyandry — 25

Chapter 2. Trajectories to House Membership — 48

Chapter 3. Fraternal Relations — 64

Chapter 4. Female Roles — 89

Chapter 5. The House as Ritual Space — 116

Chapter 6. Moral Networks and Enduring Hierarchies — 142

Conclusion — 167

Epilogue — 182
Appendix. Timeline — 185
Glossary of Tibetan Terms — 186
References — 192
Index — 203

Figures

Figure 0.1. The Panam valley. Panam is an ordinary farming area in the western part of Central Tibet, in the region Tibetans call Tsang. © Heidi Fjeld   3
Figure 0.2. A newly renovated house in Sharlung. © Heidi Fjeld   18
Figure 0.3. Harvest time. Primarily subsistence farmers, much of the life of residents in Sharlung revolved around agricultural work. Soon after we arrived in Sharlung in 2002, the harvest started; it was a hard but happy time, and school children were brought back home to help. © Heidi Fjeld   18
Figure 1.1. The Takrab house. © Heidi Fjeld   29
Figure 2.1. The bone (*rü*) and flesh (*sha*) 'lineage' (*gyü*). © Heidi Fjeld   50
Figure 3.1. In an ideal polyandrous constellation, one husband would work the land, one would herd the animals and one would bring cash income to their household. The *dzo*, the cross-breed of yak and cow, were used for farm work, including male tasks such as ploughing and threshing. © Heidi Fjeld   84
Figure 3.2. All households in Sharlung had goats and sheep, and some had *dzo* and cows. The animals had been redistributed from the communes to the individual households as part of the Household Responsibility System, in 1981, and the numbers had increased over the decades. © Heidi Fjeld   85
Figure 3.3. The eldest brother and husband is expected to become the household head (*sayön*), responsible for the running of the household, including making sure that the ritual obligations are fulfilled. © Heidi Fjeld   86
Figure 4.1. Women's workload is both broad-ranging and heavy, both in the field and within the house. Here women are winnowing using the tractor as a fan. © Heidi Fjeld   94

Figure 4.2. A nun washing clothes in the river. Ordination does not exclude domestic work for women. © Heidi Fjeld 95

Figure 4.3. Nuns from the local nunnery practising playing *gyaling*, a woodwind oboe-like instrument used for rituals. © Heidi Fjeld 96

Figure 5.1. A *lukhang*, the main shrine on the ground floor. © Heidi Fjeld 124

Figure 5.2. A *namo* on the first floor. © Heidi Fjeld 126

Figure 5.3. Offering to the *tsen* on the roof. © Heidi Fjeld 129

Figure 5.4. Numerous *lu* reside in Sharlung, and the land and water are marked by the offerings made to them. © Heidi Fjeld 132

Figure 5.5. After the harvest, the house is cleansed by monks performing *Sharnyig dütok*, an exorcising ritual common throughout Tibet. In the ritual, the negative forces – leading to illness and general misfortune – are driven out of the house, in the form of effigies called *nédak* (the owner of illness) and his protector *ngarmi* (strong person) that are carried out and left in the fields, one towards the west and one towards the east. © Heidi Fjeld 137

Figure 5.6. A harm stopper (*nöpa kak*), placed on the inner door of a house. © Heidi Fjeld 138

Figure 8.1. Resting after a long day in the field. © Heidi Fjeld 183

Preface

'You can stay with us! We have a big house with many people. It is better for you. The public house is not clean. Please come! My father is away, but I will ask him later, but please come!' A young nun was smiling a beautifully open and friendly smile, inviting us to her house – without her father's consent. We were standing in one of the narrow paths connecting houses in Sharlung, a farming village in Tsang, Central Tibet. She was on her way home, and we were on our way back to the 'public house' (*chikhang*), our shelter for the past two days. She pointed to a white house behind the stupa and repeated 'Come!' Her offer seemed very tempting indeed, not so much because of the meagre standards of our designated accommodation, but more because of my research interest in daily lives in local households. We thanked her for the generous offer and said that we would very much like to stay with her family but that we would have to ask the village leader, who, we had been told, was currently away. She laughed again and explained: 'But my father is the village leader! I will ask him upon his return tomorrow.'

We had left Lhasa three days earlier. It was with a particular combination of anxiety and excitement that we drove our loaded land-cruiser out of the city, heading for Panam county: Samdrup, my co-researcher from Tibet University; Runa, my four-year-old daughter; Mingzom, her nanny; and myself, a PhD student in social anthropology from the University of Oslo. None of us had been in this area of Tibet before, and although I had prepared myself with readings and lengthy talks with people from Panam, I was uncertain of what to expect upon arrival. My initial interests had been social mobility, hereditary divisions, artisans and skilled workers, and others classified as low ranked (*menrik*), and I had chosen Panam because of people I had met and remarks I had heard during my previous stays in Lhasa. There, while eating in small Tibetan restaurants, I had encountered musicians who would come inside to play their *dranyen* (Tibetan lute), performing for a small fee. Although people enjoyed the music, these musicians were often referred to as beggars (*longkhen*). I had noticed that many of these travelling musicians were from Tsang, and often from three villages in Panam, an agricultural valley located between the cities of Shigatse and Gyantse. Later, in Lhasa, when asking a friend from Panam if he had heard about these villages, he laughed a little and said: 'You have clearly not heard the saying: Sachung[1] is purely a blacksmith place, Bargang is purely a butcher place' (*Sachung garwé gartsang yin, Bargang shembé shemtsang yin*).[2] His birthplace was higher up the valley but, he said, 'everybody knows about the blacksmiths (*gara*) in Sachung and the butchers (*shenba*) in Bargang'. Based upon these observations and information, I decided to go to Panam for fieldwork.

Armed with travel and research permits provided by Tibet University (TU), as well as an exchange agreement signed by the Tibet Autonomous Region (TAR) government and the rectors of Norwegian universities, Samdrup and I approached the Panam County administration building. The few other researchers travelling to rural Tibet in the previous years had often ended up staying in the county seats due to administrative regulations, and it was my aim at least to be able to stay in the township centre and, hopefully, in a village. This was in the beginning of the 2000s, and looking back, it was a period of relatively relaxed policies and openness to foreign collaborations. Although it felt very restrictive at the time, and the process involved careful negotiations and manoeuvring, it was possible to get research permits for social science and humanities projects as long as they focused on what was perceived to be non-sensitive issues. For more than 25 years, Norwegian universities had a highly successful collaboration with Tibet University, exchanging students and working together on research projects. This agreement allowed me, as one of very few foreigners, to obtain a permit to conduct a longer fieldwork in a rural area of the TAR. Approaching the county authorities, Samdrup informed them about this collaboration and explained that our purpose for the stay was a study of the local history and culture and especially the work of women in low-ranked families, as this was the main topic of the research permit issued by Tibet University. After looking through all the paperwork – permits, agreements and letters of recommendations from Lhasa – the county leader asked me if Norway was part of the European Union. This puzzled me for a moment, but as I answered that 'No, we are not' and saw the satisfied smile on his face, I realised that there might have been some controversy concerning a large EU development programme that had been running in parts of Panam in the years preceding.[3] Norway's non-membership in the EU seems to have settled the question, and the county leader made his phone call to the township centre, informing them about our arrival and making sure that they would provide us with all necessities.

Driving on the dirt road from the county seat to Kyiling Township, we passed farming villages with people inspecting the ripe fields of barley and wheat. It was the beginning of harvest, and the valley seemed a fertile and relatively prosperous place. After some thirty minutes driving, we passed a larger village with the famous Sachung monastery rising above, one of the few that had remained intact during the political upheavals of the 1960s and 1970s. After Sachung, driving slowly, we passed a small village where a group of older people were sitting by the stupa, chatting and spinning wool. The place had a special feel to it, and Samdrup and I agreed that it looked welcoming.

Arriving in the township, three local leaders greeted us. Researchers had stayed in the area before, both Tibetans (Ben Jiao) and foreigners (Goldstein, Childs and Beall),[4] and they had also spent some of their time in the villages. Wöser, one of the township leaders, suggested that, due to my interest in blacksmiths and local history, we could stay in the monastery in Sachung, the village known for its many blacksmith households. Happy to be able to live outside the township centre, I agreed. However, while driving back up the bumpy road, I worried that by staying in a monastery we would be at a distance from lay families, who were intended to be the main participants in my study. When we reached the small village that we had passed earlier, people were still sitting by the stupa. Wöser explained that in this village there were many old people with knowledge of history, and he also noted that they had a very good village leader. Still hoping to be able to stay in a household, I asked: 'How about this place – would it be possible for us to stay here?' The driver slowed down, and Wöser, looking a little confused, said that he did not know if there was a proper house for us but that if we wanted we could stay in the public house (*chikhang*). The small village was Sharlung, the main location of this book – an average village in the heart of the grain producing plains of Tsang; it was the perfect place to learn about ordinary lives of farmers in Central Tibet.

Accepting the invitation of the village leader's daughter, we moved into the Takrab house. As we waved farewell to our driver, neighbours and other villagers came to help carry our things from the *chikhang*. Inside the new house, the *nama* (the in-married wife of the household) and the *achung* (her youngest husband) were busy cleaning and preparing our room by sweeping the dirt floor, sprinkling some water and blowing the smoke of incense into all corners. By the evening, we had settled in; Mingzom, my daughter and myself in one of the bedrooms, while Samdrup, with a humble thrill, accepted the offer to stay in the *chökhang*, the room where the house shrine and religious objects were kept and that is otherwise reserved for visiting monks and nuns. As Samdrup is a scholar of Buddhist philosophy, Tashi, the household and village leader, thought this to be the most suitable for him. This arrangement was ideal for all of us, and it became the start of an intense learning experience. Sharing a house with a woman and her three husbands, her in-laws and her children, learning about their daily interactions, their chores, as well as their expectations and concerns, tilted my research interest towards intimate relations, to polyandry and to the ways in which changes in marriage practices and preferences might help us not only unpack relatedness but also inform new perspectives on the constitution of Tibetan kinship. Having read Ben Jiao's excellent PhD dissertation 'Socio-Economic and Cultural Factors Underlying the Contemporary Revival of Fraternal Polyandry' (2001), describing that polyandry had again become a common form of marriage in Panam, I was already curious about the inner worlds and workings of polyandrous marriages. Despite spending considerable time visiting blacksmiths, butchers, *baru* (those handling dead bodies) and beggars, the issues of hierarchy, stigma and social exclusion proved hard to investigate in-depth in the time available. As Ben Jiao's study focused primarily on socio-economic aspects, I found my position within the Takrab house ideal for taking the return of polyandry as a lens through which I could explore in detail relationality and sociality, among and beyond humans and within and between houses in this farming community.

We were able to stay in the Takrab house from August to December in 2002, and then again in July 2004. Considering the restrictions on interaction between Tibetans and foreigners today, this seems rather remarkable. Indeed, it would be unthinkable in the current political climate in the TAR. It was during these five months that most of the data for the book was produced. For years after 2004, I tried to return to Panam, applying for travel or research permits but with no luck. The conditions had changed. At the very beginning of March 2008, only days before the protests that turned into riots, I was in Lhasa to negotiate a permit for a new project in the TAR. Since 2008, the year of more than a hundred demonstrations against Chinese rule and policies across Tibetan areas (Yeh 2013: x), the TAR has been transformed into a closely controlled space, where Tibetans live under extremely strict regulations and where access for foreign researchers is rigorously restrained, and most often denied. In 2010, the wrath that the PRC government launched towards anything Norwegian after the Nobel peace prize was given to the Chinese democracy activist Liu Xiaobo meant that access to research in the TAR became impossible for me.

I call this book a historical ethnography. As all ethnographies, it describes people and practices in a particular time and place. While the place is Sharlung village, the historical period of the book is the first half of the 2000s – that is, after the initiation of the Open up the West (Ch: *xibu da kaifa*) campaign in 2000 up to the protests in 2008 and the hardliner policies that have since been put into place. Guo Jinlong was the party secretary in the TAR from 2000–2004, and his leadership at the time was interpreted as a positive shift from the strict rule of his predecessor, Chen Kuiyuan, whose regime had focused on control and repression. Guo's emphasis was on economic development, and he was more open to foreign collaboration; the beginning of the 2000s was a time of some international cooperation in development and business and in education and research. Although it felt restrictive also then, it was a period with a certain hopeful atmosphere.⁵ The beginning of the 2000s was the starting point for an intensification of policies to bolster economic development in the TAR, focusing on economic growth, investment and consumption (Yeh 2013: 3). These policies primarily had an effect in the urban and peri-urban areas, continuing and strengthening a heavily subsidised economy and feeding large-scale construction and infrastructure projects, such as the Qinghai-Tibet railway, which opened in 2006, and the real estate projects on the outskirts of Lhasa and Shigatse. Creating an economic boom, this also increased the (already ongoing) in-migration of Han Chinese skilled and unskilled labourers (Fisher 2014). For the vast majority living in the rural areas – that is, 85 per cent of Tibetans in TAR, according to the 2000 census – these subsidies only slowly trickled down, with increased economic activity most visible towards the end of the decade (Fisher 2015). These economic policies and initiatives had little direct effect on Sharlung lives during my fieldwork there. People in the village found themselves on the periphery of state development; they were primarily subsistence farmers, some without access to electricity and running water, most without phone coverage. The local primary schools were only partly open, and few children were sent to boarding schools outside the county. There were no Han Chinese in the villages – no farmers, vendors, no cadres or leaders. Yet, the beginning of the 2000s was clearly also a period of transitions. The booming construction industry outside Panam offered new possibilities for work, and many of the farmers had started to send their sons to 'go for income', changing the economy from subsistence to a 'new mixed agriculture/non-farm income economy' (Goldstein, Childs and Wangdui 2008: 517). Although the extensive rural development projects of the 2000s were yet to be implemented in Sharlung, there was an awareness among township leaders of the importance of economic growth – their leaders assessed them based on the economic reports they produced from their township. This had consequences for, and partly explains, the relatively lenient approach local leaders had towards sociocultural practices that were both in disagreement with state laws and policy regulations and associated with beneficial economic outcome, such as polyandrous marriages.

Ending in 2004, this historical ethnography is thus situated in the years just before a new period with very comprehensive social and political schemes, in which the state again made itself strongly present in rural communities across the TAR. First, as part of the national goal to construct the New Socialist Countryside, in 2006 the TAR government launched a large-scale project aiming to provide new housing to the rural population. Through what was called the Comfortable Housing Project – a programme combining state and local subsidies, savings and private and bank loans – many farmers and herders have either (been) resettled or renovated or built new houses, reshaping parts of the rural land. The extent of the effect of this project varies across the TAR, and the government's claim that all rural residents had new housing by 2010 is clearly an exaggeration (Robin 2009; Goldstein et al. 2010; Yeh 2013: 253). Yet, the Comfortable Housing Project has had major consequences for rural life, not only changing the physical environments but also, as Yeh convincingly argues, transforming rural Tibetans into consuming subjects enmeshed in a market economy of indebtedness on the one hand, and in a complex gift economy of expected gratitude with the state on the other (Yeh 2013). Some years later, the state again came closer to farmers' lives, following the start of Chen Quanguo's period as TAR party secretary in 2011. As part of his strictly imposing control regime, 'village-based cadre teams' of four or more people were sent to live in the villages of TAR, serving a double purpose of 'improving services and material conditions' and monitoring and maintaining 'social stability', as Human Rights Watch writes.[6] Their presence was a new form of close surveillance of, and state involvement in, rural lives, and marks a distinct difference from the historical period covered in this book. Generally, the state's approach to rural lives since 2008 is very different from what I could observe in Panam in 2002 and 2004. State efforts to transform farmers and pastoralists into wage labourers have taken new forms in recent years, although these aims were mentioned already in the 11th Five-Year plan (2006–2011). In 2019–2020, the TAR government introduced a large-scale training and job matching scheme that was to be rolled out across the region, and in which 500,000 so-called 'rural surplus labourers' had participated by the first seven months of 2020 (Zenz 2020: 7). This was based on President Xi Jinping's stated goal to 'eradicate absolute poverty' (measured in cash income) by the end of 2020. This has put pressure on farmers and pastoralists to change their livelihood so they can report a measurable income and thus be declared 'poverty free' (Zenz 2020: 8).

How these changes over the last fifteen years have affected life in general and kinship and marriage in particular in Sharlung and its neighbouring villages is difficult to know. From anecdotal information garnered through occasional conversations with people from Panam and with people who have visited the area, as well as from surprisingly detailed satellite images provided by Google Earth, parts of the lives I describe seem to continue, but these are only assumptions. My aim with this book cannot be to reanalyse the ethnography within a contemporary context – being positioned outside the TAR and not being able to engage in relations with the participants is too disabling for such an attempt to make sense. My main motivation for writing this historical ethnography now, despite the time that has passed and the changes that have happened, is the dearth of research available from Central Tibet and the bleak prospects of future openings for new studies.

With the exception of the excellent monographs by Emily Yeh, *Taming Tibet: Landscape Transformation and the Gift of Chinese Development* (2013), and Theresia Hofer, *Medicine and Memory in Tibet: Amchi Physicians in an Age of Reform* (2018), as well as Goldstein and colleagues' numerous and important articles – which are all based on fieldwork primarily done before 2008 – very little research describing rural lives in Central Tibet has been published in the last decades.[7] With the years that has passed since fieldwork, I encourage a temporal sensitivity when reading this historical ethnography and hope *The Return of Polyandry* can provide an insight into everyday rural lives that have again been closed to eyes from the outside but that nevertheless constitute the majority of Central Tibetan lives.

Notes

1. All place names within Panam have been anonymised.
2. *Sa chung mgar ba'i mgar tshang yin Bar gang bshas ba'i bshas tshang yin.*
3. The EU-funded Panam Integrated Rural Development Project was aimed at increasing commercialisation of livestock and dairy production, amongst other things. I learned later that their approach to changing the local subsistence economy and scaling up production was controversial among some of the farmers, who were worried both about decrease in the quality of the products and about their ability to compete in commercial markets.
4. Melvyn Goldstein led a large project on the impact that rapid development has had on intergenerational relations in Panam, working together with the Tibetan Academy of Social Sciences.
5. See International Campaign for Tibet, 'New TAR Party Chief in Leadership Reshuffle', 12 May 2003. Retrieved January 2021 from http://www.savetibet.org/new-tar-party-chief-in-leadership-reshuffle/#sthash.zfbeURah.dpuf.
6. Official Chinese media have reported five duties of the village teams: 'building up Party and other organizations in the village, "maintaining social stability," and carrying out "Feeling the Party's kindness" education with villagers', as well as 'promoting economic development and providing "practical benefit" to the villagers'. Human Rights Watch, 'No End to Tibet Surveillance Program', 18 January 2016. Retrieved January 2021 from https://www.hrw.org/news/2016/01/18/china-no-end-tibet-surveillance-program.
7. Sienna Craig's monograph *Healing Elements: Efficacy and Social Ecologies of Tibetan Medicine* (2012) also includes ethnography from rural areas, but the parts from the TAR primarily describe Lhasa.

Acknowledgements

The ethnography in this book – with the memory of its people, stories, events – has been part of my life for more than two decades. These two decades have also been the formative years of my academic life, and naturally there are so many people who have contributed with ideas and insights that have inspired and shaped this book that it is impossible to include all.

Leaving the village in Panam in 2004, I felt a strong sense of gratitude and humbleness for the generosity of the family that let us stay with them, and this gratitude has only grown stronger with the time passed and the book now written. I was very fortunate to meet a village leader who welcomed me into his house and who took it upon himself to show me around and to teach me the essentials of rural life. I am forever grateful for the hospitality, generosity and kindness that he and his family showed me, my little daughter and the research team we came with. Thinking about all the people in and around the village in Panam who welcomed me, served me tea and agreed to spend some of their time answering what must have seemed like an endless line of questions fills me with much gratitude but also sorrow of not being able to return and to stay in touch.

The fieldwork in Panam was made possible through the Network for University Co-operation Tibet-Norway, the amazing collaboration and exchange programme that for more than twenty years enabled Tibetan students to study for MA and Ph.D. degrees in Norway and Norwegian students, like myself, to study in Central Tibet. 'The Network' and their main partner, Tibet University, provided me with research permits, and I thank Hanna Havnevik, Sissel Thorsdalen and Ingela Flatin at the University of Oslo, and Weihong and others in the Foreign students office at Tibet University, for all their efforts to secure permits and facilitate my stays in both Lhasa and Panam. I was very fortunate that Tibet University sent Samdrup, a brilliant lecturer of Budhism, to accompany me for the first four months of fieldwork in Panam. My deepest thanks go to him for being such an excellent co-researcher with his clear and curious mind, kind personality and deep respect for, and knowledge of, rural life in Tibet. In Lhasa, I am especially grateful to

Ben Jiao and Tseyang Changngopa for teaching me about Panam and Tibet, and for all their help in planning the fieldworks, and to Birte Haugen for being such a lively and friendly company in Lhasa over many visits. In Lhasa and Oslo, I am very grateful to so many Tibetan friends and colleagues, who I unfortunately cannot name here, for teaching me about Tibetan social life, culture and history, and to whom this book is dedicated.

The Research Council of Norway and the Department of Social Anthropology at the University in Oslo kindly provided me with the funding to conduct the fieldwork on which the book is based. I am grateful to my supervisor, Signe Howell, and my mentor, Marit Melhuus, for their generous support in all phases of the work, for all their analytical input, care and friendship throughout my anthropological endeavours. I would especially like to thank Tone Sommerfelt and Benedikte V. Lindskog, who have been my long-term anthropology conversation partners on all things related to this book. They have not only read and commented on earlier versions of the text but have also followed the book project up until completion, exemplifying the blessing of close long-term friend-colleagues.

Tibet anthropology and Tibetan studies is made up of not only a brilliant but also a very friendly and inclusive crowd that I feel lucky to be part of. In addition to Tibetan colleagues and friends, I am especially grateful to Astrid Hovden, Per Kværne, Resi Hofer, Hildegard Diemberger, Charles Ramble, Nancy Levine, Geoff Childs, Sienna Craig, Marietta Kind, Isabelle Henrion-Dourcy, Robbie Barnett, Nanda Pirie, Giovanni da Col, Nyingkargyal, Mona Schrempf, Toni Huber, Inger Vasstveit, Harmandeep Gill, Tawni Tidwell, Jill Sudbury, Koen Wellens, Alice Travers, Martin Mills, Melvyn Goldstein, Ken Bauer, Stephan Kloos, Carole McGranahan, Jonathan Samuels, Eveline Bingaman, Emily Yeh, Rae Erin Dachille, Elisabeth Hsu and Andrew Fisher for contributing with their insightful comments and interesting discussions throughout the years.

In Oslo, I would also like to thank Astrid Anderson for reading earlier drafts and teaching me about kinship, and Ingvill Rasmussen, Inger Skjelsbæk, Gro Ween and Tsomo Svenningsen for inspiring and insightful discussions. I am grateful to my wonderful colleagues in the Section for Medical Humanities: Anthropology and History, to Anne-Lise Middelthon for all her care and encouragement over the years and especially to Anne Kveim Lie for being the perfect writing retreat partner, for perseverance in our daily academic life and for making work so much fun.

At Berghahn Books, I would like to thank Tom Bonnington, Tony Mason and Caroline Kuhtz for all their excellent work to prepare this manuscript, and the two reviewers for their generous feedback, precise suggestions and kind encouragement.

Finally, I would like to thank my parents and parents-in-law for all their support and help and Jacob Risdal Otnes for being there and sharing (some of) my interest in Tibet and the Himalayas. I am grateful for his encouragement both during our early trips together and for the patience in the periods when I have been absent. Sharing the experiences in Panam with my daughter Runa was a joy that I will cherish my whole life, and I thank her for being an incredible little traveller – then only 3–4 years old – and for opening new worlds for me in the Tibetan countryside. Tuk jé ché!

NOTES ON TIBETAN TERMS

There is a significant divergence between the oral and the written forms of Tibetan words, and it is difficult for non-specialists to pronounce words romanised with the standardised Wylie system. For example, the term for Tibet is *bod* but pronounced *bö*. For readability, I use Tibet and Himalayan Library's Simplified Phonetic Transcription of Standard Tibetan developed by David Germano and Nicolas Tournadre.[1] Spellings are given in Wylie in the Appendix: *Glossary of Tibetan Terms*.

Note

1. https://www.thlib.org/reference/transliteration/#!essay=/thl/phonetics/s/b1.

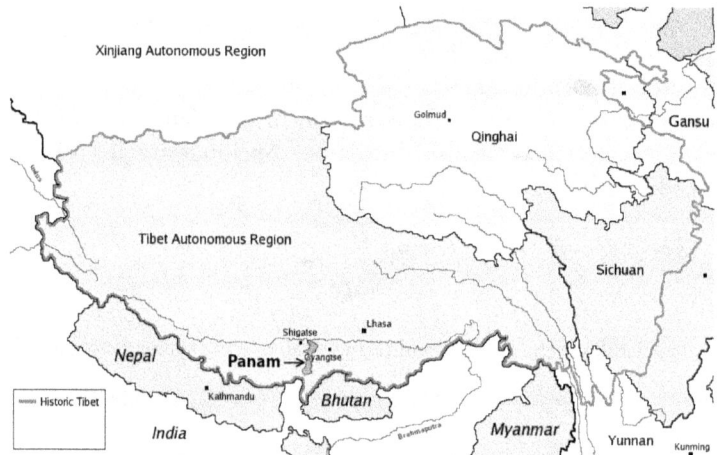

Map of Tibet Autonomous Region and the field site, via Wikimedia Commons under a Creative Commons Attribution-Share Alike 3.0 Unported license.

Introduction

One sunny afternoon in Sharlung village outside the city of Shigatse, Drolma, Mingzom and I were sitting in the porch of the Gongbo house, spinning wool and playing with the youngest baby. Drolma, the in-married wife (*nama*) of the house, explained to me: 'In my birth village, only few people used to marry polyandrously (*zasum*), but now it is widespread. Now everybody marries like this.' Outside Tibet and the Himalayas, the marriage of one woman and two or more men has been both a rarity and often ridiculed. 'Why does everybody marry like this?' I asked. She smiled and summed up: 'Everybody wants a better life.'

During this conversation in September 2002, I recognised how Drolma's story illustrates changing marriage preferences and practices in this particular place and time. Born to parents who had been labourers without land before the Chinese invasion in 1950, Drolma was the first woman to marry polyandrously in her family's history. At 22, her father had approached her with a marriage proposal from a household in a different village within the same valley. She had suspected for some time that her parents were involved in marriage negotiations, although the details had not been revealed to her. In this period, Drolma had eagerly scrutinised any unexpected visitor coming to their house, wondering if some of them might be her future husband, for she knew that potential grooms might visit in disguise. She had paid extra attention when she was serving tea to guests and aimed to present herself as humble and polite while also trying to get a closer look at the visitor. When her father finally told her about the ongoing negotiations, she was not surprised to learn that the marriage potentially involved three husbands. Several of her friends had married this way already – polyandry was common in her village – and hence the arrangement was not foreign to her. She was glad, she said, when she heard that the suitors, who were brothers, were close to her age. She realised that she had in fact met the eldest groom-to-be, who had come to her home with the pretence of being a business contact of her brother, and she had liked him. After a few days of consideration, she decided to agree to the marriage.

The preparations for the wedding began, and after four months, shortly after the Tibetan new year celebrations, she was taken to her grooms' village. They had borrowed a white car, substituting the white mare that traditionally brought the bride to her wedding, and the ride took only half an hour. Drolma was happy that she was to relocate to a place so close to home. During the wedding celebrations, she shared the podium with all three husbands; they were seated at her side, placed according to their age. The eldest husband spent the first night with her, reflecting his authority over his brothers and initiating his special relation to their wife. The second night Drolma was with the middle husband, and one week later, with the youngest one. After the wedding, Drolma moved into her eldest husband's room. He had made a tentative schedule for when she would visit her other two husbands. In the beginning, she felt shy in her new house, and although her mother-in-law had made it clear that the wife's preferences regarding the organisation of access to sexual activity mattered, Drolma did not voice her opinions. In fact, Drolma said, reflecting back, at the time she did not have an opinion or a preference, as the situation was so new to her. However, as the years passed, she found a way to organise what they call *kora khor* – going round in circle – that worked well for all the marriage partners. Through giggles and laughs, she explained that because her eldest husband often was working outside the village, she had her own room, and, with time, she preferred that the two remaining husbands visited her there. Together with her middle husband (*ajok*), she worked out a two-week schedule for the three of them, of which he then informed the youngest husband (*achung*). A large house enables this kind of arrangement, providing the wife with the freedom of a separate room.

The household Drolma had married into was relatively wealthy. Her husbands engaged in complementing economic activities; one worked as a carpenter and one as a driver, both bringing income to the household, and the youngest was in charge of the agricultural work. Drolma's chores included helping the *achung* in the fields and tending to the animals and the children, as well as sharing domestic work with her mother-in-law. Her father-in-law administered the household chores, helped with the fields and represented the household in external affairs. In this perspective, the advantages of polyandry

Figure 0.1. The Panam valley. Panam is an ordinary farming area in the western part of Central Tibet, in the region Tibetans called Tsang. © Heidi Fjeld

are clear, and the economic organisation and ambition of farms is at the core of both the emic and the etic explanations of polyandry.

In Central Tibet[1] before 1950, fraternal polyandry – the marriage between two or more brothers and one woman – was a common marital form of the upper agrarian classes, particularly those with hereditary access to land and (the often heavy) tax obligations attached. This category of farmers were called 'taxpayers' (*trelpa*). However, from 1980, Tibetan farmers of all social backgrounds, including Drolma's family and the lower ranked skilled workers (blacksmiths, butchers and corpse-cutters), had also started to arrange polyandry. When I surveyed Sharlung village in 2002, I found that almost 60 per cent of all marriages were polyandrous, and of the remaining 40 per cent, 13 per cent were the result of partitions of former polyandrous marriages. According to Sharlung villagers, all those that have more than one son in the household would attempt to arrange polyandry for them. The return of polyandry, including its new social distribution, is surprising.

Polyandry has been recognised as directly related to sociopolitical organisation in general and land tenure and taxation systems in particular. Already four decades ago, it was described as a marriage form that was particularly 'fragile in the face of external pressures [for example, from missionaries and modern nation states] for social change' (Levine and Sangree 1980: 405). The administrators of the 'modern nation state' of the People's Republic of

China (PRC) have loudly opposed the practice of polyandry. By prohibiting polygamy already in the first Marriage Law in 1950 and frowning upon polyandry as abnormal and primitive, the Chinese government has effectuated a pressure similar to that which Levine and Sangree expected would lead to 'complete cessation or decrease in the incidents of polyandrous marriages' (ibid.). Melvyn Goldstein concluded in a similar way, based not on state interventions but rather on the particular sensitivity to the economic rationale of polyandrous organisation. In 1987, he wrote: 'New opportunities for economic and social mobility in these countries, such as the tourist trade and government employment, are also eroding the rationale for polyandry, and so it may vanish within the next generation' (1987: 77). With the massive economic changes and rapid expansion of opportunities in and outside the agricultural areas of Central Tibet from the 1980s, but in particularly since 2000, we could expect a decline of new arrangements and a cessation of polyandry in rural Tibet. This, however, is not the case. In fact, in Panam valley, the pattern is opposite.

Moving into the Takrab family home in Sharlung for the first time in 2002, I was not surprised to find that the three sons in the house shared one wife. While preparing for fieldwork, I had talked to and read the excellent work of Ben Jiao, a Tibetan anthropologist who had done his PhD with Melvyn Goldstein, graduating from Case Western University in 2001. His work, conducted in a bigger village in the same valley, had shown a significant increase of polyandry since 1980 (Ben Jiao 2001). Ben Jiao identified this increase to be directly related to post-1978 economic reforms in China, which 'created a set of socio-economic conditions that has led to a substantial number of Tibetan families to choose the traditional Tibetan marriage pattern of polyandry over monogamy' (2001: xi). In his dissertation, Ben Jiao showed how polyandry was an effective economic strategy, increasing not only income of the household but also social status. Tibetans, he wrote, 'view it [polyandry] as a means-end strategy that households used to maintain or increase their economic status' (ibid.: 193). The main, and most relevant, post-1978 reform was the national Household Responsibility System (*gentsang lamluk*), which marked the end of the collective commune period and involved de-collectivisation; the village land (and animals) was divided and redistributed, providing each household with fixed plots of land to maintain over a long period of time. In Panam, this reform started at the end of 1980 and re-established the household as the central locus for production, as it did across the PRC. From a social history perspective, the renewed emphasis on the household established all farmers as structurally similar to the former 'taxpayer' (*trelpa*) category of the pre-1950 land tenure system in Central Tibet. Although they did not have the same tax obligations, through de-collectivisation and redistribution all farmers held estates, with hereditary access to land to be administered from one generation to the next. Importantly, in Central Tibet, it is normative that all sons have equal rights to inheritance of land, which means that if all sons marry independently and move out, the land will be fragmented. Agrarian societies attempt to solve the issue of land inheritance in different ways; some give the eldest or the youngest all inheritance rights, others negotiate between the entitled, while others simply identify one person to take over the farm.[2] In Central Tibet and the Himalayas, people have preferred a so-called monomarital principle – that is, to arrange only one marriage among the sons, per generation (Goldstein 1971a). As daughters usually marry out and live with their husband's family, their weddings have less effect on the future of their natal household. Hence, with the renewed status of the household and the redefined relation to land following the Household Responsibility System in 1980/81, many of the farmers in Panam found polyandry to be the best way to organise marriage and inheritance in their new situation of being in charge of a restructured type of farm.

A materialistic explanation of Tibetan fraternal polyandry, which dominated earlier research, is based on the emic wish to secure the estate across generations on the one hand, and to maximise access to male labour on the other. As such, polyandry is closely connected not only to inheritance rights but also to the traditional three-folded economy of agrarian areas of Central Tibet. Economic diversification involves members of the same household engaging in agricultural work, like herding, as well as a range of off-farm activities – traditionally trade and transport and, more recently, construction work, as in the example of Drolma's husbands. Surprisingly, starting from the 1980s but intensifying with the Open up the West (Ch. *xibu da kaifa*) campaign in 2000, the economic development policies of rural Central Tibet have confirmed and enhanced the advantages of polyandry. Incentivised by state subsidies, farmers in Panam have steadily transformed from a subsistence to a much more diversified economy as members of the households seek new forms of income outside the farm (Goldstein et al. 2003; Goldstein, Childs and Wangdui 2008). By arranging polyandry, farmers are able to participate in these economic opportunities opening up in their vicinity; polyandrous households have more members to perform new types of work, and hence bring income back home, while keeping the farm production. When talking about polyandry, people in Panam villages explained that these marriages allow them to improve the economy of their household – that is, the unit they call *khyimtsang*. Moreover, it enables them to maintain the *khyimtsang* for generations. What does it mean to maintain the household, beyond mere economy? I suggest a broader social approach to polyandry and the household as the increase and spread of polyandry in Panam not only manifests the interconnection between marriage, land and reforms but provides an opportunity to rethink relationality and sociality and how we conceptualise and understand kinship and village life in Central Tibet.

There has been a curious analytic disconnection between polyandry and kinship in previous research (with the exception of Levine 1988).[3] Thus, the title of this book both refers to the empirical return of polyandry in farming communities in Panam, and to the theoretical return of polyandry in the study of kinship. The first of two main arguments in this book is that the new arrangements of polyandry are part of a process in which farmers are (re) creating and consolidating households as fundamentally meaningful social, cultural and ontological ritual places manifested in the physical houses, with a particular social history and possible future. These houses are the loci for kin-making and constitute the core of kinship groups in Panam, hence polyandry is a kinship matter. These processes can be fruitfully analysed by engaging a house perspective inspired by Lévi-Strauss' concept of the house as a 'moral person' (*personne morale*) (1983: 174), a kinship analytic that unites contradicting principles, such as descent and residence, two organisational principles that have been a puzzle in Tibetan kinship studies. Yet, a house perspective does not necessarily imply that Tibet should be classified as a house society, and this brings me to the second argument in the book. The centrality of the house, and its interconnection with polyandry in Panam at beginning of the 2000s is an example of the flexibility and pragmatism inherent in Tibetan social organisation and can serve as a case of what I call kinship of potentiality. Across the vast and diverse Tibetan ethnographic region, a range of kinship principles and idioms are shared, albeit to different extents, based in flesh and bone, in residence and filiation, in lineage, laterality and locality. These provide Tibetans with culturally available possibilities and potentialities, when manoeuvring social and political contexts affecting the kinship sensibilities of being related; of a sense of belonging on the one hand, and the organisation of membership, rights and obligations to a collective – to the village or other communities – on the other hand. In particular places, at particular times, kinship is formed, enacted and maintained, leading to great variation but also a strong sense of continuity, as these principles, idioms and practices are foregrounded and backgrounded, depending on a range of internal and external factors, concerns and forces.

Kinship Developments: From Classification to Practice, to Pragmatism

A house perspective is one of the many approaches that social anthropologists have taken to challenge the much-criticised traditional kinship theories, aiming to move beyond classifications, rules and biocentric perspectives towards daily practices, domestic lives and the making of kinship (Carsten 2004: 16). Kinship has been at the core of the anthropological endeavour since the discipline's very beginning, and – through reinventing itself over the last four decades – it remains fundamental to our analysis of social and cultural life. Kinship is both a theoretical concept and a social category (Franklin and McKinnon 2001), and anthropological approaches to both aspects have taken many turns from its nascent start in the end of the nineteenth century. In 1870, Lewis Henry Morgan, a lawyer with an interest in native American societies as well as in evolution, published an extensive work on kinship terminology, in which he developed the first grand theory in kinship studies, the so-called classificatory and descriptive systems, and later subcategories of these (Parkin and Stone 2004: 5–9).[4] Morgan's, and his followers', theories were based on the idea that language directly mirrors culture, and hence relationship terminology was a way to understand social life and behaviour. Although the evolution theories that motivated Morgan and his associates' comparative projects were left behind rather quickly,[5] this way of approaching kinship became very influential, and continuing until today, much research effort has gone into systematic mapping of kinship terminology, also in the Himalayas.[6]

On the other side of the Atlantic Ocean, the functionalist turn in social sciences at the beginning of the twentieth century directed anthropologists' interest in kinship, and descent groups in particular, towards the political functions of kin-based institutions in small-scale societies (without states), and away from history (and evolution). Mid-century, leading British social anthropologists such as Radcliffe-Brown, Evans-Pritchard and Fortes, were very influential in their investigations of the role and function of corporate descent groups in Africa. These studies were firmly placed in Fortes' distinction between the 'domestic' and 'the politico-jural' domains of kinship (1959), and their interests were clearly in the latter. Peripheral to the corporateness of descent groups, marriage more generally was deemed uninteresting and irrelevant. In many ways, this interest in kinship as it unfolded in the political, legal and public domain continued Morgan's American project, as it developed into a technical, rather abstract endeavour, and with time also included ambitious comparative efforts by bringing African lineage models to Southeast Asia and Papua New Guinea (Barnes 1962). Early kinship theories were to a large extent detached from the complexities of people's everyday lives (Carsten 2004: 10–12). In France, Lévi-Strauss was working on an alternative to functionalism and what developed to be a competing grand theory of kinship, in which marriage, and the alliances formed between groups through the exchange of women (wives), formed the core. A structuralist approach, alliance theory was concerned with cultural logics and underlying structures – most prominently found in negative marriage rules and binary oppositions – and, by default, was even more disinterested and disconnected from people's lived lives. Much ink has been spilt arguing over whether descent or alliance was the most fundamental principle of kinship. Another, and very different theoretical approach of the 1970s, based in Marxist critique and with particular vigour in France, shifted focus away from the politico-jural domain that had dominated mid-century social anthropology towards the domestic – that is, to the household as the central unit of analysis.[7] These theorists were concerned with the household as a corporate unit of production and property and represented a turn closer to lived lives, although it was the large-scale social analysis of power relations, exploitation and economic and political change that drove their theoretical developments.

More and more removed from people's lives (with the exception of some of the (neo)Marxists), kinship left the centre of the anthropological stage in the 1970s and 1980s. Or, rather, it was helped off stage by David Schneider. Trained in the North-American school of cultural anthropology (descending from Morgan and Boas), Schneider opposed the technical and schematic way to look at kinship and the prominence given to language, and shifted his focus towards meaning and symbols – an interpretive anthropology represented most prominently by Clifford Geertz – in his seminal study *American Kinship: A Cultural Account* (1980 [1968]). Schneider argued that American kinship was based on two main ideas, namely shared biogenetic substance and solidarity that endures over time, reflecting biological and social aspects of kinship, or what he called the order of nature and the order of law (1980 [1968]: 25–30). Together with his later book, *Critique of the Study of Kinship* (1984), Schneider convincingly showed that kinship theory was permeated with Euro-American assumptions about the primacy of relations formed through sexual procreation, epitomised in the idiom of 'blood is thicker than water' (1980 [1968]: 49). These assumptions about the meaning and value of biology and substance are not universal, he argued, and hence former kinship analyses were not only wrong but the whole comparative kinship project was doomed to fail (1984). This echoed what the British anthropologist Rodney Needham had argued already in 1971, but perhaps due to the interpretive turn more broadly in anthropology coinciding with Schneider, his critique gathered more momentum, and mid-century kinship studies as we know it disappeared into the background of the anthropology debates. However, Schneider's critique was not only destructive, in the sense that research on kinship almost vanished for two decades, it came to be productive to the revitalisation of kinship theory and the development of the so-called 'new kinship studies'.

The encouragement to detach kinship from biology, to complicate the relations between nature and culture, and to include what had conventionally been classified as kinship into other anthropological themes, such as gender, personhood and the body, brought new life to the analytical kinship endeavour (Carsten 2004). Coinciding with the developments and increased availability of reproductive technologies, which so clearly challenge the distinctions between nature and culture and the biological and the social, kinship studies returned to the forefront of the discipline in the 1990s, particularly influenced by Marilyn Strathern's book *After Nature*, published in 1992. *Cultures of Relatedness*, edited by Carsten (2000), marked a new, broader approach to kinship, based on the messy, lived experiences of the everyday. This focus on what 'being related does for people living in particular localities' (Carsten 2000: 1) proved to be very fruitful, as it enabled analyses that started with a sensibility to emic terms and understandings of relationality. It captured the creativity that people bring to the production of close relations and the performative aspects of kin-making and maintaining, and it transgressed gender, class and other power relations that had narrowed perspectives (and relevance) of previous kinship theories. Importantly, a focus on relatedness enabled an epistemic dissolution of the distinction between the domestic and the political domains that had dominated kinship studies.

Many issues have contributed to '"undoing" kinship in its various classic anthropological guises' (Carsten 2004: 16), and this brings me back to the house. Together with issues such as reproductive technologies, gender and food/substances, the house brought perspectives discussed in 'new kinship studies' to old social and cultural concerns. In this book, I give the house a central analytic force, as a place where the everyday unfolds, where kinship is (re)produced and performed, and where the individual is positioned in the order of the world. The house is also a social group to which individuals belong and to which other houses relate. Hence, the house is a locus for the study of relatedness, combining social, ontological, symbolic, political and architectural aspects. I take the house, as Carsten writes, to 'embody the interconnection between the individual trajectory, kinship and the state' (2018: 103). This approach comes out of the house debates that developed in social anthropology at the beginning of the 1990s and onwards. Lévi-Strauss' notion of a 'house society' (*société à maison*) – a particular type of social organisation – was the starting point for these theoretical and ethnographic debates. What made this concept so useful was its 'symbolic unifying capacities' of kinship principles (Carsten 2018: 106), such as alliance/descent, affinity/consanguinity, matrilineality/patrilineality. This informed a new, more holistic approach to kinship in cases such as Tibet, where the role of descent is ambiguous. A house perspective is broader than Lévi-Strauss' work and intentions, as reflected in the title of the seminal volume *About the House: Lévi-Strauss and Beyond*, edited by Carsten and Hugh-Jones (1995), and offered 'a way of grasping the significance of kinship "from the inside", that is through explorations of everyday intimacies that occur there (Carsten 2004: 56).[8] Inspired by these early house studies, Elisabeth Hsu, in an article on the social and material life among Naxi and Moso in southern China, listed three aspects of what a focus on the house in kinship studies might entail: first, an increased emphasis on residence and territory; second, a focus on local concepts of house, hearth and home, which includes not only the locality but also the physicality of the house; and third, a perspective where daily domestic life is given preference as an entry into kinship issues (1998: 70–72). These three aspects are at the core of my choice to engage a house perspective in the analysis of the return of polyandry and of kin-making in rural Central Tibet.

Polyandry in Kinship Studies

Polyandry has not only remained disconnected from kinship theories in Tibetan studies; it has also been curiously peripheral in kinship studies in social anthropology more broadly. Of course, polyandry is an ethnographically rare phenomenon, although it has been practised in many corners of the world.[9] It is also a type of marriage that challenges fundamental notions of gendered sexuality and reproduction. Fraternal polyandry in Tibet implicates shared fatherhood and, as such, contradicts commonly held underlying perceptions of male sexuality and reproduction in Euro-North American culture, such as the notion of a man's evolutionary drive to spread his genes. In fraternal polyandrous marriages, men are unable to, and seemingly uninterested in, identifying and establishing biological fatherhood (in a scientific sense of the 'biological'). On the contrary, they readily accept socially validated paternity – that is, they do not make a distinction between pater and genitor.

Polyandry has also challenged the very definition of marriage. If anthropologists were interested in polyandry in the mid-twentieth century kinship theories, their main concern was with how to classify these practices, asking, for instance, whether they should be defined as 'plural mating' or 'plural marriage'?[10] If we follow Leach's classic lists of 'distinguishable classes of rights' defining marriage, namely that they serve to establish legal parenthood, they establish monopoly in the spouses' sexuality, they give right to the spouse's labour, and rights to property, provide a joint fund of property for the offspring of the marriage and establish a 'socially significant' relationship of affinity (1955: 183), polyandry would qualify as marriage. In what ways, if any, do such definitional discussions matter? Well, they point to concerns, to the taken-for-granted notions underlying a phenomenon. For instance, in principle, polyandry is not more difficult to define than its conjugal 'opposite', polygyny.[11] The unwillingness to define polyandry as anything else than cicisbeism or plural mating is an indication of an underlying androcentric bias and also that men's involvement in these types of relations has been met with suspicion. Discussing the lack of comparative studies of polyandry, Berreman sums up: 'We have tended to regard monogamy as expectable (even moral), polygyny as reasonable (even enviable) and polyandry as puzzling (even disturbing)' (1980: 378). Lévi-Strauss is another example of this, as he claimed that men's natural disposition has 'deeply polygynous tendencies' and from that assumed that polyandry would only be practised when there are no other alternatives (quoted in Levine 1988: 4; see also Cassidy and Lee 1989). Underlying and implied in this contention is the expectation that with economic improvements polyandry would be abandoned as a viable form of marriage. Using the return of polyandry in Panam as a case, I aim to challenge these underlying assumptions.

Polyandrous Houses

People who are married polyandrously live, share and belong to the same household. The household has been a central unit in the research on Tibet; it has, as Sophie Day writes, '*stood for* the Tibetan-speaking region just as caste or tribe have done in other parts of the word' (2015: 174). Throughout the Tibetan ethnographic region, villages were made up of households of different character, groups with distinct rights and obligations to each other, to local monasteries, to the village and to the polities of which they were part. Often termed *drongpa*, *khangpa* or *khyimtsang*, the status of the households depended on relations to land, ancestors and material and ritual wealth but also on biography. In some areas, such as in Ladakh in India and Humla in western Nepal, types of households were, and are, clearly distinguished by terminology where a corporate, named house is called *khangchen* or *drongchen* (large house), while a satellite, adjunct unnamed household is called *khangchung* or *drongchung* (small house) (Levine 1988; Day 2015; Hovden 2016). In theory, *khangchen* constitute the main members of the village, with clearly defined and strictly regulated rights and responsibilities in the village, while the *khangchung* either belong to the *khangchen* or has independent status but limited formal obligations in the village. The last decades of social, economic and legal changes in the Himalayas have complicated both these distinctions and the relations between the large and the small houses, as Day describes in detail from Ladakh (2015). Polyandry was associated with the *khangchen/drongchen* – the large, named houses that formed the core of the communities (Levine 1988; Day; 2015; Hovden 2016). While polyandry is decreasing in numbers across Himalayan communities, including Ladakh and Humla, this association remains.

Before the Chinese invasion and massive restructuring of Tibetan society from the 1950s onwards, the households in rural Central Tibet were also of distinct character and status, reflecting relations to land and to the administers of land – whether they were the government, monasteries or aristocratic families.[12] Among the farmers, the main household categories were *trelpa* and *düchung* – the landholding taxpayers and the landless labourers – of which the *trelpa* households shared characteristics with *khangchen/drongchen*, including the association with polyandry. *Düchung* were not satellite households of the *trelpa* but shared some characteristics with *khangchung*, in the sense that they were unnamed, more temporary units without known biographies, poorer, and often in a precarious relation to the *trelpa* or others with rights to farm land.

Marriage forms and arrangement patterns also varied among *trelpa* and *düchung*. *Trelpa* often held parent-arranged (more or less) elaborate weddings called *changsa*, while among *düchung*, informal couple-initiated marriages with small weddings, called *khathukpa* ('meeting of mouths') was most common. A *khathukpa* marriage most often led to the establishment of a new household, while *changsa* most often led to patrilocal residence, except in the cases where there were no male heirs in the receiving household, when matrilocal residence was common. The Chinese takeover made the categories of *trelpa* and *düchung* redundant. During the collective period, lasting until 1980, *khathukpa* marriage was most common across the social landscape in Central Tibetan villages.

Marriage and class is intertwined in Tibet, as elsewhere. Returning to Panam, marriage, class and state bureaucratic practices formed the households in particular ways. Before 1950, most landless farmers (*düchung*) lived in unnamed nuclear families (Goldstein 1978a; Aziz 1978a), and this was also the case in Panam. Labourers without hereditary access to land were called *yokpo* (a term that elsewhere refers to serfs), and they lived in small households, often in a rented room in one of the 'taxpayer' houses (called *genpo*). With the introduction of the first 'Democratic Reforms' in 1959, a reform much appreciated by the poor labourers, the Chinese government redistributed the houses and land from the local landholders to the former landless labourers. For administrative reasons, the local government officials encouraged the villagers to give a name to their new house, and these names came to represent the group of people living in the house as well as the attached land – that is, a form of estate (Ben Jiao 2001: 94). The Democratic Reforms lasted only one year, to much dismay, and with the collectivisation starting in 1960, the then named houses no longer had attached land; however, the names remained as house names (*khangming*) and developed as reference points for identity and belonging in the villages. Then, following the redistribution of land in 1980/81, fixed amounts of land were attached to these named groups, and hence, structurally, all households became named, corporate estates, in ways that resembled the former *genpo* in the area. This context is important for the renewed interest in polyandry, and it is within these reconstituted named estates, associated with formal plural marriages (*changsa*), that fraternal polyandry stands out as a highly valued sociocultural practice.

The return of polyandry, and the parallel transformations of the domestic that it involved, calls for a more nuanced way to conceptualise households in Central Tibet. Aziz described agricultural Tibet as a society where the place of residence was of major importance, and where the household was the prime group to which individuals belonged: 'It is not the idea of descent, but rather the concept of household which stands out as the keystone around which social relations are articulated. It is the residence principle which is central', she wrote (1978a: 117). What, then, is the relation between residence and household? A term often taken for granted in anthropology, studies of 'households' have primarily been concerned with comparing form and functions of groups of co-residing individuals who engage in common economic endeavours (Netting, Wilks and Arnould 1984; Gray 1995). However, a focus on the household, with its temporal and ad hoc connotations, can only bring limited understanding of corporate units and does not explore the full potential of 'residence'.[13] 'The residence principle', as Aziz called it, should not necessarily be operationalised as the analytical term 'household' but should rather, I hold, inspire a general focus on residence – that is, 'the fact of living in a particular place' (*Oxford Advanced Learner's Dictionary* 1995: 996). Residence, as a principle, implies the actual place of living, the people who live there and the social groups of which these people are members. An important critique of household studies is that due to a lack of holistic perspectives, the conceptual constitution of households – that is, the cultural meaning of the domestic – remains unexplored (Gray 1995: 16). This is valid point also for Tibetan households. Taking a broader approach to polyandry and the households in which these marriages take place, we might ask why it was so important for farmers in Panam to strengthen and perpetuate the household. And, related to that, what are the cultural meanings of the domestic in these farming communities?

While polyandry has often been analysed within the socio-economics of households, marriage is inherently also about kinship, and broadening the analytical frame of polyandry to kinship and relatedness opens new paths to explore. One such path is house perspectives, inspired by, but moving beyond, Lévi-Strauss. Taking European noble estates as the starting point, Lévi-Strauss introduced houses as 'moral persons', or 'corporate bodies', with names, material and immaterial wealth, biographies and reputations – that is, with social lives. The house endures over time, not only through the reproduction of its members but also through the transmission of material and immaterial wealth, which constitute the house itself. Hence, a house is more than the constellations of people living there at any particular time (the household); it is a social group that is perpetuated over time through filiation, adoption, descent and marriage, and other ad hoc arrangements. Houses make up significant social groups with which individuals identify and are identified by others, often legitimised in kinship terms, and they are ranked in a defined social hierarchy.[14] Perhaps the most productive aspect of the house perspective though, is the idea that houses are more than a domestic space and combine social, symbolic, ontological and architectural aspects of village life. As Howell noted: '[t]he house as the object of the anthropological gaze, let alone the historical, the political and the economic gazes, will, I suggest, yield hitherto unsuspected new insights into old concerns' (Howell 2003a: 33). This holds true for the study of Tibetan polyandry.

Many Tibetan households can be understood through such a concept of 'house', as has been recognised particularly in Ladakhi studies (Phylactou 1989; Mills 2000; Day 2015). Indeed, before 1950, the estates of the aristocracy and the land-holding farmers in Central Tibet can be seen as houses, in a Lévi-Straussian sense of the word, and in the case of Sharlung village, the *trelpa* and the *genpo* can easily be classified as houses. At the time of my fieldworks in Sharlung, most households were houses, albeit in different ways. Some had well-known names with a long biography, a good reputation, elaborately decorated physical buildings and ritual wealth, while others were newly established houses with limited material and immaterial wealth, but enough to consolidate a house. When exploring the status of marriage in the history of the various houses in the village, a clear pattern is evident: while we might find polyandry in all types of houses, there is more likely to be polyandrous marriages over several generations in houses with long biographies, and only among the younger generation in newly established houses.

Kinship of Potentiality

A focus on the house in Panam – and the polyandrous house – means a focus on the organisational principles of residence, which in a study of social relations in rural Tibet is not in itself new. Yet, there are unresolved contradictions in the ways that kin groups and meaning are described with reference to descent (primarily the patrilineage) and residence (primarily the household). Already in 1978(a), Aziz argued against the prominent role given to descent in Tibetan kinship studies when she described and analysed village life in Dingri, Central Tibet.[15] However, patrilineal descent has remained a strong undercurrent in studies of social organisation and clans in both historical periods, a point also made by Samuels (2016),[16] and periods closer to our time (Stein 1972; Prince Peter 1963). Despite more recent studies critically re-engaging with the concept of the 'clan', both from an anthropological perspective focusing on Amdo (Langelaar 2017, 2019) and from an historical perspective focusing on Central Tibet and its southern borderlands (Samuels 2016), the idea of patrilineages and descent groups remains strong. Also, the emic presence of patri-ideology in many Tibetan communities has blurred the analysis of other forms of social organisation, and particularly the significance of co-residency and the domestic group. In Panam too, there is a patri-ideology present, yet, the core, organising unit in which the local farmers manage their people, land, wealth and relations and in which individuals gain their rights and duties, and belonging, is the house. Lévi-Strauss suggested 'house society' as a particular kinship typology, consolidating contradictory kinship principles, such as descent and residence. Following the arguments above, we might call Central Tibet a house society; the *drongpa* or *khyimtsang* fit Lévi-Strauss' criteria of house as a 'moral person' – external relations across generation are house-based, the physical houses themselves are socio-symbolic spaces of particular cultural meanings (Toffin 2016 [1991]) – and this model allows for ranked classifications.[17] At the same time, other categories of farmers in Tibet, as well as pastoralists and urbanites, primarily activate both the patrilineage (and patrilateral kin) and, for some purposes, matrilateral relations in their kin-making practices, suggesting that if Tibet is defined as a 'house society', there are significant exceptions to this model. While recognising the value of the house in Panam and rural Tsang, as well as in Ladakh and some of the eastern borderland communities, we must also note the heterogeneity in the social organisations found across the Tibetan ethnographic region. Often in our attempts to build models and theories in anthropology, we tend to define deviant cases as merely exceptions; however, with the concept of a kinship of potentiality my aim is to bring also the 'exceptions' into the theoretical framework.

The broad range of marriage forms culturally available to members of Tibetan communities and in the borderlands can be understood as a range of socially accepted, potentially beneficial organisational principles that can be employed (or attempted to be employed) in a given time and place. The continuity and change in marriage practices depend on external and internal factors, such as household composition, gender relations, morality, land tenure systems, and political regulations and relations to the state. This leads to the dominance of certain marriage forms in certain contexts while allowing others to continue to exist in the background. For instance, while polyandry is less prevalent among Tibetan pastoralists today, or among urbanites in Lhasa, we do find a few cases in most of these communities.[18] In addition, we know that there are some cases of polyandry among Tibetans in India, initiated after arriving into exile (Grent 2002). Polyandry is a possibility to consider; it is a potential. Likewise, while polyandry was the preferred marriage form among farmers in areas of rural Tsang, polygyny remained an alternative when certain factors prevail, such as fertility problems, expressed also among younger couples in Lhasa.[19] Marriage forms are flexible, and choices are pragmatic, depending upon the perceived potential of the various forms socially and culturally available – that is, monogamy, polygyny, polyandry and combinations of these. Across the Tibetan ethnographic region, not only marriage but also kinship more broadly is formed, maintained and explained in a myriad of ways. Kinship principles, idioms and practices are (unevenly) shared, and the formation and maintenance of these is a process in flux, formed in a continuum of potential principles and practices that can be foregrounded or backgrounded – in different localities at different times. The flexibility, especially of marriages, might seem remarkable, but kinship and relatedness is always – albeit to different degrees – pragmatic and creatively produced through and for both ordinary and extraordinary days and events. The availability of this broad range of possible principles, idioms and practices that do not challenge kinship epistemologies but form, and are formed by, what can be called a kinship of potentiality is shared – although differently distributed – in Tibet and its borderlands.

Panam Valley and Sharlung Village

The fieldwork for this book was done in Panam (Tib. Pa snam, Ch. Bai nang), a valley located in Tsang, the vast area in west-central Tibet, between and to the south of Shigatse and Gyantse towns. The origin of its name can be traced back to two Buddhist scholars of the thirteenth century, Badra Nyima Drapa and Nalang Dorje Denshong, who practised in this area; their two names combined are Ba Na, which with time has turned into Panam (pronounced locally as *Bena*) (Ben Jiao 2001: 34). Panam is a central area for grain production in Tibet, located between the Himalayan mountain range and the Yarlung Tsangpo river (the upper stream of Brahmaputra). A river valley, it covers some 120 km from north to south, and its width varies from the narrow and high-altitude (semi-)pastoral areas in the north-west to wider areas of well-irrigated land in the south-east. Farmers produce the five main grains – barley, wheat, buckwheat, peas and rapeseed – as well as potatoes and radishes. Due to the harsh climate, with cold winters and uneven distribution of rainfall, the fields only produce a harvest once a year, as in most of the high-altitude farming areas in Tibet.

Panam County (Ch. *xang*) is an administrative unit under Shigatse prefecture, including eleven townships (Ch. *xiang*), out of which Kyiling *xiang* is an average place both in terms of scale, population and economic position. According to the *xiang* leaders, in 2001 there were 4,512 people in the township, and these belonged to 595 households. Kyiling *xiang* consists of eleven administrative villages (Ch. *cun*) varying in size and basis for livelihood. Three of the villages are located in the narrow upper valley, located at some 5,000 meters, where there is little arable land or access to irrigation, and where people are semi-pastoralists (*samadrok*). In the mid-2000s, Panam was ranked number 6 of 18 counties in in per capita income in Shigatse prefecture (Goldstein, Childs and Wangdui 2008: 518, n11). However, Kyiling township was, according to the local leaders, one of the poorest in the county, and most of the *samadrok* villagers depended on help from the local government for food security throughout the year. In the lower parts of Panam, at around 4,000 meters, where Sharlung is located, people were farmers, with relatively small numbers of livestock. Further east towards the county seat, the farmers to a larger degree engaged in off-farm income activities, working in the construction industry, renting out trucks or other means of transport (Goldstein et al. 2003, 2010; Goldstein, Childs and Wangdui 2008).

Sharlung village is located in the narrower part of the valley with limited arable land and irrigation options. During our stays in the early 2000s, the village seemed far away from the urban centres in the area, despite the rather close physical distances. For instance, despite the intentions from the regional government to introduce electricity to all the villages, due to some unfortunate events, Sharlung was excluded from the installation process and was therefore without electricity. Electricity poles had been built from the county seat, but, according to the township leaders, lack of wires caused the project to come to a halt between Sharlung and the neighbour village, pointing to the precariousness of development initiatives in the area.[20] As in most high-altitude places in Central Tibet, wood was limited; hence, people primarily used dried dung from yaks, cows, sheep and goats for heating iron stoves for cooking. There was no mobile phone coverage, and to make a call, people used the public phone in the township. Yet, Sharlung was not an isolated place; people socialised with those in immediate neighbouring villages and with others from across the valley, and many had relatives in Shigatse or Lhasa. Through marriage, work, pilgrimage, business and the search of various services, people moved easily in and out of the villages, mostly using three-wheel tractors for transport.

Before 1950, land tenure in the area surrounding Sharlung followed the same general structures as we know from elsewhere in Central Tibet, dividing the land between aristocratic families, monasteries and the government (Goldstein 1989; Fjeld 2005). An influential aristocratic family administered the land to the west of Sharlung, and Sachung monastery managed the land to the east. Sharlung and their closest neighbours to the west were villages of government serfs (*zhung gyukpa*), which meant that the fields belonged

18 • The Return of Polyandry

Figure 0.2. A newly renovated house in Sharlung. © Heidi Fjeld

Figure 0.3. Harvest time. Primarily subsistence farmers, much of the life of residents in Sharlung revolved around agricultural work. Soon after we arrived in Sharlung in 2002, the harvest started; it was a hard but happy time, and school children were brought back home to help. © Heidi Fjeld

to the government (and not the monastic or aristocratic estates) and were administered and worked by taxpayers (*trelpa*). Some *trelpa* also hired landless labourers to perform agricultural work on their farms. In Sharlung, there were two houses that served as government representatives, also referred to as *genpo*, and they were the only houses with some affluence. The majority of the population was very poor, calling themselves *yokpo* (serfs). In addition, Sharlung and the neighbouring villages were served by a number of blacksmiths, butchers and those handling the dead (*baru*), who were lower ranked than *yokpo*, endogamous and lived on the outskirts of the villages.

During our first stay in 2002, Sharlung village consisted of forty-four households, counting some 350 individuals. These numbers are obviously fluctuating, not only reflecting demographic processes of birth and death, marriages and divorces, but also household demise and new establishments, as well as outmigration. Most households consisted of three generations sharing a house and cooperating economically. However, there were great variations in household compositions, including single men and women with or without children; monogamous couples with children and/or their parents; as well as plurally married partners with children and/or their parents.

Sharlung is approximately one and a half kilometre in length and one kilometre in width – it is a small place. Agricultural areas of Tibet are recognisable by the vernacular architecture; two- or three-storey fortress-like houses built from handmade dried earth bricks and limited amounts of wood, and these houses were also common in Sharlung. Moreover, most houses were surrounded by a courtyard, in which farming implements and other valuables, such as a tractor or a horse were stored. Some houses were whitewashed with black door frames with bright paint above it; others were yet to be painted. The roofs were flat, some framed with black paint as well, and some with visible shrines on the roof – painted red or white. A tall stone wall framed the courtyards and reinforced the impression of isolation. When walking around the village, the economic and social differences were apparent simply by looking at the houses. The materiality and structure of the houses not only gave an indication of its social status and wealth but the history and distribution of marriage forms.

Doing Ethnography in Tibet

I felt very fortunate to be able to stay with a family in Sharlung for almost five months. Given the sensitive nature of both doing social science studies in the TAR and exploring intimate relations and everyday lives, this gave me the chance to engage informally and over a prolonged period with people there. My methods are ethnographic, and I combine observational and conversational data, including interviews and informal conversations. I started by conducting a survey and visited most households in the village. The survey not only gave an overview of household composition, social background, and family history, marriage and economic organisation, including off-farm activities, but it also gave me an opportunity to make kinship charts and memorise names and connections, which was a productive way to start conversations later. I focused on participation and observation among two main categories of interlocutors: farmers of *all* backgrounds in Sharlung, and farmers and non-farmers of hereditary low-rank background in Sachung, the neighbouring village. As it turned out, these categories of people included all households in Sharlung and twelve households in Sachung. Following the survey, I had extended and repeated conversations with residents of fifteen particular households. Of these, I put emphasis on five key interlocutors in addition to the eight people in my host household. These five people were: one *nama* (in-married wife) with young children; one older unmarried woman residing with her brother's family; one young polyandrously married man with a newly established household; one monogamously married man with adult children; and one younger nun from the local nunnery. Further, I spent time in the nunnery and also interviewed township leaders, village leaders and deputy leaders in Sharlung, leaders of the two closest villages, and monks in Sachung monastery. Of the low-ranked households of skilled workers in Sachung village, I repeated my visits as often as possible, in particular to one blacksmith household. Further, I visited and interviewed ritual experts from several villages in the area, including several *ngakpa*, one diviner (*mopa*), one hail protector (*ser sungpa*) and one medium (*lhapa*). Despite the relatively short time I was allowed to stay in Panam, I consider the data to represent a broad range of people and perspectives in Sharlung and its vicinity, much because of the excellent co-researcher I shared the experience with.

Our days in the villages consisted of more or less the same routines. In the morning we – my co-researcher Samdrup, my daughter Runa and nanny Mingzom – ate breakfast together in my room, sharing tea and *tsampa*. At this point, the grandmother in the house had often already joined us, chatting about everything and nothing. We always asked her about the happenings of the day in the house and around the village, and she always asked us who we were going to visit. Samdrup and I would then walk to one house in the morning, usually coming home for lunch, and visit another house in the afternoon, heading back at around six or seven in the evening. At the beginning of our stay, Mingzom and Runa spent their days playing in the house and in the garden and helping with chores such as fetching water, collecting dung and dusting. After about one month, Runa, wanting to be together with other children, joined first grade in the local school, with Mingzom accompanying her. In the evening, while Mingzom prepared our dinner, I wrote fieldnotes and, together with Samdrup, transcribed interviews. If we were at home during the day, I would often sit with some of the women in the house, and, together with Mingzom, we could discuss issues that were taboo to mention in the presence of males (relatives in particular), such as women's work (burden), pregnancy and sexuality. Being there with a child opened many conversations, and particularly the women were curious about my experiences with motherhood and marriage. Often in the late evenings we would join the rest of the family around the stove in the main kitchen/living room (*taptsang*). These hours proved to be of value not only as an occasion for discussing relevant issues with the family but also for learning about other villagers' concerns. Tashi-la, the Takrab household head and a highly respected village leader, was often called upon as a mediator for conflicts in the village, and often times people came to consult him in the evenings. On many of these occasions, I was present and able to observe their discussions together with the rest of the household. Tashi-la became engaged in my learning, and he was quick to understand my interests in cultural and social affairs; often he would inform me of events in the village that he thought would be useful for my research. These were often connected to religious events, and included household rituals of neighbouring families, special offerings to the local protector (*yul lha*) or other protectors, trips to the medium (*lhapa*), or readings and rituals in the nunnery. Just before our departure from Sharlung in 2002, he even changed the schedule of the performance of the ritual for cleansing the house so that I would be able to take part in it.

In addition to the more general participant observation approach, my main methodological strategy was to follow leads. This included to follow and following-up information provided by villagers in our talks: the terms and terminology used, people's concerns and their plans, and the ongoing events in the village, be it village meetings, public work, slaughtering, or household rituals, or travels to neighbouring places. This following-up involved asking additional questions, probing, revisiting and pursuing points of friction.

The value of closely cooperating with a local scholar cannot be underestimated for the effectiveness of the fieldworks and the possibility of producing ethnography within the very restricted frames of the Tibet Autonomous Region. All foreign students and researchers with a research permit were obliged to work together with a local scholar, and this person has many – muted and conflicting – roles, including research assistant, interpreter, gatekeeper, observer and a companion for the trip. As the representative of the government institution providing the permits to the foreign visitor, the local scholar is personally responsible for making sure the research is conducted within acceptable frames. During the first four months in Sharlung, I was accompanied by Samdrup, who was then a teacher of Buddhist philosophy and history. His knowledge about Tibetan culture, religion, history and society was very impressive. Samdrup had grown up in a farming village in a different part of Central Tibet and was in all ways accustomed to village life. He had also studied the history of anthropology, through which he had developed an interest for local cultural practices. His main field of expertise was Buddhism, but during our stay he became increasingly interested in both social organisation and local ritual practices, and he served as a mentor not only to me but also to villagers who had a particular interest in scholarly Buddhism. After our stay in the village, he remained in touch with some of the people in Sharlung, serving as a Lhasa contact for them, which reflects his kind and caring personality.

Access to people for only a short period of time, surveillance and the changing political climate make writing ethnography from TAR challenging. Also, both the intimate nature of the topics of marriage and domestic lives and the eighteen years that have passed since the fieldwork complicate the process. In addition to using pseudonyms for all place names in Panam, all participants have been anonymised. To secure an ethically sound ethnography, I have made small adjustments in the presentation of my interlocutors, adding and removing some information to facilitate anonymity. I have occasionally combined persons for the same purpose. I have done this carefully in order to keep the general impression and the main points accurate.

The Chapters: Moving Into and Out of the House

The book explores village life from the entrance into a house, through its internal organisation, to the ontological and symbolic aspects of the house, and finally to inter-house relations. Chapter 1 narrates the coming-into-being of a polyandrous marriage arrangement in the Döling house – that is, the considerations and dynamics involved when parents plan their children's futures. It presents a range of local explanations of polyandry and discusses the sociocultural constitution of the domestic unit within which polyandry is preferred. In Chapter 2, we are in the process of moving into the house, as it discusses the pathways to becoming a member. Membership possibilities open up critical analysis of kinship ideologies and practices and their discrepancies, and this chapter makes a distinction between lineages as constituting personhood and as constituting social groups. In Chapter 3, we start exploring relationality within polyandrous marriages, starting with brothers being husbands, and focus on relative age, masculinity and fatherhood. Detailing distribution of sex, authority and leadership, and the collective handling of marital conflicts, we see the encompassing role of the eldest brother in a polyandrous house. In Chapter 4, we remain within a marriage setting, situated in a multigenerational house, as we look at polyandry from the wife's perspective, through her relations to other women and to her husbands. It looks at gender models, possibilities for gender alternations and the fascinating phenomenon of the biological sex of a baby changing during birth. Chapter 5 takes us away from the marriages, but we stay within the house, exploring it as a meaningful, ordered place. This chapter details the architecture of the house, its interiors and the openings to the outside and show how the house is a bounded ritually efficacious space in which humans and nonhumans can interact in an orderly fashion, properly separated in domains, in ways that enable a prosperous and safe life. In Chapter 6, we leave the protected space of the house, change perspectives and examine relations among the houses and the inherent limitations of these. It describes relatedness in networks of mutual assistance and explores enduring social hereditary hierarchies and new forms of dependencies among the houses. The Conclusion draws attention to the temporality of the book and situates Panam as a case study of a flexible and pragmatic approach to, and enactment of, marriage and kinship – a kinship of potentiality that I argue characterises communities in Tibet and its borderlands. The book ends with an epilogue that reports a serendipitous encounter during my last visit to Lhasa.

Notes

1. After the Chinese invasion, Tibet's borders were redefined, complicating the terminology describing territory before and after the 1950s. By 'Central Tibet', I mean Ü and Tsang (when describing political administration and official categories, I use Tibet Autonomous Region (TAR)); by 'Tibet', I mean all three regions (*cholka sum*) – that is, Ü-Tsang, Kham and Amdo; and by 'ethnographic Tibetan region', I mean communities in the borderlands of Tibet where people speak Tibetan (dialects) and identify as Tibetans, or closely related to Tibetans.
2. When I have talked with Norwegian small-scale farmers about polyandry, they immediately see the benefits, as they have often been through a complicated process of transfer, based on the old Nordic allodial right called *Odelsrett*, which, based on primogeniture, gives any family member the right to buy the land, if it is to be sold.
3. See, for example, Steward (1936); Mandelbaum (1938); Berreman (1962); Otterbein (1963); Prince Peter (1963); Goldstein (1971a, 1978b); Haddix (2001); Ben Jiao (2001).
4. In a classificatory terminology, kinship categories are expanded to include persons with the same lineal connection – that is, lineal kin is merged with lateral kin if linked through the same connection. For instance, a father and father's brother is termed 'father' because they are both connected through father, while mother's brother is not, and parallel cousins are classified as siblings, but cross-cousins are not. Morgan took these to represent a 'primitive' organisation; an early stage in the evolution of societies. In descriptive kinship terminology, on the other hand, the relations between parent and child is distinct, and lateral kin is coined in common categories independent of lineal connections – that is, uncles, aunt, niece, nephew etc. (Parkin and Stone 2004: 5–6).
5. In the nineteenth century, kinship was a way to explore (pre-Darwin) ideas of social

evolution, focusing on language and terminology, and through a large network of collaborators, Morgan started a global comparative project in which he and others aimed to identify what they saw to be the development of human societies. Their interest in kinship terminology of the Others was primarily to look for similarities with their own past. While the ideas of the nineteenth century, seen also in evolution theories of 'family formation' – from primitive promiscuity, to group marriage, to matriarchy and patriarchy, to nuclear families – have been abandoned, occasionally we see traces of similar ideas in the Chinese scholarship of marriage in general and polyandry in particular.

6. See, for instance, Benedict (1942); Allen (1976); Hildebrandt, Bond and Dhakal (2018) for Tibet and Himalaya examples, and Ball (2018) for a review of current work in linguistic anthropology on language of kin relations.
7. See, for instance, Meillassoux (1984); and Goldstein (1978a) for an example from Tibet.
8. See also Waterson (1990); Joyce and Gillespie (2000); Sparkes and Howell (2003).
9. In addition to Tibetans, the Irava of Kerala, Todas (Kodas) of southern India (Mandelbaum 1938) and Pahari in the Indian Himalayas practised fraternal polyandry; Kagoro in northern Nigeria (Sangree 1972), Sinhalese peoples (Tambiah 1966), indigenous groups in north America (Steward 1936), as well as Marquesan islanders in the Pacific (Otterbein 1963) practised what was termed 'associated polyandry'. There was also the rather particular case of Nayar marriages, simply termed 'Nayar polyandry' (Gough 1959).
10. Fisher concluded in his much-cited work that all known cases of so-called polyandry were forms of polykoity or plural mating (1952), and thus he denied the very existence of polyandry as a marital form. His argument was that in the known unions of one woman to two or more men, she would only truly be married to one of the husbands because he alone would be sufficient to legitimate the offspring of such union.
11. As both polygyny and polyandry are arranged from a male position, they are not opposite practices.
12. According to Chinese accounts, monastic estates held 37 per cent of arable land, while aristocratic estates held 25 per cent, hence leaving 38 per cent to be held by the government (and used by taxpayers) (Epstein in Goldstein 1989: 3). These figures should only be taken as indicative of land distribution.
13. See Yanagisako (1979); Gray (1995); Carsten (2018).
14. House societies, Lévi-Strauss suggested, are societies that can be placed between kinship and class organisation; however, this evolutionary undercurrent of his house concept was dismissed early on (Carsten and Hugh-Jones 1995).
15. Aziz produced her ethnographic material by conducting extensive interviews with Tibetan refugees settled in Nepal, due to lack of access to Tibet.
16. For instance Davidson (2005); Van Schaik (2011); Dotson (2012).
17. Yet, 'société à maison' was introduced by Lévi-Strauss to solve the theoretical puzzle not of lineage organisation but of cognatic kinship, a characteristic different from the earlier descriptions of Tibetan societies.
18. Personal communication in Lhasa with Tibetans from pastoral areas, between 2001–2016.
19. In 2008, I was talking with Tibetan couples about fertility problems, aiming to investigate the use of reproductive technologies. Several couples mentioned the possibility of inviting a sister of the wife into the marriage before trying medical technology.
20. In Sachung, each household paid 800 yuan for the preparation of electricity introduction; however, by 2004, people were complaining that for the past two years there had been a complete halt in the process, with no indications of continuance.

Chapter 1

THE RETURN OF POLYANDRY

There is an impressive diversity of Tibetan marriage forms, including monogamy, polygyny and polyandry, and combinations of these. The distribution of marriage form has followed social hierarchies. Before 1950, monogamy was found in all social strata, polygyny was largely found among the wealthy upper classes (primarily the aristocracy), and polyandry was predominantly found among the landholding farmers.[1] In the debates referred to by Charles Bell (1928), the British special ambassador visiting Lhasa in 1920, Tibetan intellectuals agreed that monogamy was the prevalent marriage form in Tibet, yet both polyandry and polygyny were commonly accepted. Different forms of polygamy served distinctive purposes; while polyandry was beneficial for keeping the farm estate undivided, polygyny was advantageous for initiating or maintaining political alliances. Plural Tibetan marriage forms, and particularly polyandry, were not only foreign to the new Chinese rulers but also strongly detested by them, yet these practices continued in various ways. Shortly after the revolution, China's Communist Party (CCP) did focus their attention on marital practices throughout the country. The new Marriage Law of 1950, reflecting gendered relations in Chinese society, banned multiple wives, concubinage, child betrothal and the sale of sons or daughters (into marriage or prostitution), and cadres and village leaders encouraged modest wedding arrangements. While being successful in the Chinese cities, the new polices on marriage were only partly incorporated into rural areas, and villagers continued parent-initiated elaborate weddings. However, concubinage, marriage of minors and polygamy were rapidly more or less eliminated as cultural practices in inland China, mostly due to these changes in the law (Davis and Harrell 1993). Later, in 1980, a renewed Marriage Law was implemented, and this placed an even stronger emphasis on the prohibition against polygamy, banning what was called 'mercenary marriage', which refers to both polygamy and concubinage. These prohibitions were stated clearly in Article 2, which ends strongly with: '"Bigamy is prohibited"' (Engel 1984: 956). Reflecting the harsh rhetoric when describing the so-called old society in Tibet, the media, presenting the views of the CCP, frowned upon polygamy, and particularly polyandry, depicting it as an ancient tradition that is physically and emotionally harmful: a 'tumour left over from the feudal farmer-slave system of old Tibet'.[2] At the same time, the Chinese government showed a pragmatic approach to the issue. Engel (1984) cites the *Beijing Review*: 'In Tibet, an "autonomous region" of China where polygamy is still common, the law has been modified to allow continuation of those polygamous marriages that were contracted before the 1980 law took effect.' Such a pragmatic approach continued in rural areas of Tibet, and until the beginning of the 2000s, the various Chinese marriage laws had, as we shall see, a limited effect on local marriage practices. Since the 1980s, township leaders have been given generous space to negotiate local policy implementation on plural marriages, allowing for a continuity of polyandry.

A First Time for Polyandry

Lack of implementation of the marriage laws not only enabled continuity, but in the period after 1980, polyandry spread to new segments of the villages, as more and more farmers found it to be beneficial for their concerns and aspirations. Drolma's story, introduced this book, is one example of a new post-1980 polyandry arrangement. Also, in the house of our hosts, the household leader had arranged polyandrous marriage for his sons for the first time in his family's history. Moving into the Takrab house in Sharlung, we were welcomed by Lobsang Drolma, the in-married wife (*nama*) of the house, and one of her husbands. She showed Samdrup into the 'room of religion' (*chökhang*), where he would sleep, and then she took Mingzom, my daughter and me to the room above the entrance – a spacious room with large windows, a stove in the middle and carpet-covered benches along two of the walls. It was the room of her youngest husband and also a room for storing clothes. The *nama* had three husbands, but the eldest one, she told us, had gone to work in Western Tibet and was only home a few months a year. I asked where the youngest husband would stay, if we occupied his room, but she simply pointed in the direction of the kitchen-living room (*taptsang*). The Takrab was a big house, but not all the rooms had been completed. In addition to the *taptsang*, the grain storage (*norkhang*) and the room for religion (*chökhang*), the *nama* had her own room that she shared with her eldest husband when he was home, while the middle husband shared the *taptsang* with his parents and his non-nursing children.

This arrangement was similar to what I saw in other houses too. Below I describe one such process of arranging polyandry for the first time, using the house of Döling as an example that can serve to illustrate the concerns, possibilities and limitations – and the decisions involved – in the coming into being of a polyandrous house in the recent history of Panam. Dargye and Chökyi, the household leaders, had married monogamously, and they could not recollect any polyandrous marriages in their respective family histories. As such, their story illustrates the changing marriage practices that Ben Jiao described in 2001, namely that there had been a significant increase in polyandry in Panam since the 1980s. From his study in a larger village in Panam, he showed that more than 30 per cent of the marriages were polyandrous. Most of these marriages had been arranged after the decollectivisation of land in 1980/81, pointing to the strong correlation between land tenure and marriage forms (Ben Jiao 2001: 125). At the time of our fieldwork, Döling was in many ways an ideal household composition in Sharlung, with a large marriage and access to substantial land. Its members included Dargye and his wife, Chökyi, their three sons and one daughter-in-law, their one unmarried daughter, and their three grandchildren. While the three sons were conjointly married, the daughter was an ordained novice nun in the local nunnery. Due to a lack of living quarters in the nunnery at that time, she also stayed in the house. This pooling of labour and people enabled Döling to consolidate a strong household and, in the context of sociopolitical reforms, to engage in a process that involved a transformation of the household towards what we, based on Lévi-Strauss, can explore as a 'house'.

Many afternoons, I found Dargye sitting in the open space that connects the living quarters of the house, preparing wool and drinking tea or *chang*. This was the calm period of late autumn, when the harvest was completed, and people spent more time on leisure. The sun still warmed the air, and many people enjoyed moving chores outside or simply socialising. During some of these afternoons, and later in the evenings after the chores of the day were completed, Dargye shared the story of his family with us. Told on many occasions over a period of four months, I have compiled the parts into one chronological narrative, starting from the 1950s, to the marriage arrangements for his children at the beginning of the 1990s, until the formation of what I have chosen to call the Döling house.

Dargye and Chökyi were both born as landless labourers (*yokpo*). Chökyi originated from a village south of Sharlung, born into a poor family with thirteen children. When she was around seven years old, a relative of her father adopted her, and she came to the Sharlung house. In the past, this was an old, powerful and wealthy house from which the village had received its name. At one point in time, the Sharlung house had been struck by misfortune and multiple deaths, leading not only to suffering but also to labour shortage. Chökyi was one of several from the outside that was sent to help. Dargye's family rented a room in Sharlung village, and his parents and siblings worked for different landholders in the area. Dargye and Chökyi met while working the fields of Sharlung house. It was at the beginning of the 1960s, Dargye reckoned. The marriage was *khathukpa*, initiated by themselves and something like a love marriage, and his parents did not object. Dargye was the eldest of his many siblings – four sisters and three brothers. Three of his sisters were sent as a *nama* to another village, and two of his brothers as a *makpa*, moving into and becoming a household leader in the wife's household. After marrying, Chökyi moved in with Dargye and his parents (as well as one of his sisters and one of his brothers).

They were very poor when they married, Dargye explained. It was during the Team Period (*loré tsok chung*), he believed, and although they had some land, they had to pay heavy tax to the leaders and were only able to keep a little grain for themselves. He recalled it as a difficult time. Chökyi was also unhappy in the house of Dargye's parents. They were often quarrelling. One day, after their second son was born, she told Dargye that she wanted to take the children and move out, claiming that Dargye's father did not treat her and the children well. Their basic needs, such as enough food, was not covered in the household. Struggling between filial and marital obligations, Dargye was unsure what to do. Chökyi's advice to him was that because it is difficult to find parents but easy to find a new wife she did not want to pressure him to leave with her. Eventually, Dargye decided to go with her, and his team leader found a small room for them. This move did not change their team membership, and thus it did not affect their access to land or work. After some time, the team helped them to build a small house. They called it Norshar – because it was located east (*shar*) of the old Nor house.

Time passed, and Dargye became a member of the political committee in the township. Reforms also changed farm life. As already mentioned in the Introduction, the Household Responsibility System reform (*gentsang lamluk*) and the following decollectivisation in 1980/81 divided the village fields and animals equally among all villagers above 18 years of age – property that was to be administered by the households were these individuals belonged. The decollectivisation, Dargye recalls, were happy times. At the point of division, they were five people in the household (Kelsang, the youngest son, was not yet born), and they received fields for all five people. Dargye had been promoted to a political position, and while this did not provide him rights to more land, he was given a horse for transport to meetings, which came with an extra field

Figure 1.1. The Takrab house. © Heidi Fjeld

for fodder. Hence, he ended up with fields for six people. At the same time, Dargye's parents' household also received fields for five people, and after some complicated years, he inherited these too. After Dargye and Chökyi left, his parents shared the household with one son and one daughter, as well as one grandchild, who also remained in the household and inherited the land when the parents passed. Soon after, Dargye's sister also passed, and his brother, whose health was declining, moved to the city; they agreed that Dargye would take over the land in his absence. In exchange for the land, Dargye was obliged to take care of his brother's son. So, Dargye, summed up, they had been very lucky. All together, they were able to attach land for twelve people to their household. They built a new large house on some of the land – a two-storey building identical to the old, formerly affluent houses in the village. Because they felt so lucky, Dargye and Chökyi asked a lama to give the house a new and auspicious name. He called it Döling, a place (*gling*) of success (*don*).³

Weeks later, sitting in the kitchen-cum-living room drinking tea and *chang* and chatting about the happenings of the day, I asked Dargye to continue his story. The room was lit only by the small oil lamp hanging on the pillar by the stove, and the children were already asleep, lying between us in their home-made wool bags. Kelsang, their youngest father, was making *pag*, clumps of barley flour eaten together with soup and much else, in preparation for a three-day trip to the mountains to take food and drinks to the herders. Sonam

Wangmo, the *nama*, was boiling eggs for him to carry while at the same time serving tea to Dargye, who was resting from a trip to the country seat.

I asked him about what had happened after they had received all the land. He repeated that they felt very, very happy to receive so much. This, he said, put them among the biggest landowners in the village. At the same time, they were only six people to feed; himself and Chökyi, their three sons and one daughter (his brother's son had moved to Lhasa for education). A bit later, he said, guessing it was around 1983, an old nun from one of the neighbouring villages started approaching many households in the area. She was the former abbot of the local nunnery, and, following the open policies of the 1980s, she wanted to rebuild the nunnery that had been destroyed during the Cultural Revolution. She needed girls to help her. Many households in Sharlung and other villages decided to send one daughter for ordination, including Dargye and Chökyi. Their daughter was then thirteen, interested in religion and excited to join the nunnery. After her ordination, Dargye and Chökyi had the three sons' futures to consider. Jamyang, the eldest son, was approaching marriage age. Kelsang, the youngest, was still a teenager, and he was also interested in religion, always saying prayers and reading religious texts. They decided to send Kelsang to Sachung gompa (the monastery in the neighbouring village). He stayed there for some years and then left, Dargye said, so they arranged for him to join Jamyang and the middle brother, Jigme, who were by then in an established marriage. Finding a good *nama* had been easy because, Dargye explained, they had many fields and he knew many people through his position as village leader. Sonam Wangmo, the *nama*, is from Sakya, and because Dargye knew the leader in her village, it had been easy for him to make an initial inquiry about her. Dargye had heard that she was good woman – with a good personality, and, he said, her age was very compatible with his two eldest sons.

I asked him why he chose polyandry (*zasum*) and not a one-to-one marriage (*changsa réré*). Dargye started to explain the need for labour to work on their many fields. With polyandry, his sons could stay together, and they would not need to hire labour (*milak*) for the tasks. It is very good to keep many people together, he told me, especially when there is much land. The two eldest sons had a good relationship, and both preferred polyandry because they did not want to be poor on their own with only one field – that is, the fields are spilt when children move, which, Dargye said, nobody wants, and he continued, repeating, 'you know, *zasum* is a very good way – you can see it here and many other places.'

Dargye's smile seemed to signal the close of the part of the story concerning polyandry, and he moved back to Kelsang joining the monastery. It is a very good deed to send a son to the monastery, he reminded me, and they were very happy that Kelsang was able to join Sachung monastery. Sachung was a highly venerated gompa; it was old and had remained intact through the Cultural Revolution (due to its use as a military depot); it was an important place for people in the valley. Kelsang stayed as a novice for a few years; he did not like it much. It seems they spent too little time in the gompa, only performing rituals on the 10th and the 25th day of the month, so Kelsang moved back home. Kelsang, who had finished packing his travel bag when Dargye told me this, added that they had also lost their teacher, which led many monks to decide to leave, and he found it difficult to keep the vows. When Kelsang came back from Sachung, he was simply added to the marriage of his brothers. This was the best way, Dargye said, and Kelsang did not comment any further. At eighteen, Kelsang was the right age for marriage, and being incorporated into the established marriage, he did not have to leave his natal home. Also, he was not much younger than the *nama*, which made the process easier. Dargye consulted both Kelsang and Jamyang, the eldest husband (but not Sonam Wangmo or Jigme), and they both agreed. With this arrangement, the household would be able to send one person out to make money, to the benefit of everyone. Dargye said this worked out very well, as Jamyang found work in Ngari and brought back cash income, while Kelsang worked the fields and Jigme herded animals. Ani, the nun daughter, helped with domestic chores, which was good for Sonam Wangmo as Chökyi was getting old.[4]

The story of Döling firstly illustrates the changing process of marriage in the period from the 1950s to 1990s. It shows how the two main entrances into marriage, initiated by the couple (*kathukpa*) or the parents (*changsa*), are associated with the older and the younger generation respectively. There has been a surprising alteration in the nature of marriage for the families of former landless labourers; from first being an event mostly involving the couple to being a collective household concern, as illustrated by Dargye's narrative. Before 1959, the majority of the farmers in Sharlung were married monogamously in *khathuk* unions. These marriages were informal, often couple-initiated unions with very limited ceremonial elements and could be described as a type of cohabitation that was culturally recognised and served to legitimise children. *Khathukpa* marriages most often led to the establishment of new households and affected the respective natal households' land only to a limited extent. Dargye's case illustrates how parent-initiated polyandry was arranged for the first time in the period after his household was provided with new land, a pattern seen in many Sharlung houses.[5] After decollectivisation of land in 1980/81, the majority of farmers in Sharlung married in a more formal way, described as *changsa gyak*, a term that translates both as 'marriage' and 'wedding'. These are parent-initiated unions within which the two households and their representatives play important parts. Following an elaborate wedding ceremony, *changsa* involves post-marital patrilocal residence, except in cases where the wife has no brothers and thus is the heir to her natal household. Most importantly, with *changsa*, the newlyweds move into an already established household and become the next generation of household leaders there.

Secondly, the story of Döling illustrates domestic change and development among former landless labourers in Panam, a change that has strongly influenced considerations of marriage. Dargye's story is both typical and atypical; it describes a process in which the various parts are shared by many while at the same time depicting an unusual life. Dargye held political positions in Sharlung village, positions he had occupied since the 1970s, and in that sense his biography is unusual. Further, the inheritance history of his family deviates somewhat from the experiences of many of his co-villagers, as he possessed not only the fields distributed to him through the land reform in 1980/81 but also fields that he inherited in an ad hoc way from his relatives. The Household Responsibility System has had an arbitrary effect on the various households in Panam as it has elsewhere (Yeh 2004), and compared to other former landless labourers (*yokpo*) in Sharlung, Dargye and Chökyi were lucky to end up with more land than the number of people in the household indicated. Before 1980, the married unit was a less intricate part of the household as a social group. In the 1960s, living together with Dargye's parents was primarily for practical reasons due to extreme poverty. As a group, they did not share inheritable wealth, and when the disagreement between Chökyi and Dargye's father was resolved by moving, it had primarily emotional and not organisational implications. Dargye and Chökyi did not leave his parent's household economically impaired. Among the landless labourers, the household as a unit was only to a limited extent embedded with cultural meaning beyond the individual family, and the establishment of new households was not disfavoured as such. When they married, Dargye and Chökyi saw their arrangement as an agreement between individuals rather than between social groups. During the collective period from 1960, when group formations other than the state-operated communes were frowned upon, such notions of the marriage institution were widespread. Looking at the distribution of marriage arrangements in the older generation in Sharlung, post-marital, neolocal residence was common for people of all backgrounds during this collective period. There was a significant shift in emphasis when Dargye talked about his children's future and marriage, as he linked these to the social reproduction of the household. After the decollectivisation in 1980, all households, independent of social background, became structurally similar to the former landholders in agrarian Tibet – they had access to fixed plots of land that were to be managed across generations. It was with this new status as corporate estates, albeit with unequal number of fields, that the former landless labourers made their decisions on managing household resources and future possibilities, including those of marriage.

Household futures involve considerations of two main human resources options; marriage and non-marriage. Concerning marriage, there are, schematically, three alternative possibilities: first, inviting a *nama* to the son(s) or sending a daughter as *nama* to another household (patrilocal residence); second, inviting a *makpa* to a daughter or sending a son a *makpa* to another household (matrilocal residence); third, approving or not approving a couple-initiated marriage (neolocal residence). In Sharlung, these three options were somehow ranked in terms of preference, where the marriages implying patrilocal residence were seen to be most fortunate, followed by marriages implying matrilocal residence, which in most cases was due to the lack of male heirs, and lastly marriages resulting in the establishment of new households, which were not only seen to be less fortunate but were clearly disfavoured.

Considering the future for his children and for the group to which they belong, Dargye and Chökyi both chose marriage implying patrilocal residence, and non-marriage. The two sons married together secured the reproduction of the household. This was imperative to Dargye's allocation of the human and material resources and reflects the centrality of sons in the domestic organisation in Sharlung. For those outside these central positions, there were several options, of which Dargye and Chökyi initially chose celibacy for both the youngest son and their only daughter but ended up bringing them back into the household.

While in many other societies non-marriage is problematic and, in some cases, even incompatible with the adult personhood, this is not the case in Tibet. Non-marriage might involve enrolment into a monastic institution or simply imply a – more or less – celibate life in one's natal home. When Dargye sent two of his children to enrol in monastic institutions, he did so for several reasons. One significant implication of the ordination of Kelsang was that he relinquished the inheritance he was entitled to. Moreover, monastic enrolment was a highly valued and well-established option for both men and women, and celibate sons or daughters reflected well on their family. This was particularly the case with monks, although the status of nuns was improving. Dargye saw his daughter's ordination as a contribution to the rebuilding of the local nunnery and to the production of local ritual expertise in general. At the same time, the nuns in Sharlung spent less time on ritual chores in the nunnery than they did on domestic chores in their natal homes. As such, the ordination of a daughter had a double implication; the continuous contribution to daily work in, and the positive reflection back on, her natal household, and the contribution to the highly valued efforts to rebuild religious institutions.

The third point that Dargye's narrative can serve to illustrate is the value of polyandry in domestic development and planned futures, including the inherent flexibility of these marriages. With four children, Dargye and Chökyi chose to arrange only *one* marriage. With one polyandrous marriage, they were able to pool labour resources while keeping the newly acquired estate undivided for the next generation. As all sons had equal rights to inherit land, every marriage potentially divided the estate, and aiming to arrange only one marriage per generation – what Goldstein termed the 'monomarital principle' (1971a) – was a well-established strategy to avoid fragmentation of Tibetan farms. Polyandry, as polygyny, is also inherently flexible, which contributes to the value of these marriage forms. Once established, these marriages could be altered rather easily; adding and removing partners was common. When Kelsang returned from the monastery, there were several options available to him; to marry independently and establish a new household; to marry as a *makpa* into another established household; to join the already established marriage in his natal household; to settle outside the village (working for income); or, which was less likely, to remain as a bachelor in his natal home. Of these options, it was only the establishment of a new household in the village that involved an activation of his inheritance rights, and hence, by implication, fragmentation of the farm land. This was one of the reasons for the general disfavouring of post-marital neolocal residence practices. The inclusion of Kelsang into the already established marriage was in no way dramatic, as it did not alter any structural arrangements in the domestic organisation; rather it maintained the status quo.

A fourth, and last, point that Dargye's story illustrates is the significance of governance, beyond economic reforms, to the spread of polyandry and domestic transformations in Panam. As mentioned, despite Chinese marriage laws, local leaders had since the 1980s been able to maintain a lenient approach to local variations of marriage, basically allowing all types of arrangements.[6] However, in this period, the government was also maintaining and further developing registers and statistics of the local population which influenced the nature of domestic units, and thus marriage practices. These unintended consequences pertain to the houses people live in and to changing naming practices. Starting already in the 1960s, the houses in the villages were redistributed from landholders to the landless labourers. These landholders' houses were named estates and often had long genealogies. These house names (*khangming*) served as identifiers, as family names, of its members. The places – the rooms and small houses – where the labourers lived were, however, not named, and those residing there were simply identified by first names. The redistribution of houses brought an increase in the living standard for most villagers, except the former large landholders (*genpo* and some *trelpa*). Later, the farmers started to build new houses too.

Before the Chinese invasion, Dargye's parents had settled in a small room in the Lungko house (one of the *genpo*) that they worked for at the time. During the Democratic Reforms in 1959, when land and property were first redistributed, Dargye's parents received a separate part of a house that had belonged to Dagpo, another large *genpo* in the village. They kept this house for some ten years, then they built their own simple house close to the Dagpo house. Although the first house might have had a name, nobody could remember it; the name was insignificant. Similarly, when Dargye and Chökyi moved from his parents' house, the government provided them with a room in one of the public houses (*chikhang*) at the time (this was the collective period, when most property and land belonged to the government). This place also did not have a name, but when they built a separate small house they named it Norshar, the place east of Nor (a *genpo* house). During the collective period, each individual belonged to a team; hence, in terms of governance, each citizen was registered (and controlled) through team membership. However, with the decollectivisation and the introduction of the Household Responsibility System reform, the households replaced the teams as the connecting units between individuals and the state. For bureaucratic purposes, the state encouraged the farmers to name their households as part of the ongoing social and cultural changes of the domestic units. While previously it was only the *genpo* houses – that is, the former corporate estates with known genealogies – that were named, after the Household Responsibility System reform all households, small or large, were given names. In the beginning, simple descriptive names were used, such as *Khangser* (new house) in Dargye and Chökyi's case. However, with time, many people in Sharlung renamed their houses. Having firmly established a corporate estate, Dargye and Chökyi invited a lama to name their new house properly, and hence Döling was founded. Together with land and household composition, these new names, coming from a culturally meaningful source, effect, as we shall see, the very constitution of the domestic units. The example of Döling illustrates how, in summing up, it is within these transforming households that former landless labourers found polyandry – for the first time in their family biographies – to be meaningful and favourable.

Increase of Polyandry in Panam

The return of fraternal polyandry (*zasum*) in Panam is significant in numbers, albeit it is difficult to produce statistical evidence of increase. There are no national or regional marriage statistics available for Tibet before 1950. Indeed, the (lack of) registration of polyandry in public records also complicates statistical overviews. In Tibet, polyandrous marriages was commonly registered as a union between the eldest man and the wife, while his brothers (co-husbands) remained registered as living in their natal household.[7] This practice has continued with the Chinese administration as seen in Kyiling township, and therefore the incidents, and hence prevalence, of polyandry is difficult to establish. Aziz suggested, through interviews with exiled Tibetans from Dingri conducted in the 1970s, that some 30 per cent of marriages in (Central) Tibet before the Chinese invasion were polygamous, of which the clear majority were polyandrous (Aziz 1978a: 137–38). Goldstein's calculations from the Gyantse area (which is close to Panam) indicated that 60 per cent of the landholding families (*trelpa*) married polygamously and that in the remaining 40 per cent the families had only one son of that particular generation, thus being unable to arrange a polyandrous union (1978a: 209). The percentage of landholding farmers who were able to marry polyandrously resembles the situation in the Panam villages that I describe here.

During my first stay in 2002, I registered 51 marriages located in the 44 households in Sharlung. Of these, 21 were monogamous, 29 polyandrous and one was polygynous. These numbers are similar to what Ben Jiao registered a few years earlier, writing from a larger village of 90 households, where he found 54 per cent monogamy, 31 per cent polyandry, 11 per cent polygyny and 4 per cent polygynandry, the latter being a union of two or more wives and two or more husbands (2001: 125). When investigating more closely the 21 marriages registered as monogamous, I found that seven of these were *khathukpa* (out of which five had been established before 1980). Additionally, four were *makpa* marriages (matrilocal residence, often when there is no male heir), and seven marriages were the result of partitions of polyandrous marriages. As polyandry in Tibet is of the fraternal kind, its arrangement preconditions more than one son of the same generation to enter into it, hence we need to also take household composition into consideration. The remaining three monogamous marriages were found in households with only one son; in one case, the second son had established a new marriage outside the village. The numbers give a clear picture of polyandry as a preferred marriage form in Sharlung. When we discussed the high numbers of polyandry with people in Sharlung and its neighbouring villages, they were adamant that this was typical for the agricultural regions of Panam.[8]

The ideal constellation of a polyandrous marriage is three brothers and one wife, and people in Sharlung believed that three co-husbands was also the most common constellation. When surveying marriage distribution, I found that the average number of co-husbands was close to three; however, most of the marriages were unions of two husbands and one wife. Three marriages involving five husbands, but only one of these involved that all co-resided at the same time. In the two other, some of the husbands were either too young to participate actively, or attended schools or worked outside the village for longer periods. In practice, then, most – indeed with only one exception – polyandrous marriages in Sharlung involved three or less husbands. Although a large number of co-husbands is advantageous for the household in terms of labour, constellations of four or more co-partners were recognised to be very demanding marriages, not only for the wife but also for the younger brothers, whose age would be significantly lower than their wife. Therefore, in these cases, off-farm activities were encouraged.

Looking at the numbers, polyandry does indeed appear to be widespread in Sharlung. This impression is strengthened by the fact that of the many monogamous marriages registered, one-third of these were couples divorcing from a larger polyandrous union, indicating an even higher percentage of arranged polyandrous marriages in the village.[9] Differing from pre-1950, polyandry was not restricted to a certain category of people but was rather distributed widely across social divisions and hierarchies.

Local Explanations

Despite being common and appreciated, perceptions and explanations of polyandry differ, not only in the villages around Sharlung but also outside the area. Particularly in Lhasa, young Tibetans conveyed some curiosity, and also animosity, towards the practice of polyandry. During a talk about marriage in Panam that I gave at the *English corner*, a language initiative operative in Lhasa until 2008, some of this disapproval became apparent. Tsepun, a then 35-year-old teacher who grew up in a village in Central Tibet but had lived in Beijing and Lhasa for the last 20 years, had a view on polyandry that I found to be rather typical among Tibetans in the cities:

> Polyandry is an old custom, something that we need to change. There are many good customs in Tibet that we should work hard to maintain, but some are not so good, and we don't have to continue to do something just because we have always done so. Polyandry is so strange; I don't know why anybody would like to be married in that way anymore. Maybe in the village this is still useful, but at least in the city we don't need so many people in the family. If there is one father and one mother, and two children – then that is enough.

In Lhasa, I often got the sense that people talked about polyandry with a certain sense of embarrassment, as if trying to conceal this practice from me, thinking it might leave a negative impression of Tibet. In Panam, on the other hand, my experience was rather the opposite: people were eager to talk about polyandry, and conversations often turned towards what they saw to be the advantages of such marriages.

The local explanations of polyandry I heard in Panam were materialistic, expressed as a strategy to strengthen the household. Basically, polyandrous marriage prevents land fragmentation and maximises male labour within the *khyimtsang*. In addition, normative polyandry limits the population growth in the village. People in Sharlung emphasised different aspects of polyandry; most often, however, they addressed one or two of the above-mentioned points. Below are six ways that people in Sharlung talked about polyandry, illustrating some of the variety of local explanations.

> Some people think that those married as *réré* ('one to one', monogamy) are happy. But this is not always the case, because they have very hard work. It is better with *zasum* because then we have more hands. Three [husbands] is the best – one to work in the fields, and one to work with the *ralug* (sheep and goats) and one to bring income. It is much better when each person has less work – that makes everybody happier. (Lakyi phala, the household leader of a previous *yokpo* and now a relatively affluent house)

> In Sharlung, some people have always had *zasum*. Mostly, earlier, it used to be the wealthy, but now it is the same for everybody. It is always good to be many people, and with *zasum* it is very easy. Even during the land division [1980/81 reform], those with many people got more land. For instance, some butchers in Bargang – they had *zasum* with two wives and one husband before the division, and therefore they had many children and received much land from the government [due to the per capita distribution of land]. Then in the next generation, the five sons married together, and therefore they have few children. So now they have land for many people without being many people – this is the smart way to go about this. (Gomchang Dadul, fifty, married *khathukpa* monogamously with one woman and, after her death, remarried with her sister)

> Polyandry is very popular here now. This is for its economic reasons. The wealthiest *khyimtsang* have polyandry, right? For example, in the house by the foot of the mountain, Dagpo, five brothers share one wife. This is good because the problem in the village is that the number of people increases, but the land remains the same. In 1981, there were 200 people here; now there are around 300 or 400. But despite the increase in people, the land will not be redistributed in some 100 years. (Ösel, forty, deputy village leader)

> *Zasum* is the marriage in the very, very old *drongpa* (*drong nyingba nyingba*). In the history of this place, it is those with *zasum* that have been prosperous and famous in the valley. The Dagpo, Lungko, Lampo, right? They were powerful in the old society, and they are still important. All of them have polyandry. They never had to split the land or the people. They stayed together, and the *zasum* was successful [no partitions]. So Dagpo are still powerful and wealthy (Longchang achi (elderly woman/grandmother), sixty)

The problem with monogamy (*changsa réré*) is that there are too few people, so it is not possible to make a household grow. *Changsa réré* are not so stable, because if something happens to the one husband it is very difficult for the wife and the children. Also, if the husband has to travel outside to make income, it is difficult for the wife because she has to depend on *milak* [paid assistance] for ploughing and doing the rest of the heavy field work. (Norshön Migmar, thirty-five, in a newly established household with his wife and one brother after a long-term conflict with his parents)

Ha, ha, here, brothers do everything together – they even share mistresses. Look at the woman (*ama*) by the river, for instance, and her lovers; the two are married together, and still have the same mistress! Why should they not be married together if they can have the same mistress? (Lobsang Drolma, thirty-five, *nama* in Takrab)

Central to these explanations is the economic rationale for polyandrous marriages, not for each individual but for the whole group. Such groups are residence-based and referred to as *khyimtsang*, *dütsang* or *drongpa*, which all translate to English as 'household' although of various kinds. Strengthening and perpetuating the household is essential in the preference for polyandry in Panam. The economic rationale of polyandry is based on the combination of post-marital patrilocal residence norms, equal inheritance for all sons, and the household administration of material and immaterial wealth, including farmland, animals and fortune (*nor*), as well as (re)productive forces (*yang*, *sönam*). As mentioned, because all sons hold equal inheritance rights, every son's marriage could potentially lead to fragmentation of the parents' land, and people saw this as very unfortunate, not only for the group to which they belong but also for each particular couple and individual. Further, motivations for polyandry were closely connected to the three-folded economy of the area; namely, agricultural production, animal husbandry and wage labour. The fixed, but limited, amount of land is best utilised by dividing the requisite labour among the household members themselves, thus avoiding the expense of external workers.

The demographic aspect of polyandry – the interrelation between population size and the amount of land available – was only mentioned to me by people in leading positions. Increasing population numbers is a concern among village leaders, as fertile land cannot be expanded. With a high occurrence of polyandry, fewer women marry, and this reduces the birth rates in the village. This is, however, an effect of polyandry, rather than reason. More often, people would rather actively compare polyandry to other forms of marriage – mainly to monogamy – and assess the advantages and disadvantages of the marital forms, particularly in terms of male workload, security and the possibility of growth. The association of polyandry and (former) wealthy households, the landholders (*genpo/trelpa*), was explained to me repeatedly, and for good reasons. Several of the historically affluent households in the village had, for as long as anyone could remember, arranged their marriages polyandrously. Polyandry was associated with these households and their history of wealth accumulation and growth; polyandry was historically proven, so to speak, to be intimately linked with a successful and higher ranked socio-economic position. I think it is important to note that the conceptual association of the landholders and polyandry had connotations beyond economy. As the quote from the older woman above says, the polyandrous *genpo* houses had a history of being powerful and well-known. The perception of polyandry as a marriage of the 'upper classes' indicates an ongoing process within which alteration of marriage practices is one aspect, and where former servants and labourers (*yokpo*), as well as the low-ranked skilled workers (*menrik*), incorporate cultural practices associated with the former landholders.

A different kind of explanation emphasises interpersonal relations between the co-partners in a polyandrous union, and, as stated with a chuckle in the last quote, the close relation between brothers more generally. The consubstantial sameness of brothers creates both physical and mental resemblance, which, according to some of my interlocutors, implies an expectation of similar preferences, also sexually. More generally agreed upon in our conversations in Sharlung was an expectation of solidarity among brothers (or siblings, particularly of the same sex). Still, the materialistic aspects remained crucial in the local explanations of polyandry. These explanations were made rational in close relation with the social organisation in the domestic groups (*khyimtsang*) into which villagers defined themselves and others. The cultural logic of polyandry is closely related to the inheritance practice, where all sons hold rights to equal shares of land. However, other peoples across the world experience similar challenges concerning the transfer of immovable goods from one generation to the next, and, yet, rather than arranging polyandry, they practise inheritance rules such as primo- or ultimogeniture. When discussing polyandry with villagers in Sharlung, such alternative practices were not very attractive, because, as one elderly man said, 'brothers want to stay together'. Moreover, and close to his statement, a young woman's noted a wish to stay together: 'if we could choose, then all children would remain with their parents,' indicating what can be seen as a centripetal orientation of domestic organisation.

The Corporate Household

These local explanations are reflected to varying degrees in theories of polyandry. More particularly, interpersonal relations and cultural values on the one hand, and socio-economic aspects on the other, have been at the core of anthropological analyses of Tibetan polyandry, represented by Nancy Levine and Melvyn Goldstein's work. Mapping marriage and family organisation in pre-1950 Central Tibet, Goldstein employed a socio-economic rather than a purely economic model. He emphasised social stratification and land tenure, pointing to the monomarital principle of the land-holding households: 'one whereby for each generation one and only one marriage should be made, the children of which are considered members of the family unit with full jural rights relative to their sex' (1978a: 208). This is an alternative principle to the more common ultimogeniture or primogeniture, aiming to result in a so-called stem family to take over an undivided estate. Polyandry is, according to Goldstein, 'a functional analogue of other wealth conserving kinship mechanisms ... which operate to reduce the frequency of, or preclude, divisions of family patrimonies' (1978b: 335). During the social and political system of Ganden Podrang, the Dalai Lamas' rule, polyandry was particularly beneficial to those households with hereditary access to land, and with that, heavy tax obligations. For the landholding farmers – the *trelpa* – the tax burdens necessitated a broad labour pool within each corporate household in order to be able to fulfil these obligations in general, and the corvée taxes in particular. Goldstein noted that the two main 'goal-oriented factors' (1978b: 326) of polyandry were the wish to prevent land fragmentation in order to enable fulfilment of tax obligations and the wish to maximise male labour; of these, he places emphasis on the former (1971a: 72–73). Hence, he saw the efforts to preserve and perpetuate the corporate household across generations as the core motivation for choosing this potentially demanding marriage form – a theory that is very close to local explanations as found in Panam too. Polyandry, then, is a means to an end (Goldstein 1990: 619), rather than a goal in itself.

Nancy Levine's classic 1988 monograph *Dynamics of Polyandry* brought additional elements and a different perspective to fraternal polyandry, based on ethnography from Nyinba, a Tibetan-speaking community in Humla, Western Nepal – that is, outside the tax system of the Dalai Lamas' rule. She critiqued a materialistic (and deterministic) approach, arguing that 'the importance of polyandry extends beyond the economics of it' (1988: 159).[10] Levine presented five elements as crucial to the explanation of polyandry in Nyinba communities: first, polyandry had a special cultural value due to the cultural representation of the past in which ancestors are portrayed as brothers linked by polyandry and characterised by their family harmony;

second, fraternal solidarity was one of the core kinship ideals; third, the corporate household (*drongpa*) system presupposed polyandry and its economy; fourth, the Nyinba village, as a corporate unit, was structured around polyandry and non-proliferation of member households, making polyandry 'structurally pivotal'; and fifth, most men and women found polyandry a personally comfortable form of marriage and the one that 'suits culturally defined practical goals' (op. cit.). Hence, Levine concluded that polyandry has an economic rationale but that in the earlier literature this has been 'overemphasized at the expense of its kinship, political and symbolic correlates' (op. cit.).

Central to both Goldstein and Levine's analyses is, however, that the *corporate household* presupposes polyandry. Moreover, Levine's point that polyandry is 'structurally pivotal' within the village organisation concurs to a large extent with Goldstein's conclusion that polyandry in Tibet is oriented 'toward the social consequences of economic productivity, rather than toward subsistence per se' (1978b: 329). While Goldstein is primarily concerned with the external relations of the residence group, and particularly with the state (in terms of tax obligations), Levine focuses on both the politico-jural (political, economic and religious obligations) and the domestic (interpersonal relations) aspects of the residence group. They both argue that polyandry is closely intertwined with the corporate nature of Tibetan households. Neither Levine nor Goldstein define 'household' analytically, and it seems that they use it as an emic term. Also in Sharlung, people highlighted that to strengthen and continue the domestic unit was the most important motivation for arranging a polyandrous marriage, because such marriages enable accumulation of wealth through economic diversification, as well as maintenance of the unit across generations. The word they commonly used in Panam was *khyimtsang*, usually translated in dictionaries as family and/or household (Das 1902: 162; Goldstein 2001: 135). Breaking down the word, the etymological meaning of *khyim* is 'home', while *tshang* is 'nest' or 'dwelling'. Other words also used to denote these domestic units are *thempa*; people (*pa*) of the threshold (*them*) and *dütsang*, where *dü* (*dud*) translates as 'smoke' and *tshang* as 'nest' or 'dwelling' – that is, the dwelling place around a hearth. *Khyimtsang*, as well as *thempa* and *dütshang*, refers directly to the place of dwelling; the house that people belong to that defines their social identity, and through which they gain their rights and obligations in village affairs.[11] Acknowledging the relevance of the physical house to the social unit, exploring the *khyimtsang* enables us to better understand the efforts that many Tibetan farmers put into strengthening and perpetuating it. The *khyimtsang* is not a house in the simplified sense of a physical structure (called *khang*) but a domestic corporate unit in a certain social organisation that holds value beyond household activities. Moreover, a *khyimtsang* as a house can consist of several, or no households, and the constitutional nature of two terms differ in significant ways.

Anthropologists engagement with Lévi-Strauss' house perspective not only developed into a heuristic device for reframing studies of kinship, including kinship principles and practices but also socio-symbolic approaches to the domestic (Carsten and Hugh-Jones 1995). Lévi-Strauss' much-quoted definition takes a house to be a 'corporate body holding an estate made up of both material and immaterial wealth, which perpetuates itself through the transmission of its name, its goods, and its titles down a real or imaginary line, considered legitimate of kinship or of affinity and, most often, of both (1983: 174). He calls the house, in this sense, a 'moral person', which indicates that the house is much more than a physical structure for dwelling; it is a social institution that is a property-holding unit that endures through time, often with ritualistic elements (Carsten and Hugh-Jones 1995: 14). The house is a subject with agency, rights and obligations. It incorporates not only the people living there, and hence constitutes the group in a particular time, but also the property itself – names, titles and other prerogatives of its identity. Seeing Tibetan *khyimtsang* as moral persons, or corporate bodies, holding material and immaterial wealth points to the significance and meaning of polyandry, beyond merely economic advantages. In the economic, social and political context of Panam (at the time of this study), a polyandrous marriage was one of the most effective ways to enable perpetuation and a strong transmission of name, wealth, reputation and identity over generations.

As mentioned in the Introduction, some Tibetan-speaking communities, houses and households are made distinct, and this helps clarify the status of the different domestic units. The two different types of households (*drongpa*) in Ladakh are clearly of different status – *khangchen* (the large house) constitutes units that have rights to land and obligations to village work, and *khangchung* (the small house) is an offshoot household consisting of individuals in a non-reproductive state, such as unmarried daughters or retirees, or a small household without land or village obligations. A village would consist of a fluctuating number of households (*khangchung*) and a fixed number of what can be termed houses as moral persons (*khangchen*) – that is, those houses that are stable and constitutive to the village (Phylactou 1989; Day 2015). As Day shows, 'these houses and households are sometimes distinguished, sometimes conflated and sometimes merged' (2015: 179), and during the last 50 years, these domestic units have in Ladakh come to share most characteristics, albeit with an awareness of difference. This has led to some local frustration over potential loss of identity, as there is an expectation that the *khangchen*, and their house names, 'fashion and convey a stable, lasting and even "timeless" series of social identities and positions' in the village (ibid.:

190). One of the ways that *khangchen* fashioned such stability was through fraternal polyandry, before it was effectively prohibited in Ladakh.

Childs' analysis of 1958 Kyirong shows that two types of households were distinguished: one hearth (*tap chik*) households in which all members resided together and cooked over a single fire, and two hearth (*tap nyi*) households that included both the main household and a subsidiary residence (Childs 2008: 71). The latter were termed 'adjunct house' (*zur khang*), or residence for the elderly (*gentsang*) (op. cit.). In Panam it was uncommon for a named house to have offshoot houses such as the *khangchung* or *zurkhang*, as all generations co-reside in one house. In fact, it was an explicit goal to only have one household per house, for the same reason as the monomarital principle. The common empirical overlap of household and house should not, however, lead to an analytical concurrence of the two terms.[12] Some local homesteads indicate how household and house might also be distinguished in Sharlung. One of these homesteads was a run-down and poor-looking building located to the west of the village, called Lampo. It was an uninhabited house, with no household activities but where the ritual presence maintained the status (and the power) of the house. The Lampo house used to be an influential house with a large household. In the last generation, ten children were born into the house; however, due to personal conflicts they had all moved out successively. Since 1995, the house had been empty of people; hence, empty of a household. It was not, however, empty of meaning. Because Lampo had a long history, it hosted a house protector (*namo*) considered to have significant power. The protector was the *kyelha* ('natal deity') of those connected to the house by filiation, who continued to perform offerings either in the house or through 'long-distance offering'. Lampo had been a well-established house in Sharlung for as long as people could remember and its historical high rank and ritual power were maintained through such continuous offering to the house protector. Much due to the protective powers of the *namo*, the Lampo house remained the loci of belonging for the individual members, and it would continue to be so until the *namo* was moved or people for other reasons stopped making offerings in the house. As such, this empty house illustrates the distinction between a household and a house; it was the house without a household.

Seeing the *khyimtsang* as a house rather than merely a household offers a broader perspective on polyandry, and particularly on its return and increase since the 1980s. What was at stake in the local efforts to strengthen and perpetuate the established domestic unit, the *khyimtsang*? People living together as members of the same house in Tibetan communities do share economic endeavours. However, more than that, I argue, the *khyimtsang* is also a physical house of social, symbolic and cosmological nature that provide belonging, protection and connections to its individual members.

Unintended Consequences

The renewed emphasis on houses among farmers seems to have been an unintended consequence of Chinese policies, which had started already during the late 1950s when the houses of the *trelpa* were redistributed to people of *yokpo* status, and continued throughout various reform periods, culminating in the post-1980 period when the homesteads were given corporate status through the Household Responsibility System.

The state-initiated socio-economic changes had led, and continued to lead, to a stronger local emphasis on the house as residence, as a structuring orientation in the village. With the changes in marriage forms, the characteristics of the domestic units were also negotiated. As Day (2015) describes from Ladakh, sociopolitical changes have blurred the distinctions between houses and households, leading them also to sometimes be conflated; the domestic units in Panam were also fluctuating. Before the 1950s, there was a clear distinction between the houses of the landholding farmers and the aristocracy, and the households of the labourers, servants and others of lower rank. The former were named corporate estates with long genealogies, connected in webs of inter-house networks and often hosting plural marriages that had involved elaborate weddings. These were clearly demarcated physical houses; defined, as we shall see, as cosmological orders and protective ritual entities, and material and immaterial wealth passed in these houses from generation to generation. The latter, on the other hand, were unnamed households that can perhaps best be negatively defined in the sense that they were households of various sizes that did not have a known biography and that had not perpetuated themselves as corporate units through generations. They were domestic groups that shared a common economic endeavour, married monogamously and lived in dwellings that did not enable the transfer of material or immaterial wealth across generations. Chinese social and economic re-engineering has changed the base of these distinctions and allowed for new negotiations, formations and alterations of the domestic realm. New access to land has enabled former *yokpo*s to organise themselves polyandrously and, by doing so, engage in a transformation of unnamed households into named houses, in the manner associated with the former landholders and high-ranking houses of the Panam region. As polyandry and *trelpa/genpo* are conceptually connected, inherent in the organisation into houses is an expectation – and value – of polyandrous marriages. Hence, the increased preference for polyandry is part of a shift towards a social organisation in which the farmers belong to named, corporate estates; houses that are meaningful units far beyond economics.

A theoretical emphasis on houses implies a new approach to the conceptualising of what in many ways is a conundrum of residence and descent in Tibetan kinship. Throughout Tibet and the Himalayas, the contextual relevance of patrilineality varies, and in rural Tsang these descent groups has very limited organisational force. In the next chapter, the distinction between kinship as constitutive of personhood, on the one hand, and of local groups, on the other, shall inform the exploration of the meaning and impact of linearity, laterality and residence, as we turn to the sources of membership in houses of Sharlung.

Notes

1. See Bell (1928); Stein (1972); Goldstein (1971a, 1978a). The distribution of polyandry in traditional Tibetan society has been an issue of some discussion. Rockwell and Combe, both writing from eastern Tibet, held that only farmers practised polyandry. Bell, however, argued against this and claimed that polyandry was common among both the peasantry and the pastoralists (1928: 159–61). He concluded, referring to his conversations with the Lhasa aristocracy and his broad reading, that 'all agreed that, taking Tibet as a whole, monogamy was more prevalent than either polyandry or polygamy [polygyny]' (ibid.: 161). Also, he noticed, Tsang, where Panam valley is located, was as an area with an 'exceptional prevalence' of polyandry (op. cit.).
2. Macartney (1994).
3. Döling is a fictive name, chosen to reflect common types of house names (*khangming*) in the area. It has a connotation of auspiciousness. Other common names reflect a sense of happiness, topographic location, cardinal direction from a large house, or temporality.
4. Chökyi unfortunately passed away only one year later.
5. In the literature of Tibet, marriage (*changsa*) is often described as accompanied by elaborate wedding rituals and strong participation of the groom's and the bride's household members. This, I believe, is due to the dominance of upper-class informants in earlier studies of Tibetan societies (see Fjeld 2005: 22–23) and does not reflect all forms of weddings and marriages.
6. This was reflected also in the township leaders own marriages, which included both polyandry and monogamy.
7. Ramble, personal communication, Vancouver, 2013.
8. According to my interlocutors, polyandry is less common in the higher altitude villages in Panam where people engage in semi-pastoralism (*samadrok*).
9. That some monogamous marriages were arranged as polyandry also reminds us that the configuration of marriages can change over time, especially in the case of plural marriages, and thus, the marriage distribution presented here – reflecting a particular moment in time – cannot address this important diachronic dimension, as discussed in detail by Berreman (1975).
10. Levine relegates Goldstein's analysis, based on the economic rational, to only a sophisticated version of the earlier assumption that 'without polyandry, Tibetans would be reduced to poverty' (1988: 158). This seems to be a reading of Goldstein that is based on an exaggerated notion of difference. Moreover, it does not discuss Goldstein's later work on polyandry (1978a and b), where he gave the social aspects of economic considerations the main attention; hence, he developed a socio-economic and ecological rather than a purely economic perspective. The material Levine presents does not, to the extent that she maintains, disclaim Goldstein's argument that polyandry is oriented towards mini-

mising land fragmentation and maximising male labour in order to secure the economic growth of a landholding household.
11. While in other Tibetan communities *trongpa/drongpa* is used to denote the households of corporate character (Aziz 1978a; Levine 1988), this is not widely used in Sharlung.
12. The anthropological history of the two terms diverges extensively, indicating not only different connotations but, perhaps more importantly, different analytical potentials. The 'household' was traditionally employed to describe groups based on co-residence. Yanagisako writes: 'Generally the term refers to a set of individuals who share not only a living space but also some activities. These activities, moreover, are usually related to food production and consumption or to sexual reproduction and childrearing . . .' (1979: 165). Due to the extensive practice of the same activities in groups of people not residing together, several suggestions to separate the 'domestic' activities from the term 'household' have been suggested (see Seddon 1978); however, production/consumption and reproduction seem to remain at the core of the household descriptions. The household is analytically distinct as a category based on common economic endeavour at a particular time and in a particular space.

Chapter 2

TRAJECTORIES TO HOUSE MEMBERSHIP

Houses, as physical buildings and social units, host individuals who are often related by agnatic kinship. Yet, the role of patrilineal descent is not obvious. Exploring kin-making and its informing principles, trajectories to membership are an analytical opening as they illuminate the often confusing relation between residence and descent in Tibetan social organisation. Membership pathways indicate how patrilineal descent is an ideology – rather than a practice – in social life, house constitution and continuation.

The Trouble of Descent

Social organisation in communities across the Tibetan ethnographic region has been described through a range of principles and concepts, such as patrilineality and residence, unilateral and cognatic/bilateral kinship, or clans and households. While Tibetans often talk about the patrilineage (*rü gyü*) as significant for belonging and identity, I found that it had few, if any, practical implications for village life in Panam. In practice, *rü gyü*, which literally translates as the 'lineage (*rgyud*) of the bones (*rus*)', denotes the more general patrilateral kin in Central Tibet. Likewise, *sha gyü*, which literally translates as the 'lineage (*rgyud*) of the flesh (*sha*)', refers to matrilateral kin. These differences of lineage and laterality closely relate to the significance of clans among many Tibetan-speaking peoples in the Himalayas, and the absence of these in Central Tibet. Moreover, the practical use of the terms *rü gyü* and *sha gyü* points to significant differences in kinship ideology and practices of relatedness on the one side, and of kinship as constitutive of personhood and of social organisation on the other.

The ideological significance of patrilineal descent might suggest an organisation closer to unilineality with significant complementary filiation; yet, as in many ethnographic cases, in daily life a range of practices suggest other more relevant criteria for group formations. As with Central Tibetans in general, the villagers in Panam did not express much interest in their family's ancestors; they did not keep long genealogies of lineages. This does not mean that they were uninterested in the past, or in biographies. On the contrary, they kept a record of, discussed and emphasised the biographies of the named houses.

While people recognise different strengths of relatedness depending upon male or female links, for all significant purposes, links through both men and women, laterally and lineally, are important in Central Tibet. This is particularly apparent in the negative marriage rules, which, in principle, exclude all relatives as potential marriage partners; all those called *pa pün* (father's relatives) and *ma pün* (mother's relatives).[1] These are generic terms that include those related by *rü gyü* and *sha gyü*.

Kinship theory can be complex and perhaps confusing, but two points on the interconnections between the house and descent in Panam are most important in the following. First, the role of patrilineal descent as the language through which continuity of the corporate named houses is expressed, hence, the lineage does not generate the perpetuation of the group. Second, the strong presence of agnates within a house is caused not by patrilineal descent but by a cumulative past of patrifiliation.

Kinship Idioms of Flesh and Bone

Fundamental to the description of relatedness in Tibetan societies are the two elements in the folk theory of procreation, namely *rü* (bone) and *sha* (flesh). Of these, *rü* is considered most important, both in terms of the biological constitution of the body, as well as the social implications of the sharing of bones. *Rü* is a polysemantic concept that refers not only to the physical bones but also to patrilateral kindred and in some cases hereditary status.

Male Connections

It is difficult to find an English equivalent to the concept of *rü*, but the various levels of meaning could be fruitfully explained in terms of kinship and in particular patri-biases in Tibetan notions of relatedness. In an article from 1981, Levine discusses the interrelations between the various meanings of *rü*, pointing to the multilayered character of the term. Her descriptions from Nyin in Nepal share many similarities with how villagers in Panam explain the fundamental meanings of the concept. As Levine notes, the root concept is 'bone' (of humans and animals), and, through the local theory of procreation, the bones form the basis for the other meanings of the term (ibid.: 55). The bones are transferred via the sperm from the father during intercourse and are manifested in the bones of the conceived child's body. This is also described in the second chapter of the Explanatory Tantra, one of the four tantras of Tibetan medicine: the father's reproductive fluids (*khuwa*) produce the bones (and a major part of the brain (*rüpa lé*)).[2] This implies that *rü* is transferred directly from one generation to the next. The whiteness of the sperm is identified with the white bones and is transferred from father's father to father to children – that is, defining the patrilineage as constituted by those with the common *rü* (*rüpa*, ('bone people'), *rü chikpa,* ('one bone'), *rü gyü* ('bone lineage') or combinations of these).

Rü and its opposite *sha* have metonymic significance for the kinship categories for Tibetans. While Levine and others find the *rü gyü* to denote the patrilineage and in many cases named clans in various Tibetan communities in the Himalayas (Levine 1981; Fürer-Haimendorf 1964; Ramble 2008), this is misleading in Central Tibet. When talking to people in Panam, they did hold that *rü gyü* was exactly what it says, the lineage (*gyü*) of the bones – that is, patrilineage. In daily life, the terms *rü gyü* and *rü chikpa* and *pa pün* (father's relatives) were used interchangeably, and in the very few (ritual) cases where agnates gathered as a group, they did so as the generic *pa pün* – that is, as the patrilateral kin. Hence, while the *rü gyü* is both constitutive of personhood and an important organisational element in other Tibetan

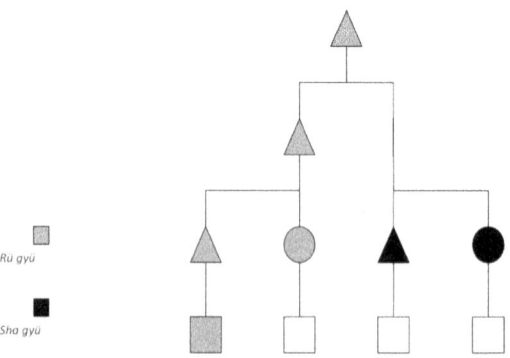

Figure 2.1. The bone (*rü*) and flesh (*sha*) 'lineage' (*gyü*). © Heidi Fjeld

communities, its organisational force was very limited in the Panam case. The bones constitute the matrix of a person's body, and is foundational for a person's physical and mental abilities. Hence, the sharing of bones implies an expectation of similarity both in the physical features and in personality. This similarity is also central to the arrangement and organisation of fraternal polyandry.

Female Connections

While bones make up the matrix of a person's body, flesh (*sha*) is less constitutive of both personhood and social relations. The solidarity and emotional closeness that is expected among those sharing bones is less relevant when sharing flesh. Moreover, while those of common bones can inform group formation, although it does so in very few situations, common flesh does not.

The links formed through *sha* are less clear, and therefore, perhaps explanations of female connections are more diverse and divergent. The *sha*[3] is the manifestation of the (red) menstrual blood of the mother in the child's body, which is also clearly described in the same chapter of the Explanatory Tantra: the mother's reproductive substances (*datsen*) produce flesh and blood (*sha trak*) and the vital and vessel organs. However, while a child receives the bones from the father and the soft substances from the mother, in Panam, the notions of transfer differ. These differences have organisational implications, and it was in the context of discussion of kin groups that the issue of transfer came up. In this understanding, bones are transferred in a direct line through the male links, but the flesh is transferred only indirectly: the menstrual blood of the mother is a manifestation of the bones that she received from her father. In this perspective, flesh is transmuted *rü* from the mother's father, via the mother's menstrual blood, and thus her menstrual blood does not originate from her mother's flesh. This understanding differs from theory of conception in Tibetan medicine, as seen in the Explanatory Tantra, where a woman's menstrual blood is clearly described as coming from her mother's menstrual blood and should be seen as a local lay interpretation.

The indirect transfer of bones through *sha* can help us understand the *sha gyü* and its potential organisational aspect. The *sha gyü* does not have lineal character and should be understood as denoting laterality only. In the case of an indirect transfer of flesh through the menstrual blood of the mother from the mother's father, the *sha gyü* cannot continue after the third generation. If we take one individual as the starting point and trace those of common flesh, we find a very limited distribution of people: namely siblings and siblings of the mother. These all share the transmuted *rü* from the mother's father.

If each woman indirectly transfers her father's *rü*, the *sha* will from the next generation come from elsewhere (from a new father's *rü*), and the common *sha* can thus not continue. Therefore, although *gyü* translates as 'lineage', the *sha gyü* should not be understood as a descent lineage as conventionally used in anthropology.[4]

When asking people in Sharlung about the meaning and relevance of the *sha gyü*, I often received vague answers. One woman told me that just as the *sha* does not inform the character of a person in a strong way, the *sha gyü* is also not very important to a social life of that person. The local notion of women's limited contribution to a child's body and its identity in terms of descent should not, however, lead us to overemphasise the importance of patrilineal groups. Tibetan kinship categories are patri-dominated in the emphasis put on *rü*, but the women, too, transfer *rü* by providing the flesh. Regardless, traditional principles of substance composition of the body should not be taken as evidence of agnatic organisation. Rather, this patrilineal emphasis is an indication of a significant distinction made between relatedness as constitutive of personhood, on the one side, and relatedness as informative to social organisation, on the other. While *rü* predominated in the notion of personhood, it did not generate significant group formation in Panam.

The *rü gyü* and the *sha gyü* are thus of different character, as the *rü gyü* can be termed a descent lineage in anthropological terms, while *sha gyü* cannot. They are, however, equally important to keep track of. While agnates often are of immediate relevance to each other in daily life, those belonging to the same *sha gyü* are not. There are several obvious reasons for this; first *sha gyü* consists of very few people, who are often separated by significant distances due to post-marital residence patterns, and second the emphasis put on the internal strength of the group that shares residence in the house. Because a woman usually moves in with her husband(s), she joins a group of house members (*nangmi* (family, insiders)) who are siblings of the same mother(s) and father(s) (*pachik machik*). Polyandrous marriages therefore increase the number of people related by patrilineal descent in a house.

I came across very little concern with pedigrees and genealogies among people in Panam, beyond lateral relations. Patrilineal descent was used as an expression of continuity and a legitimisation, in the sense that an influential house should ideally manifest an unbroken patrilineage. The consequences of lineal ruptures were few, if any. The lineal implications of a *makpa* marriage can serve as an example. While in some Tibetan-speaking communities in the Nepal Himalayas, such as among Sherpas, the lineage of the household into which *makpa* marries changes upon his arrival (so that his children share his patrilineage), this was irrelevant in Sharlung. Rather than descent, then, residence – the fact of sharing a house – forms close relations, not only in the everyday but also in questions of filiation, inheritance, rights and duties. Trajectories to house membership enlighten these connections and consequences.

Membership by Virtue of Filiation

Independent of sex, all those born into a house gained formal membership and had the right to remain in that house for life. When asking about rules, I was told that those born into a house should ideally share the same bones (*rü*), through patrifiliation. However, patrilineal descent was not the only decisive factor for membership, and there were many exceptions to this ideal pattern. Matrifiliation and other bilateral kinship relations were easily accepted as a legitimate source of membership, and both sons and daughters could remain as members so long as they were not incorporated into another house. In fact, being the offspring of a house member automatically granted membership.

Again, normatively, a house should consist of an unbroken patrilineage where at least one son had remained in his natal home and produced male heirs. However, membership by virtue of bilateral filiation included not only the male heir but also his unmarried sisters and their children. This pattern was evident in all generations; so that (from a male ego) the father's unmarried sisters and children might also be full members in his house, despite not sharing the bones (*rü*) with their co-house members and belonging to a different patrilineage. These relations were not seen to be problematic. Because a woman indirectly transfers the bones of her patrilineage through her menstrual blood, transmuted into the soft substances (*sha*) of her child's body, her child is (indirectly) connected to the patrilineage and, as such, also to the house. Nevertheless, when asked about the membership of an unmarried woman's children in her natal house, people in Sharlung told me that these children's membership depended not on the *sha* connection to *rü* but was rather by virtue of being born by a member (man or woman) of the house, again highlighting the value of bilateral filiation over lineage.[5]

Daughters of a house gained membership by birth, and they remained members until they married out. High incidents of polyandry logically imply a surplus of unmarried women in a specific area of study. This was also the case in Sharlung and its neighbouring villages, where the majority of houses hosted an unmarried daughter. I was not able to get sufficient data to provide figures of unmarried women in Sharlung, but Ben Jiao found that in the township centre, '30.6 % of the women aged 30 years or older were unmarried and 21% of these were never married' (2001: 121), and Childs, Goldstein and Wangdui reported that when they surveyed three villages in

Panam in 2006, 27% of women aged 25–39 were unmarried (2011: 7). By contrast, Ben Jiao notes that only three men had not married by the age of thirty: one celibate monk, one man with a disability and 'one man that never married' (2001: 121).[6] In Sharlung, there were three main categories of unmarried women: spinsters residing in their natal home, nuns ordained in the local nunnery and single women (widows, divorcees or never-married) that lived in a household alone with or without their children.

As a source of house membership, filiation is not differentiated according to gender, and women transfer rights to their children. Matrifiliation is effectuated not only in situations when there is no male heir but also in cases where a sister shares residence with her brothers and their family.[7] Spinsters residing in their natal home often complicated household dynamics, and although they remained external to the reproductive core of a house, they often held an authoritative position by maintaining close relations with natal kin, particularly mother, sometimes leading to conflict with the sister-in-law, the *nama* in the house. Some of the unmarried women residing at home in Sharlung were nuns, ordained in the local nunnery but living at home. The word for nun, *ani*, is also the word for father's sister, indicating a long history of overlap between these two categories of unmarried women. In 2002, fifteen out of the 44 households in Sharlung hosted an ordained nun. This is a high number, also compared with the neighbouring villages, and reflects the rebuilding of the local nunnery. After ordination, all the nuns in Sharlung remained as members of their natal houses, independent of degree of participation in household activities or their actual place of living.

For Panam, then, filiation both describes more accurately the process of recruitment into the local corporate groups and indicates the relation between descent and these corporate groups. The idea of filiation, rather than descent, as an organising principle is a long-term concern in anthropological kinship studies; however, it has not solved the challenges of describing an organisation over time.[8] Already in the 1950s, Fortes pointed out that filiation denotes merely the 'relationship created by the fact of being a legitimate child of one's parents' (1959: 206), while descent is the ideological rule that 'states which of the two elementary forms of filiation and what serial combination of forms of filiation shall be utilized in establishing pedigrees recognized for social purposes' (ibid.: 207). This distinction is still useful. In Panam, house membership was defined by virtue of bilateral filiation, and in the case of patrifiliation this was also expressed as patrilineal descent. However, while filiation describes the process of membership, it cannot properly explain the development of an organisational pattern in which the corporate groups perpetuate themselves. In similar ways to what Barnes (1962) suggested in his classic study of the patri-dominated groups in the highlands of Papua New Guinea, also in Panam people stated a cultural preference for the father's group, and at the same time, a cumulative past of affiliations (what Barnes called 'cumulative patrifiliation') have resulted in the co-residence of agnates. There was an emphasis on the importance of father's group (*pa pün*) also in Panam, and in addition, patrifiliation had been strengthened in recent history. The increasing emphasis and preference for patrifiliation informs and is informed by the re-emergence of polyandry, leading to a process of cumulative patrifiliation, which again implicates the co-residence of individuals belonging to the same patrilineage. At the same time, the surplus of unmarried women in a community with a high percentage of polyandry also affects the composition of the residence groups, as these (unmarried) women occasionally give birth to children (belonging to a different patrilineage) who also become members of their mother's house. These parallel processes indicate an analytical perspective that goes beyond descent and cumulative patrifiliation to a more holistic perspective that encompasses the various aspects of kinship and group formation. A remaining important question is the relation between descent and residence in Panam. If we take the value of the patrilineage to be primarily ideological to the continuation of the house, the role of unmarried daughters is peripheral. Yet, when recruiting new members and considering the household composition of a house, descent is given some importance beyond the issue of belonging. These new members are primarily incorporated through marriage, or in some cases, by adoption.

Membership by Virtue of Marriage

Independent of the type of marriage arranged, the new partner became a formal member of her or his new house. Although personal relations persisted after marriage – including the continued offering to the natal deity (*kye lha*) – the relocating partners renounced their previous house membership. Membership by marriage involved participation in both production and reproduction and was, as such, an important way to secure the perpetuation of the house and to maintain and develop the estates connected to the household. As elsewhere in Tibet and its borderlands, all three post-marital residence options were practised in Sharlung. Patrilocal, matrilocal or neolocal norms can be ascribed upon a marriage arrangement; it depends on the motivation for marriage, the people involved, and from whom the marriage initiative has come. People in Sharlung described that patrilocal residence was the most common, whereby the woman becomes a member and takes the name and identity of her husband(s)' house. Hence, when Yangchen, a young woman from another village in Panam valley, married into the Kyiling house, she was from then on referred to as Kyiling Yangchen (or Kyiling *nama*), and Potri, marrying into Norkhang house, was referred to as

Norkhang Potri, etc. Other practices exist, people said, but these were ad hoc solutions to unfortunate situations, such as lack of a male heir (resulting in matrilocal residence) or a young couple that has fallen in love and initiated their own marriage (which most often resulted in neolocal residence). In spite of the sense of exception that people expressed concerning matrilocal and neolocal residences, these were nevertheless traditional practices fully valid and constitutive of legitimate marriages and households. In Sharlung village, of the 51 marriages registered, 55 per cent were residing patrilocally, while 15 per cent matrilocally and 30 per cent neolocally. These figures indicate that although patrilocal residence was the ideal, it was still only describing little more than half of the cases. However, these numbers do not reflect the original arrangement of the marriage, as many of the neolocally residing couples had moved away as a result from conflicts in a former patrilocal marriage.

When, then, is matrilocality practised? *Makpa* marriages are very common the Tibetan ethnographic region. In some border areas, such as Gyethang in Yunnan, post-marital matrilocal residence is normative (Corlin 1978), but in Tibet, *makpa* marriages are most often arranged in cases where a family has no sons, or, occasionally, when parents decide to transfer the land to a daughter and her husband. While an in-marrying wife (*nama*) marries one or several men who reside with their parents and who are the legitimate heirs to the house estate, a *makpa* marries a woman with no resident brothers, and he becomes the legitimate heir to his wife's house estate. Although not the ideal, *makpa* marriages were an unproblematic event for established houses in Sharlung. A *makpa* did not in any ways weaken the (sense of) continuity of a house. In fact, while the introduction of a new patrilineage has some consequences for internal house dynamics, it does not in any substantial way influence social standing, reputation or external inter-house relations.

A *makpa*, like a *nama*, became the legitimate heir to household leadership in his generation. For *makpas*, there are usually no other men of his generation present in the house, and as such the power relations differ greatly from those experienced by *namas*. The *makpa* is invited to become the new household leader, and once included into the house, his origin as an outsider is seldom made relevant. A *makpa* is often referred to in the literature as an 'adopted bridegroom'.[9] In Sharlung, however, a *makpa* was not described as 'adopted' (*butsap*), and there were no attempts to conceal his different patrilineal origin. Rather, as in the case of the *nama*, his natal house was a source of potentially valuable reciprocal relations. Moreover, with unaltered lineage status, sexual relations with his patrilateral and matrilateral kin remained incestuous also after his inclusion into a new house. However, the name of the house into which he marries became his upon inclusion, in similar ways as a *nama*.

Ideally, gender is crucial to the continuity of an estate in the sense that only men hold the right to inherit land. The various marriage alternatives reflect the drive to find a male heir to the house, which can be done by filiation, inviting a *makpa* or, as we shall see, by adoption. Generally speaking, men inherit houses, women do not.

Membership by Virtue of Adoption

As in many societies, replacement of children, either for fostering or adoption, is a common and accepted practice in Tibet. The word *butsap* refers to those children who have permanently relocated to non-biological parents and who, upon inclusion into a new house, have gained full inheritance rights. *Bu* translates as 'child' and 'boy' and *tshab* as 'replacement' or 'substitute' (Goldstein 2001: 876), which indicates the secondary or solutional character of the arrangement. Earlier sources indicate that pre-1950 adoption was particularly common among the upper classes – that is, the aristocracy and the landholders (Petech 1973) as well as within the families of monk officials (Goldstein 1989: 8–9). In Sharlung, adoption was often found in the poorer households. While succession, and the continuity of the house lineage, was an important motivation for adoption among the upper classes pre-1950, in Sharlung people talked about adoption as a way to change household composition, and as a source of labour and care.

While fostering conventionally involves parents looking after someone else's child, adoption in addition involves 'kinning' of the child into the fostering parents' kin network (Howell 2006). Adoption as practised in Central Tibet is an in-between category that involves incorporation into a social group but kinning only to a limited extent. More precisely, upon adoption in Sharlung a person became a full member of a house – that is, he or she gained formal, unlimited inheritance rights. However, this inclusion did not obscure the biological origin of the adoptee, and relations were not expressed in kinship idioms.[10] Howell defines adoption to be 'the practice whereby children, for various reasons, are brought up by adults other than their biological parents and are treated as full members of the family amongst whom they live' (Howell 2006: 52). This definition is broad and only differs from fostering in the latter point of the children being 'treated as full members of the family amongst whom they live'. Membership, and the process of becoming a formal member, is of crucial importance for understanding adoption, and Howell suggests elsewhere that such a study would fruitfully focus on what she calls 'kinning' (2003b). She defines 'kinning' as 'the process by which a foetus or new-born child (or a previously unconnected person) is brought into a significant and permanent relationship with a group of people that is expressed in a kin idiom' (2003: 465). 'Kinning', Howell argues, is a universal process that ensures intersubjective relatedness. Central to this is what she calls transubstantiation – that is, 'the substance (biological body) remains; the social essence (being, self) is changed' (ibid.: 470). By such transubstantiation, she argues, an adoptee is kinned, and their relation is expressed in an idiom of kinship.

In Panam, there were adoptees in several households, the majority of whom were adopted at the beginning of the 1960s. This reflects the political events of that time whereby the local monasteries and nunneries were forced to close and many monks and nuns were subsequently adopted into households of relatives. Adoption was then a way to secure household membership while being able to refrain from marriage, and hence not break their monastic vows.[11] Later, these former monks, and particularly nuns, formed their own small satellite households (*khangchung*) within the house that they were adopted into. In order to form a viable household while at the same time continuing celibacy, many preferred adoptions as a solution to the need for household expansion. These cases point to the value of adoption as a strategy to increase labour capacity and care, in addition to the more well-known motivation of securing an estate by succession. In the more recent cases of adoption, arranged after 1980, these motivations worked together. The Magnub house in Sharlung can serve as an example.

Managing Poverty

Magnub was a very small household, consisting of one monogamously married couple with little land. The woman, Drolkar, had been a *yokpo* before the Chinese invasion, working for different landholders in the village. Around 1960, she married Dawa, a former monk of Sachung monastery who was forced to disrobe during the first reforms in 1959. Dawa was a relative of Dagpo, the *genpo* house that Drolkar had worked most for. This was the period of the Democratic Reforms redistribution, and the couple received a small house in the western part of the village (called Magnub) and some arable land from the local government (that was shortly after reorganised into collectives). Years passed and Drolkar did not become pregnant, and because they needed assistance for agricultural and domestic work, they decided to try to adopt a child. To give away a child was seen to be a loss, and a gift, and should therefore ideally be a transfer between people of close (*nyebo*) relations. In practice, a relocation of a child primarily happened between relatives. Drolkar had few relatives, and the only ones she felt she could ask had three sons but were not willing to relocate any of them. Thus, the only option they had was to ask Dagpo, Dawa's matrilateral relatives and Drolkar's former employer, who had twelve children (five sons and seven daughters).

To ask for a child, Drolkar and Dawa brought *chang*, tea bricks and *kathak* (white ceremonial scarfs) to the leader of Dagpo. According to Drolkar, the process went smoothly, and Dagpo agreed that they could have Tendöl, his twenty-year-old unmarried daughter. Tendöl, bringing only some new clothes provided by her parents, moved into Magnub shortly after. She stayed with them for several years and was also recognised as part of the household during the Household Responsibility System, a reform that then provided Magnub with fields for three persons. Because they needed cash income at that time, Drolkar and Dawa decided to send Tendöl to find work in Lhasa. While in Lhasa, she met a man, they married, and she settled in the city. With Tendöl disconnected from Drolkar and Dawa, they found themselves in need of labour and help in the house again. The two were getting older and concerned about their health, so they decided to ask Dagpo to adopt another girl. The leader of Dagpo, having six unmarried daughters still living at home, agreed to the relocation of Sedön, one of his younger daughters, to Magnub. They were very happy about this, Drolkar told us, as Dawa's health was declining, and Sedön was a kind and caring person.

After two years, Dawa unfortunately passed away, and Sedön remained with Drolkar. Drolkar wanted to arrange a marriage for her, but because they were poor, they could not afford to invite a *makpa*. At this particular time, Drolkar's relatives, who had already arranged a polyandrous marriage for their three sons, went through some difficulties. The youngest husband, Tsering, was unhappy and wanted to split from the marriage. Drolkar suggested to her relatives that she could adopt him, and, if they liked each other, he could marry Sedön. They agreed, and Tsering moved in with them in Magnub. Although marriage was intended, they defined him as an adoptee (*butsap*) rather than *makpa*. A year later, however, Tsering and Sedön did marry, and they later had three children.

Two purposes for adoption can be accentuated in this case: that of labour and care (Sedön) and that of marriage and succession (Tsering). While the first type was common, the latter was less so. As already described, the 'adoption' of a husband (*makpa*) to marry a home-residing daughter was both a widespread and well-established practice, but there is a nuance of difference between a *makpa* and a *bustap* who later becomes a *makpa*.[12] The distinction lies in the intention, in the structural implication of the relocation, and in the exchange of gifts involved. In the process of negotiation and relocation, the type of relation manifests, either as affines or adoptees. While affines have a formal and agreed upon relation informed by a morality of mutuality (by gifts and structures of assistance), adoption involves a time-specific and one-directional relation – that is, the biological parents transfer the child, and the giving and receiving part has very limited formal obligations. The inherent power structures of a wife-giver and wife-taker relation, on the one side, and of the biological and adoptive parents, on the other, significantly differ. Marriage is arranged among (ideally, and often in practice) houses of equal rank, but in Sharlung adoption was often a transfer from an affluent to a poor house. The example of Magnub and Dagpo illustrates social inequality between those adopting and those providing an adoptee – also an aspect of the local rationale of the monomarital principle and economic diversification. In a social organisation informed by these principles, certain individuals are structurally peripheral (unmarried women and excess sons outside the core marriage of the house, for instance, as I will return to in Chapters 3 and 4), and for these, adoption can be one strategy for house membership. In Sharlung, houses with a large group of children tended to be wealthier, as a large household enables economically diverse strategies for income. Occasionally, and in times of crisis, the resource-poor adopters could ask the natal house of the adoptees for help, however, they were not obliged to respond, and in many cases they did not. As such, inviting a *makpa* and asking for an adoptee was different in the temporal and formal aspect of the relation between giver and receiver. While an affinal relation was formal and long-term, and included expectations of mutual assistance, an adoption relation was not. Yet, as a one-time transfer, adoption was formal and recognised by both families involved and by the village leadership.

The Limits of Adoption

Butsap was clearly a means to balance labour. An adoptee was recognised as a full member of the house into which he or she moved, including the entitlement to inheritance. Adoption was also socially and culturally accepted. However, adoption in Sharlung involved limited efforts to kin the adoptee into a network of relatives of the adoptive parents, and their relations are not clearly expressed in kin idioms. Tendöl and Sedön were not kinned, in Howell's terms; Sedön and Drolkar did not use daughter-mother terms to address each other, and in the same way, Tsering did not call Drolkar mother; they both used the term for 'elderly woman' (*achi*), in the same way outsiders would. Being included into the social group through kinning (into the kin network) involved, in the case of Sedön and Tsering, a process of what we can perhaps call 'housing'– that is, of being incorporated into the house (and the house network). As house membership is exclusive, Sedön and Tsering were formal members in Magnub only, and as such, the past memberships of their natal houses were no longer of significance. Upon inclusion, the new members are 'housed' in the sense that their natal belonging is made irrelevant for the present identification with a local group. When Tendöl, Sedön and Tsering moved into Magnub, this became the name by which they identified themselves and were identified by others. Upon inclusion, and with time, the new members (and particularly Tsering) came to represent the house in external affairs, such as the village meetings, participation in mutual aid networks, and in labour exchange. Indeed, they became formal house members.

Adoption potentially represents a challenge to the epistemology of relatedness in Tibet, as the idiom of kinship is grounded in a biological connectedness of shared substance (bones, and to a lesser degree, flesh). However, this biocentric idiom of kinship does not exclude other forms for incorporation into a house, and kinship understood as filiation is only one of several sources of formal membership. Cohabitation formed their group identity and sense of belonging, and it is interesting that so little effort was made to kin their relations through language; the process of kinning but did not involve an effort to make an adopted relation resemble a relation of bones (shared substance). Although they were fully incorporated into the Magnub, the fact that Tendöl and Tsering did not violate the incest taboo by marrying each other illustrates the limited degree of kinning in the incorporation process. Lack of emphasis on biological resemblance, or transubstantiation, is another indication that inconsistent lineage relations are unproblematic for kinship epistemology and practice. In the *butsap* process, this biological connectedness was never challenged, and no ritual activities were performed to mark the transfer of parenthood.

There was no negative stigma associated with adoption. Yet, there were significant efforts to incorporate the adoptee into the house. The daily activities of a common economic endeavour – co-residence (including nurture and participation in ritual activities of the house), inclusion into a network of kin (for mutual assistance and other houses) and, most importantly, the defining of the adoptee to be the legitimate heir to the house – are all signifiers in terms of a kinning process. Although not expressed in a kinship idiom (such as mother/daughter/son), those residing together, the adoptee and the adopters, shared a house name, which served as the most important marker of identity and belonging. Moreover, the post-adoption position was permanent and identical to that of being an heir by virtue of filiation, and their individual rights (most importantly inheritance) were not contested; neither within the household nor outside. As Howell has pointed out: 'adoption is what adoption does' (2006: 77), and in the case of Panam, *butsap* enables the transfer of rights and obligations associated with a formal membership to a previously unconnected person. By doing so, *butsap* is juxtaposed with filiation and marriage as a trajectory to house membership.

Sources of Membership and Structural Positions

The source of membership is contextually relevant in the intra-house organisation and must be understood as closely connected to the structural position of the individual, gender and relative age. Social organisation in agricultural Tsang is ideologically patri-dominated, but filiation provides the structurally central positions within a house in Sharlung – that is, sons of the male household leader are entitled to the house by succession. This is particularly true for communities with a high incident of fraternal polyandry, where the cultural rationale is that of maximising male labour within the established unit by limiting the centripetal effects of new household establishments in each generation. Further, fraternal polyandry keeps a group of brothers together, a highly valued concern that reflects local perceptions of consubstantial relatedness. At the same time, marriage and adoption can also provide structurally central positions for the individual. Depending upon life phases, women and younger brothers share the fate of being in potentially peripheral positions and thus depend more upon personal attributes and abilities to make alliances with influential house members. Hence, the positions of members from all sources are vulnerable in some periods, albeit to varying extent. In the two chapters that follows, we move into polyandrous marriages and look at how relative age and gender is crucial in the individual negotiation and consolidation of positions in these rather complex ways of life.

Notes

1. See Samuels (2021) for a critical discussion on incest taboos and negative marriage rules in Tibetan history.
2. I am grateful to Tawni Tidwell for the references to, and comments about, the stanzas on bone and flesh in the Gyüshi.
3. In some Tibetan-speaking communities, such as Nyinba, identify the substance from the mother's body to be blood (*trak*) (see Levine 1981). In Panam, *trak* has no metonymic significance in terms of kinship recognition.
4. See Levine (1981); Diemberger (1993) for more details.
5. Membership by bilateral filiation was also expressed in the post-birth treatment of the placenta. The placenta of all children born by members of the house is buried into a hole in the courtyard; as such, each child was anchored to the house and physically connected to their same-house relatives – that is, to the 'insiders' (*nangmi*) (see also Carsten 2004: 44).
6. In her study of Chumik in the Nepal Himalaya, Schuler (1987) argued that the high percentage (44 per cent) of unmarried women cannot be explained only as an implication of polyandry. In Chumik, a surplus of unmarried women was also an implication of patrilineality and primogeniture, various forms of endogamy and the categories of legitimate and illegitimate birth, rendering women as peripheral in the social and economic contexts.

7. When an unmarried woman became pregnant, she commonly established a new household with the child's father. Because most men were married in a polyandrous organisation, in such a situation he thus left his brothers and wife in order to start a new household.
8. See, for instance, Barnes (1962).
9. See Bell (1928) and Stein (1972) for early examples. Among Sherpas in Khumbu, the in-marrying man is called 'adopted groom', *makpa butsap* (Diemberger, personal communication, Montreal, 2011).
10. In addition, fostering also occurred, although for shorter periods, but because it did not involve membership, I leave out the topic here.
11. According to one former monk in Sachung, the vows must be 'returned' (through a particular ritual) upon disrobing, in order to avoid the multiplication of the effects that the robes provide. This was particularly important when breaking the vows, as the negative effects of this sinful behaviour would be increased if done with the vows. Returning the vows was not allowed in the 1960s; thus, many of the former monks and nuns refused to engage in sexual activities. In Panam, some of the former Sachung monks collectively returned their old vows in the mid-1980s.
12. In *The Navel of the Demoness*, Ramble describes similar, yet different, blurred lines between adoption and marriage in Te village in highland Nepal. In Te, due to a concern about the lack of availability of marriage partners in the future, it was common to arrange 'child marriage', a process in which the child also relocated to her/his future partner's parents' house. The child, Ramble notes, 'will be brought up as a member of the family, and a relationship between playmates will evolve into a marital union'. 'Child marriage (more accurately, perhaps, child betrothal involving a change of residence)', he continues, 'is a means of ensuring that a household has heirs who will themselves produce heirs' (2008: 115).

Chapter 3

FRATERNAL RELATIONS

Polyandrous marriages involve complex constellations of people. They entail close cooperation among numerous individuals and ask each and every one to accept and prioritise a collective goal. The role distribution is relatively clear in a polyandrous marriage, based on the principles of gender and relative age. Yet, through navigation and negotiation, roles are adjusted and altered, enabling individuals to make their own way in married and household life. In the history of Tibet and the Himalayas, polyandry has been arranged for two or more brothers. There are no moral prohibitions against including non-related co-husbands as such; however, belonging to the same house is at the core of the cultural logics of polyandry and hence motivates the arrangement itself. In addition, by being of the same bones and flesh and thereby constituted by the same essential substances, brothers are very closely related, and brotherhood is associated with loyalty and solidarity, something often mentioned when people in Sharlung talked about polyandry. However, consubstantiality (i.e. being of the same substance) does not exclude the possibility of hierarchy, and rank and authority among brothers are clearly structured, both in the case of co-husbandship and beyond. The basic structuring principle within a same-sex sibling group is relative age, and while there are contextual possibilities for role formation and negotiation, the superior position of the eldest brother is largely undisputed. These hierarchies are internalised, embodied and enacted through childhood, and rarely questioned.

Siblings from the same mother and father are, by the precreation theory of flesh and bone, are the closest relatives, and especially those of the same sex in a sibling group are expected to have strong emotional connections. Perceptions of brotherhood, then, are important to polyandrous practices. Levine argued that fraternal solidarity was pivotal to the motivation for polyandry among Nyinba (1988: 9, 278),[1] showing that the relation between brothers has its roots in stories of the past; the myths about their ancestors portrayed these as brothers who were linked by polyandry in a time characterised by family harmony (ibid.: 159). Perceptions of consubstantiality and the following expectations of sameness, closeness, solidarity and common interests were also evident in Panam, seen in daily life practices of friendship, affection and care, inside and outside married life. Brothers are not only co-husbands; they can also share extra-marital relations.[2] Similarly, Levine found that young Nyinba brothers shared premarital sexual relations (ibid.: 9). 'Brothers', an elderly woman told to me, 'like to stay together'.

Among brothers, relative age is made apparent as a principle for rank from early childhood. The superiority of the eldest son is seen in many aspects of domestic life, such as in distribution of food during meals, clothing, in expressed affection – cuddling and attention – and in access to healthcare (see Levine 1987a, 1987b). When arranging a marriage, relative age and the superiority of the eldest was reflected in the various stages leading up to the wedding and further into married life. In the initial period of marriage negotiations, the eldest brother (*genshö*) often visited (in disguise) the potential *nama* and investigated, accepted or rejected his parents' suggestion on behalf of his brothers. The younger brothers did not have this opportunity, and in the case of the *genshö* being absent, the task was simply not performed. During the wedding ceremony, the *genshö*'s dominant position was acknowledged with the *nama* being seated on his left side and his brothers on his right side, again organised according to relative age. The eldest husband can thus be seen as the mediator and connector between the *nama* and his co-husbands. Moreover, on the night of the wedding, the *nama* stayed with the *genshö*, who initiated sexual life of the marriage. Often the *nama* would stay the following nights with the younger husbands, also organised according to age. Later, it was the *genshö*, in cooperation with the *nama*, who decided the frequency and the distribution of the younger husbands' sexual access to their wife. While it was the responsibility of the *nama* to make everyone feel equally well-treated, there was an expectation that she would be closest, in terms of emotional bonds and frequency, to her eldest husband.

In early scholarship on polyandry, the different roles of the men and their relations to the married woman was a topic of much concern. This was due to the interest in marriage definitions mentioned in the Introduction, and it was often argued that these plural unions should not be termed marriage but should rather be seen as 'cicisbeism' (the married woman having a lover outside marriage) or 'polykoity' (or what we would now call polyamorous relations). Fisher (1952), for instance, claimed that the wife was married only to the eldest man in the fraternal group. The younger brother, Fisher argued, were merely co-residing with the monogamously married couple of their eldest brother. Today, however, there is no disagreement over defining these unions as marriages and all men included are recognised as husbands. However, it is clear that the positions of the co-husbands is ranked, their relation to the shared wife is different, and the younger husbands are thoroughly subordinated.[3] Although personal qualities and skills might be given preference in certain contexts, a husband could nevertheless always claim his rights based on his position in the age hierarchy.

Relative Age and Encompassment

Robert Hertz's classical article on 'The Pre-eminence of the Right Hand' (1973 [1909]) can help provide some insights on brothers as co-husbands, as parts in a whole. A central point Hertz made was that the relation between right and left is one of qualitative difference, and that fundamental aspects of these differences can be found not only in nature but also in religion and in the body. The different qualities of the right and the left hand are based on organic symmetry, wherein the right hand is in a position to stand for the whole body, and thus incorporates also the left hand. Hertz argued that this ability of the right hand to *stand for the whole* is crucial to its superior position. Louis Dumont, working on forms of hierarchies in South Asia, expanded on these ideas and suggested that the relations between the oppositions – that is, the relations of incorporation – should more precisely be seen as a particular kind of hierarchy. Dumont argued that the oppositions – the right and the left – cannot be defined in themselves but 'only in relation to a whole' (1979: 810). What Dumont called a hierarchical opposition is the opposition between a set and an element of this set, where the element is identical to the set of which it forms a part (ibid.: 809). Further, the element is also a contrariety to the whole, and as such is a double relation. This double relation connects to the nature of hierarchical opposition and informs Dumont's well-known conclusion that 'essentially, hierarchy is the encompassing of the contrary' (op. cit.; see also Dumont 1970: 66). Encompassment is a value, not in the sense that it is what is considered good but as 'that which structures the relations of elements in the whole' (Robbins 1994: 28). What Dumont calls the 'dominant value', then, is, Robbins writes, that 'element which in general encompasses its contrary' (op. cit.). A dominant value often comes to symbolically represent the whole – that is, the set of parts incorporated.

In Tibetan fraternal polyandry, we can conceptualise the eldest husband as the dominant value of the marriage. Co-husbandship is a hierarchical relation, in the Dumontian sense of the term, where the eldest husband encompasses the younger husbands, not only in the internal marital organisation but also in terms of symbolic representation. The eldest husband is not only the 'ultimate value' of the marriage but also of the social group they together constitute – that is, the house. Such encompassment could be seen in various contexts; in the wedding process and in the organisation of daily life, in distribution of labour and sex, and in the recognition and terminology of paternity. Moreover, in polyandrous marriages, the notion of encompassment provides a useful perspective on the handling of conflicts and resolutions that unfold in different ways when involving the eldest or the younger husband (Fjeld 2008a).

Distribution of Affection and Authority

Central to the success of a polyandrous marriage is a fair distribution of affection, including sexual access. Maintaining fairness was the common responsibility of the *nama* and the eldest husband but also a concern of the household leaders – that is, the parents (in-law). In Sharlung, it was the *nama*s who were commonly blamed for marital failures.

Upon marriage, a system for sexual distribution (*kora khor*) is defined. In this initial period, the *nama* often has only limited influence on the details of the arrangement. Many women described this as a period of feeling shy and embarrassed. *Kora khor* translates as 'going around in circles' and is the basic principle of sexual access in a polyandrous marriage. In cases, and phases, where the *nama* had a weak position, it was her eldest husband who administered the *kora khor*. However, after the first initial marital period, the *nama* was expected to participate in making these decisions. My interlocutors assessed that in Panam an arrangement where the *nama* had close cooperation with her eldest husband in the periods when he was present in the house and where she made independent decisions when he was absent was most widespread. There were, however, exceptions to this, depending on interpersonal dynamics.

There are several patterns into which sexual access can be distributed, depending upon the labour division among the co-husbands, structural elements of the interior of the house, the nature of the relations of the partners and the preferences of the *nama*. In the larger houses in Sharlung, the co-husbands and the wife had private sleeping rooms, while in houses with less space, the husbands often alternated where they slept. It was common for the *nama* to share a room with her eldest husband; indeed, this was a sign of a successful – a good – marriage. When discussing this with women, indeed many felt sad for *nama*s without their own room, indicating the vulnerability of their position and relations in the house. Below, I describe the four main ways to arrange *kora khor*.

The first type of *kora khor* was found in the many marriages that involved only two husbands, and where one of them worked outside the village for several months per year. In such cases, the husband that travelled would often stay with the wife in the whole period that he was home, while the home-based husband and the wife shared a room when they were alone. When both husbands were there, she would also visit the home-based husband but not frequently. More complex systems evolved when two or more husbands co-resided for the majority of the year. The second type of *kora khor* commonly practised in the early phase of a marriage involving two husbands was that the husbands and the wife each had separate rooms, and the wife alternated between sleeping in her room and the husbands' rooms. She might or might not decide how to alternate. Dikyi, a young woman in the village, told me that her two co-husbands worked together during most of the day (in the field, or elsewhere) and that they at some point during the day decided on the nightly arrangement, if any. When the evening set in, the designated husband would take his blanket to the wife's room, and, by recognising the blanket, she would know who she would be with. Moreover, Dikyi explained that although she did not dislike this system, she expected that in a few years' time – when her children were older and her position in the house more strongly consolidated – she would administer the *kora khor* on her own, although, she pointed out, she wanted to make sure that both husbands were content. In the third, and most common type of *kora khor*, the *nama* shared a room with her eldest husband (who may or may not work outside the village). Dikyi's neighbour Phundröl, had a more active role in defining the *kora khor*, despite also being in an early phase of her marriage. She had a strong position, both in relation to her parents-in-law, and to her three husbands, and came across as a confident and outgoing person. In her house, the spatial arrangement was such that Phundröl shared the sleeping room with her eldest husband while the other two husbands each had their own room. The eldest husband worked outside the village for more than four months per year, and in these periods, Phundröl would sleep alone and define the *kora khor* on her own terms. When he returned back home, she stayed with only him for two weeks, before returning to the regular *kora khor*. According to Phundröl, it had been she who suggested this system: 'of course I did', she said, and she had then asked her eldest husband if he agreed with her, which he did. Phundröl chose to move around her husbands' rooms. She was nursing one child, who slept in her room, while the other children slept in the kitchen/living room (*taptsang*) together with the grandparents. Independent of breastfeeding, Phundröl always returned to her (and her eldest husband's) room after completed intercourse with one of the younger husbands. When I asked if she had wished to share a room with her other husbands in the period when the eldest was travelling, she said: 'No. I have a better relation with the *genshö*.' The fourth type of *kora khor* is the clustering of sexual activities; a system where the *nama* visits all husbands during one night. This was rather uncommon, and talked about as an exception, and only practised in marriages with no more than three husbands. According to hearsay, two *nama*s in Sharlung preferred this system, and although it is accepted, other women did chat about it with some curiosity.

Despite being a collective concern in the household, sex was private. Some of these types of arrangement, particularly the arrangement where the husbands are visiting the *nama*'s room, were potentially embarrassing for those involved. Hence, there were several more or less discreet ways to indicate on-going sexual activity in a particular room, enabling others in the house to keep a distance. Two strategies can serve as an illustration. In Darkhang house, for instance, when the *nama* and one husband entered a room for sex, she put either the strap holding up her boots, or the belt on her *chuba* on the door, signalling the need for privacy. In other houses, women would put their boot straps on top of the blanket, indicating the same. Because there was no electricity in Sharlung at the time, the rooms were very dark at night; thus, the strap on the blanket was for people to be warned by touching the blanket if they had already entered the room. The practical signalling of on-going sexual activity did not only avoid what was seen to be an embarrassing situation but also displayed performance of *kora khor* for the others in the house, providing an indication to the household leaders.

To sum up, the distribution of emotional and sexual connections also reflects the special relation between the *nama* and the eldest husband. Women openly revealed having more affection for the eldest husband. The two held particular position with regards to the future, as the next male and female heads of the household. Their cooperation was crucial for the future of the house, and much emphasis was put on enabling this, both between themselves and among the parent generation. Fair distribution of *kora khor* was an important part of affection and a collaborative sensibility also outside the conjugal unit.

The position of the eldest husband and his special relation to the *nama* was also reflected in the issues of paternity, although in a different way. The hierarchy and the symbolic relation between the brothers and co-husbands came to the fore in the question of paternity. The eldest husband symbolically stands for the group of fathers, and he is called '*pala*' (the conventional term for 'father' in all marriage forms). However, this did not mean that the other husbands were called *akhu* (father's brother/uncle).

Social Fatherhood but One *Pala*

In the known cases of fraternal polyandry, paternity is defined biologically, classificatory or socially, which, as Levine and Silk have argued (1997), very much influences the conflict level of polyandrous marriages. Levine's Nyinba ethnography indicates that a high level of conflict is found among those who openly identify biological paternity among the co-partners. The potential conflicts in this is based in the per stirpes inheritance system, where the land is transferred from a father to his biological child regardless of age hierarchy. These inheritance rules are also evident in Panam. In Sharlung, it was, however, taboo to identify openly the genitor of a child, and all children were recognised offspring of the marriage – that is, of all the husbands. Socially validated fatherhood, combined with internalised age hierarchy, contributed to a relatively low conflict level among co-husbands in Sharlung. The eldest husband's encompassment of the younger was reflected in the terminology used to denote paternity. The eldest is the classificatory father (*pala*), and his co-husbands are termed according to age, *ajok* (the middle) and *achung* (the younger). Thus, the younger husbands were not conceptually linked directly to fatherhood but rather to brotherhood yet clearly distinct from father's brothers outside marriage, called *akhu*. These terms that the children used for their fathers did not fully describe the relation between the eldest husband, his brothers and their offspring, because although only the eldest husband was termed 'father' by the conventional term, all husbands were recognised as not only social fathers (pater) but as genitors. This is also based on the flesh and bones idioms and consubstantiality of brothers.

All husbands were considered to contribute with male substance in the creation of a child born to the wife. Because male substance manifests in the bones of a child, and because the co-husbands are (ideally, and most often in practice) of the same patrilineage, the substance transferred from the co-husbands is seen to be the same; they are biologically identical. Thus, the explanation of fatherhood is connected to local understandings of biology on the one hand, and the constitution of a child's body on the other, emphasising consubstantiality of siblings of the same mother and same father(s) (*pachik machik*). *Pachik machik* is commonly used to describe siblings in monogamous marriages; however, siblings from polyandrous marriages, and thus children of different genitors, were also referred to by these same terms. Hence, the group of brothers/fathers were '*pachik*', suggesting socially validated fatherhood. Fatherhood is, however, more complex. All children of a particular marriage were seen to be 'fathered' by all their mother's husbands, not only socially but also in terms of providing the crucial genealogical matrix of the children; the precondition for this being that the mother (although she often knows) will not disclose who among her husbands is the genitor of a child.

Local procreation theory does not explicate plural genitors. Women are perceived to be fertile in a period of around five days (the fifth to the tenth day) in the menstrual cycle, which means that in a situation with several husbands present, the genitor cannot always be determined. My interlocutors shared the understanding that one intercourse is sufficient for conception; there were no notions of nurture by additional sperm for a successful impregnation (see also Diemberger 1993). Thus, each conception recognises only one genitor, however his identity was not revealed, neither in private nor in public. Being unaware of the genitor of a particular child is more than a lack of knowledge. Efforts were made to produce this ignorance about genitors. In the anthology *Anthropology of Ignorance*, High et al. (2012) argue that ignorance cannot be explained simply as negative, as the absence of knowledge, but rather as something that is produced through specific practices. Cultural production of ignorance is rather the 'production, out of the infinite sea of things that people happen to not know, of culturally recognized and elaborated units, fields, modes of ignorance' (2012: 33). The unknown genitor of polyandrous unions is an example of a culturally and socially produced ignorance. I often heard people talk about resemblance – which child resembles which father – however, always in playful and joking manner, and never confirming a connection. Although women did hint about likely genitors among themselves, they put much effort into keeping this information vague and away from men, and from becoming known in the public. They did not name the likely genitor within the house nor outside. In cases of two husbands only and where one was absent during parts of the year and therefore biological fatherhood would be easy to deduce, women could tell stories about the time of conception, a husband's travels and visits, or other activities that produced some, even if little, uncertainty. Even when, at some level, it would be rather obvious that only one of the husbands could have been the genitor, this is not explicitly produced to be a fact but rather undercommunicated and actively ignored. Several women told me that in daily life they would point to particularly strong emotional ties between one father and a child or hint about resemblance, often to emphasise other-than-genitor relations and also to produce ambiguity and uncertainty. As one man of a marriage with three husbands said: 'There is no way to know.' The production of ignorance is an important, and shared, effort to control jealousy and maintain a collective sensibility. Not even during divorces was this ignorance challenged, and I am not aware of any cases where fathers or mothers violated this norm.

Throughout my stays in the Takrab house, I tried to systematically observe father-children interactions, looking for indications of special bonds between what I found out were the biological fathers and their children. I have come to conclude that in the cases I was able to observe, having contributed male substance to a particular child does not define or affect father-child relation in a substantial way compared to relations to other children of the marriage. In some cases, the mother whispered to me who she held to be the genitor, and observing those father-child relations unfold, I found no signs of them being more emotionally attached to their children (see also Levine 1987b). All husbands were 'one father (*pachik*)', a group represented by the eldest, the *pala*. As such, the *pala* encompasses the *ajok* (the second eldest) and the *achung* (the younger), and he is not only a part of the whole ('one father') but his relation to the whole is of a particular kind. The *pala*, I suggest, symbolically stands for the whole. The paternal terminology thus refers indirectly to the relations between fathers and children, and directly to the relation between fathers, or co-husbands, and the house, as the eldest husbands not only encompass their brothers as co-husbands but also as the household leaders, and by that, the whole house.

Transfer of Leadership

The principle of relative age is confirmed in leadership relations and power transfer processes. Although there is always the possibility to negotiate and influence the ascribed positions within hierarchical relations, the foundation of the distribution of authority in polyandrous marriages remains for the most part unchallenged.

The leadership structure of a house was formalised and organised around a male (*sayön*) and a female leader (*nangma*), of which the former had general authority. The *sayön* ('the leader of the place)' or *khyimdak* ('owner of the house') was publicly recognised by the house members and the community. He was the ultimate leader of the house, who organised not only the daily (male) tasks, such as farming, herding and other off-farm activities and projects but also, for example, the future planning of the next generation's marriage. He acted on behalf of the house, maintaining mutual aid networks for funerals and weddings, and he represented the house in village obligations, including partaking in community work. In Sharlung, there was an unchallenged arrangement whereby house leadership was transferred from the *sayön* in one generation to the eldest man in the next generation. House leadership preconditioned marriage, and should the eldest son refuse a married life, he would not be eligible for the leader position. In an organisation based on a monomarital principle and following one household per house, the eldest husband also held a dominant position in the one and only marriage in his generation.

As with most stratified arrangements, age hierarchy between siblings is a cultural norm and is naturalised in Tibet. In our conversations, people simply explained the difference in influence and authority among brothers with the tautological truism that the eldest is more highly valued because he is more important, and further that it is natural that he is more important because he is the eldest. Age hierarchy sensibility is doxic, in Bourdieu's term – that is, a learned natural and social order that appears self-evident (1997: 164). From birth, the eldest son is placed in a superior position and taught to lead, while the younger brothers are placed in an inferior position and taught to look to the eldest for leadership and advice. During childhood, their parents explicitly show more affection for the eldest son; when the mother has cooked, he receives food first. Their sisters cuddle him often, listen to his stories and give him compliments for his achievements. Only seldom do younger brothers challenge the legitimate authority of the eldest; in cases of extreme incompetence, due to disability or addiction, or long-term periods of absence, it is acceptable for a younger brother to take over the *sayön* position, however this was said to be rare. I did not see examples of male household leaders who were not the eldest living member of their generation in Sharlung, although there were some female household leaders.

Polyandrous Masculinities

When brothers are co-husbands, certain types of masculinities are culturally produced and socially encouraged, particularly a type of collaborative masculinity. Yet, polyandrous relations, and co-husbandship, have not been explored in gender or men's studies. One might wonder why polyandry and polygyny are so seldom compared in the social sciences, and particularly why cross-gender comparisons in plural marriage are non-existent. Broadly speaking, both marriage forms include plural partners, both are justified through household composition and wealth (and labour or land, with the exception of Mormon polygyny), and both involve complex emotional and personal relations. Much has been written about co-wives but less about co-husbands (Goody 1982; Ember et al. 2007). One of the reasons for this difference is, of course, that the number of women who are co-wives in the world is much higher than the number of men who are co-husbands. In addition, I think the status of 'co-husband' challenges gender norms in ways that make us think about this phenomenon as an exception, especially in men's studies. Although men's studies are developing theories about different ways to enact maleness, to which co-husbandship could be a relevant case, the main interest in these studies has been the effects that different enactments of maleness have had on gender difference and inequality (Gutmann 1997). For instance, explorations of so-called hegemonic masculinities – normative masculinity that 'embodied the currently most honoured way of being a man' (Connell and Messerschmidt 2005: 832) – have remained focused on relations between men and women or, more concretely, the practices that legitimate 'the global subordination of women to men' (op. cit.). The notion of hegemonic masculinity implies a hierarchy that includes subordinated and alternative masculinities and a dominant position based on an internalised form of power. Co-husbands are, as we have seen, related through enactment of hierarchies, of naturalised dominance and authority, and the role of the eldest brother could in that sense be interpreted as an enactment of hegemonic masculinity.[4] After much critique, Connell and Messerschmidt suggested that a revised version of this concept recognises, first, the plurality of masculinities and, second, the hierarchy of masculinities – ideas, they argue, that have survived two to three decades of criticism. Certain masculinities, they write, 'are more socially central, or more associated with authority and social power, than others' (ibid.: 846). This hegemony is socially and culturally produced and continuously changing, challenged also by alternative masculinities, and leading to various constellations of gender relations. Women, and relations to women, are also central to the process of constructing these masculinities, as is clearly evident in the case of the husbands and their shared wife in polyandrous marriages too.

In the little research done on Tibetan masculinities, one type that is often described as hegemonic, or perhaps better termed a dominant masculine ideal, is a 'heroic' masculinity (Makley 2007), a potentially explosive masculinity that needs to be tamed. Hillman and Henfry (2006), interviewing Tibetans and Chinese living in Dechen (Kham, Yunnan province), found that the term *pho khyokha* was readily used in discussions about Tibetan masculinity, translating as something like a 'manly man' (ibid.: 261). Both heroic masculinity and *pho khyokha* are closely connected to the imaginary of a young nomad; wild, physically strong, virile and passionate, as well as loyal. Makley, exploring gender and masculinities in the rapidly urbanising Labrang, a monastic power centre in the mostly pastoral Amdo region in north-eastern Tibet, found that (among other complex forms of lay and monastic masculinities) 'the most basic aspect of heroic masculinity in practice was the assumption that young men were naturally compelled to engage in violent competitions with other young men, and to pursue sexual encounters with women' (2007: 243). In Labrang, young men were expected to 'learn to channel' this 'explosive potential', and this taming is achieved through homosocial and patrifilial relations, which are expressed in loyalty (op. cit.). Male superiority, Makley argues, is less about the ability to control women and more about the ability to move out of the domestic sphere and connect (the household) with larger (translocal) networks – networks that are formed through homosocial relations and activities. Monkhood, which has been an alternative status for Tibetan men, is also a channelled masculinity, she argues, tamed through the ritualised transition performed through ordination. Hillman and Henfry also found that monks were perceived to be *pho khyokha* – the physical strength associated with lay masculinity was then interpreted as the strength of the mind, and in being able to 'abstain from certain worldly pleasures' (2006: 266). Both Makley's study and Hillman and Henfry's studies are from Tibetan areas close to, or associated with, nomadic communities – areas that are far from Panam, not only in geographical distance but also in ways of life. However, these masculinities are produced in a broader context, too; a context that is partially shared by Tibetans across the PRC. Perceptions of Tibetan masculinities are (in)formed by the context of the official transcript of Tibetans as the ethnic (minority) Other, also among farmers in Central Tibet, and the 'young nomad man' is very close to the Chinese representation of Tibetanness (especially since the end of the 1990s) (Louie 1992; Makley 2010). As Connell and Messerschmidt argue, broadly speaking, masculinities are produced through the interplay of local, regional and global levels, and indeed, the (regional) representations of not only 'Tibetan' as an ethnic minority in China but also 'Tibetan man' in Tibet as *pho khyokha* – the sturdy, untamed nomad – provide a cultural framework that might come into play in daily lives and interactions (ibid.: 849) – that is, as gendered practices in particular localities, such as in agrarian Panam.

The dominant ideal in the context of polyandry is a collaborative masculinity, in which the enactment of maleness maintains both amicable homosocial relations within and outside the household, as well as with the wife. Yet, there are multiple masculinities at play – including what could be termed heroic, on the one hand, and caring, on the other – all of which were normative ways of being a man in Panam. Yet, the sense of a tamed or channelled 'explosive' masculinity prone to violence and sex, as described from Amdo and Kham, does not resonate strongly with dominate masculine ideals in Panam. The image of the horse-riding wild nomad circulates there too, but more as a figure in films and stories, and serves, in some ways, as an Other. Especially Khampa men are talked about as wild, unpredictable and difficult to trust – based also on experiences with business interactions in Panam villages – and are examples of a masculinity that would undermine polyandry. The eldest brother, the person of doxic authority, enacts maleness in a way that emphasises control and decisiveness – enabling collaboration – which could be seen as the dominant masculine ideal in Panam. The production of collaborative masculinity is inherent in the treatment of boys while growing up, yet this is associated with both a heroic and caring masculinity. Naughty boys were seen to be funny, and this wildness was also encouraged, indicating the need for some process of taming into adulthood. Yet, this wildness was less associated with a potential to 'engage in violent competitions' and to 'pursue sexual encounters' (Makley 2007: 243) and more with being unruly and free, forming an alternative heroic masculinity. A caring masculinity, especially in relation to children and wives, was subordinated; it was a recognised way to be a man, however, it was less explicitly appreciated. The plurality and hierarchy of masculinities inform polyandrous relations and brothers as co-husbands, and the acceptance of various ways to enact maleness was closely connected to relative age and to roles in a marriage. The handling of conflicts in a polyandrous arrangement can serve to illustrate the significance of relative age, of roles and the ideal of a collaborative masculinity.

When Things Get Complicated: Polyandry-Specific Conflicts

Throughout the years, both scholars and popular media have engaged with conflicts in, and partitions of, polyandrous marriages, reflecting perhaps the underlying notion of polyandry as going against a Western idea of male sexuality.[5] Also, in Lhasa, Tibetans often talked about polyandry as potentially ridden with conflict. It is worth noting that although many polyandrous marriages had been divided at some point in time, many remained together either in the original constellation or with a reduced number of people. In fact, according to local registers referred to by the township leaders in Kyiling, the conflicts leading to divisions in the area were often not specific to polyandry but rather intergenerational disagreements, such as between the *nama* and her mother-in-law.

Nevertheless, also in Sharlung, people acknowledged that polyandry was a more demanding form of marriage, as compared with monogamy (yet less demanding than polygyny due to the competition between sets of heirs in the latter). Three main polyandry-specific conflicts were prominent: first, an unfair distribution of affection and sexual access (the *nama* disrespecting one or more of the husbands); second, an unfair contribution to, and distribution of, economic resources; and third, the youngest husband's lack of interest in the *nama* (particularly in cases of significant age differences between the two). In addition, conflicts between the *nama* and her sister-in-law were common, and although these cannot be defined strictly as polyandry-specific, they were more prominent in polyandrous houses.

In Sharlung, I was told that most of the conflicts were of the first type; namely the distribution of affection and sexual access, reflecting the responsibility given to the *nama* in polyandry. However, in the various cases of conflict escalation and divorce, the *nama* and her eldest husband often operated as one union. In the situations where the *nama* had a difficult relation with one or more of the younger brothers, the eldest husband would often side with her. Similarly, the *nama* would most often support the *genshö* during conflicts with his brothers (or with parents, as was often the case).

Conflicts that involved either the *genshö* or the *nama* often resulted in divorce and establishment of a new household; there were only a few cases where the *nama* and a younger husband had moved and re-established themselves elsewhere. As in the Norkhang case I describe below, domestic conflicts that involved the *nama* and *genshö* were perceived to be highly problematic and a potential crisis, and serious efforts were made to mediate. When mediation failed and division occurred, the eldest son's parting from a house was morally and materially sanctioned, often leading to disrupted relations and limited inheritance.

The Partition of a House: Norkhang versus Norshön

A house-based community like Panam emphasises sibling unity. With patri-ideology, this particularly concerned brothers, but in the context of a high incident of polyandry and a surplus of unmarried women, sibling unity also often included a sister. Classical conflicts in kinship relations are that between siblingship (filiation) and that of conjugal relations (affinity). The siblingship is at the core of the polyandrous house in Tibet, and the *nama* was seen to be the one that potentially could threaten the harmony of the sibling group, and particularly the position of an unmarried sister-in-law, in cases where they shared a house.

The following example shows several aspects of co-partnership on the one hand, and the superior role of the eldest husband on the other.[6] Two dimensions of polyandrous conflicts are central: first, the foundation for the conflict and the internal power relations in a sibling group; secondly, the handling of domestic conflicts and the sanctions against the eldest son for threatening the perpetuation of the house. During my stay in Sharlung, several domestic conflicts were on-going. Some of these had started more than twenty years before and had never been resolved; others had a shorter history and negotiations were still sporadically occurring. The following is an example of a partition of one of the larger houses, called Norkhang. The division was the result of several failed attempts to reach an agreement within the original house. The split from the house had been very dramatic, and four years after, the two parties still avoided each other. Although this particular partition had some unusual elements to it, it can serve to illustrate common basic problems leading to partitions of polyandrous marriages in Sharlung.

The Norkhang household had been divided when the two eldest sons, their shared wife and only child moved and established a new household on their own. The three young adults had borrowed money from the wife's natal house in the neighbouring valley and had received financial help from friends in Sharlung to build a small house on one of the less fertile plots of land that the two brothers had inherited from their natal household. They called the new house Norshön – the 'little Nor'. Remaining in the original Norkhang house were the men's mother and father, one brother, who had also been part of the conjoint marriage, one nun sister, as well as three younger siblings and the mother's sister.

We enter their story when the *sayön* of the Norkhang house, the *makpa* Dawa Tsering, and his wife had suggested to their three eldest sons that they would arrange a marriage for them.[7] The three sons were at the time 26, 23 and 18 years old and had agreed to marry together. Through his affines in the neighbouring valley, Dawa Tsering had been told about a woman called Sökyi, who was of the right age and was also from one the wealthiest houses, and he decided to approach her father. They easily came to an agreement of a possible marriage. Dawa Tsering travelled with his eldest son, Migmar, in the guise of businessmen, to meet Sökyi. During the visit, Sökyi served tea and *chang*, as is usual when receiving guests, and according to Migmar, her way of serving, showing a kind and humble personality, and her striking beauty and suitable age convinced him that she was a good match for him and his two brothers.[8]

The role of the eldest as a representative for the group of future husbands is uncontested in this first phase of the marriage negotiations, as already mentioned. When I asked Migmar's younger brother, Namgyal, if he could have travelled to see Sökyi that first time, he told me he could have visited her, but his opinion would not have mattered. That assessment, he said, is the privilege of the *genshö*. We can take this as another example of how the *genshö* encompasses the co-husbands, and as an indication of the hierarchical arrangement being made evident from the very beginning of a polyandrous marriage. The *genshö* is the one 'part' of the 'whole' (group of brothers in marriage) that has the particular embracing character that is embedded with the ability to act in accordance with the will of the other encompassed parts. The encompassing status of the *genshö* was reflected in wedding preparations, the daily organisation of domestic life and in the escalation of conflicts.

The problems in Norkhang started shortly after the wedding. Sökyi, the *nama*, did not settle with ease into the house. In particular, she was unhappy and uncomfortable with the way her sister-in-law and mother-in-law treated her. Dawa Tsering and his wife, on the other hand, had two main concerns in this early phase: first, that Sökyi did not manage a good *kora khor*; and second, that Migmar contributed too little to the household economy. These conflicts between in-married and resident women and between generations were not uncommon in Sharlung. They often involved the *nama* but were not driven by jealousy among co-partners (as is often described in studies of polygyny). According to Dawa Tsering, they experienced a dramatic change in cooperation and co-residence relations after Sökyi moved in. Their claim was that Sökyi did not treat the three brothers equally; in fact, they said, she did not like her youngest husband. Observing how the marriage unfolded, it was their opinion that Sökyi did not 'love him' (that is, did not include him properly in the *kora khor*). The parents and their eldest daughter (who was a nun but lived at home) encouraged Sökyi to connect better with the youngest husband, but, according to the nun, Sökyi got angry with everyone except Migmar and Namgyal, her two oldest husbands.

Migmar and Sökyi, on the other hand, denied any unfair distribution of affection and held that the youngest husband had in fact been included in the *kora khor*. They claimed that the accusations from the parents (in-law) were simply redefined after the conflict had escalated, in an attempt to legitimise their position after the fact. Moreover, they argued that the parents' critique of Migmar's (lack of) contribution of his off-farm income to the household came up only after it was apparent that Migmar took Sökyi's side in her conflict with them. Lack of economic contribution and unfair distribution of affection were indeed two problems that could legitimise a divorce in a polyandrous house. The main point of interest here is the immediate support that Migmar gave to Sökyi when it became clear that she was unhappy in the house. Initially, the quarrels had occurred between Sökyi and her sister-in-law, in particular, but also with her mother-in law, and he sided with her regardless of the moral sanctions he could expect if he chose to break with his own parents. This choice consolidated a particularly close relation between Migmar and Sökyi, the *genshö* and *nama*. From then on, Migmar tried to convince his brothers to side with them against the parents, and after some time, Namgyal did. However, the youngest husband did not.

After some time, two constellations emerged in the household: Sökyi, Migmar and Namgyal on the one side and Dawa Tsering, his wife, the youngest son in the marriage and the nun, ani Lobsang, on the other. The younger household members were not involved in the conflict. The disagreement between the two parties kept escalating, and at some point it turned into a physical fight between Migmar and his father (of which the context remains unclear). After the fight, Dawa Tsering stated that he did not want Migmar to remain in his house, as he said he no longer trusted him. For the first time after the conflict had started, the two parties agreed, because Migmar and Sökyi also wanted to move, although for different reasons. Migmar convinced Namgyal to continue to be part of the marriage and to move with them. Independent of the conflict level, the splitting of a household was a complicated process in which the inheritance of immovable property was a major concern for all involved parties. This was particularly the case for the eldest son, as will be made clear in the following. Before that, I want to describe the process of negotiation, the parties' claims, and outcomes, to show how material and moral sanctions are interconnected when the eldest son decides to split from his natal house. This is even stronger when he is joined by his wife and a brother.

After the decision to move was made, the negotiations of dividing immovable and movable property started. Migmar and Namgyal were entitled to equal inheritance of land, while the *nama* was entitled to, in addition to her original dowry, compensation for the work already performed in the household. They claimed: two individuals' shares of land (that is 2.4 *mu* (0.4 acres)) each in line with the ideal inheritance norms, and land instead of cash as compensation for the *nama*'s work (the amount set to be land for half a person, that is 1.1 *mu*). Dawa Tsering refused both claims. His position was that the two sons should inherit no more than 1.5 *mu* of land each, and the *nama* should get compensated for her work in barley (*né*). One could expect that inheritance of land would have been easier after the Household Responsibility System, as the redistribution so clearly defined the amount of land per person to be attached to the household. According to the National Inheritance Law of 1985, each child of a household is entitled to inherit a full share of land upon exclusion or partition (Palmer 1995), and in Sharlung this was 2.4 *mu*. Although being the normative practice in other parts of Central Tibet,[9] age neutral inheritance rights among sons was primarily an ideal in Panam, and in practice, the transfer of land was negotiated in every individual case. Within the village, some of Norkhang's *ganyé* relations – a network of mutual assistance that I return to in the final chapter – and later Tashi-la, as the village leader, tried to mediate between the parties. They all agreed with Dawa Tsering's claim that because Migmar would severely damage the strength and the future of the house upon moving – a moral misconduct – he should be materially sanctioned and receive only 1.5 *mu* of land, and that the *nama* should receive her compensation in barley rather than in fields. 'We have to consider the situation for the parents,' Tashi-la explained to me, 'and for them, it is a great disadvantage that their two sons move. They have to make a new plan for the future. That is difficult because they are getting old,' he continued.

Being unhappy about the village leaders' decisions, Migmar and Sökyi went to the township leaders and asked for their assistance. Two leaders looked at the case and decided that Dawa Tsering should respect the standard set by the Household Responsibility Reform and give 2.4 *mu* of land to the two sons, as this was their full share provided by the government. Further, the leaders set the compensation to be given to Sökyi for her work in the household to one *mu* of land, as well as cash payment – five yuan per day of work. After two years of marriage, this meant 3,600 yuan, a substantial amount of money at the time. Needless to say, Migmar, Sökyi and Namgyal were satisfied with their suggestion. But Dawa Tsering refused to pay because, he claimed, the township leader was biased towards Sökyi as they originated from the same village. Moreover, he argued, the decision was not made in accordance with local norms of division and inheritance in polyandrous houses. Dawa Tsering brought the case to the county court, which was the highest legal authority in the area. There, three judges decided that he should give two full shares of land to his two sons, but only cash or kind compensation to the *nama*. This was set to be 1,800 yuan – that is, five yuan per day for one year.

Looking at the two lowest levels of mediation, the *ganyé* and the village leader, it is evident that the mediators put a strong emphasis on securing the elder generation, and by doing so, they sanctioned those who moved. Both the *ganyé* and the village leader disagreed with the claim of full land inheritance for the sons. A central element in their concern with the eldest generation was obviously the loss of labour. In addition, the handling of the move of Migmar, Namgyal and Sökyi should be seen in relation to the house. This is particularly explicit in the cases of polyandry. Moving out in order to establish a new household was morally and economically sanctioned by both the *ganyé* and the village leaders, not only due to their concern for the older generation but also because a split undermined the normative order of a house-based social organisation. This conflict was dealt with in the context of an increasing emphasis on perpetuating named houses, or corporate estates. Despite the ideal of equal inheritance rights amongst sons, the practice of unequal inheritance rights in polyandrous houses was well-known from the landholding estates before 1950. Although equal inheritance rights of all sons is an important part of the cultural rationale of polyandry in Sharlung, individual sons that move out are sanctioned with the restriction of inheritance rights for the sake of maintaining an estate as much as possible. This is particularly clear in the case of the eldest son(s). Younger sons who are not part of polyandrous marriages have alternatives to claiming their land inheritance; in the early 2000s in Sharlung, these were primarily to enrol in school and later settle outside the village, to marry out as a *makpa* and thus become a *sayön* elsewhere, or to seek work in the construction business and move from the village. These options were more limited for eldest sons.

Migmar's (and Namgyal's) separation from the house left the Norkhang significantly impaired. Firstly, the estate was smaller, both in terms of land and labour. Secondly, Norkhang lost its future leader and representative, who was the person who had, through childhood, been raised to be the authority in his generation. Thirdly, because the wife and a child moved with Migmar, there was a setback in terms of time, as a new marriage had to be arranged, hopefully resulting in new grandchildren. Lastly, as in most cases involving the *genshö*, the process of parting was also very difficult and led to hostile relations between him and his natal house. This was not only emotionally challenging but also had a significant impact on future work exchange and mutual aid systems central to the organisation of village life. The Norkhang example illustrates how conflicts involving the *genshö* can be heated and are thus sanctioned both morally and materially. The particular handling of conflicts that involved the eldest son reinforced and reconfirmed the position of the *genshö* as having the most value within a marriage and, in that, the future house. The *genshö*, encompassing his wife and his co-husbands, was critical to the succession of the house and was given a responsibility to represent, not only formally in terms of local political processes but in terms of the social group to which he belongs.

Encompassing the Brothers, and Representing the House

When talking about conflicts, people in Sharlung held that the most common division of polyandrous marriages occurred when the eldest husband and the *nama* established a new household on their own. However, when looking at the household survey, this seems to be only partially accurate. Mapping household constellations over time, it appears that the most common reason for partitions of polyandrous marriages in Sharlung was the youngest husband leaving. Such discrepancy between the survey and what I was told indicates the perceived social implications of the youngest separating from a house compared to that of the eldest husband for the continuity of the house, and hence how these conflicts are noted, remembered or ignored.

As the Norkhang case shows, conflicts that involve the eldest husband of a polyandrous marriage are serious and can lead to public discussion and mediation in order to minimise the risk of partition. In the cases of partition and re-establishment, the relations between the eldest husband and his natal house very often remain strained for years after. Contrary to this, problems that involved the youngest husband only very seldom developed into full-blown conflicts, and post-partition relations remained good. This makes sense when looking at the context of the relations that the younger husbands have to the group of husbands as a whole and the group's relations to the house as a unit. Because the younger husbands are encompassed by the eldest in terms of their belonging, the implications of their departure are less severe for the continuity of the house. While they, and particularly the youngest husband, constitute significant parts, they do not manifest the whole. Age was relevant not only for the internal organisation of co-husbands' roles but also for the relation between the wife and her partners. In marriages with a large age gap between the co-husbands, and thus between the youngest husband and the *nama*, the youngest's discontentment often concerns lack of sexual attraction. Such problems were solved pragmatically and with ease. When arranging a marriage, the ideal age of the wife should be younger than the eldest but older than the second husband. In the large polyandrous marriages of four or five co-husbands, the youngest husband will thus often be significantly junior to his wife. For instance, in the marriage in the Dagpo house where five husbands share the *nama*, the youngest brother is fifteen years younger than his wife. Because of this significant age difference, he has partly been raised by his wife, something recognised to be potentially problematic for future sexual relations. When I visited them, the boy was thirteen and had enrolled in middle school in the county seat. It had been made clear to him that after he had got to the proper age (they indicated 16), he would have to decide on whether to actively become part of the established marriage in the future, or not. However, there was a clear alternative open for him; to live, work and remarry outside the village.

The discontentment that involved the eldest or the youngest husband was handled in very different ways, for while strong moral and social pressure was put on the eldest to remain in his natal house, a smooth transition was facilitated when involving the youngest husband. In many of the large polyandrous marriages, the youngest husband had parted from the marriage and relocated elsewhere. Most of these were talked about as being unproblematic partitions, where solutions had been found that were acceptable to all parties. Important to such resolutions was the issue of inheritance and, particularly, the transfer of land. While a young husband settling outside the village could not and did not claim land from his natal house, those who remarried and remained in the village had to activate their inheritance rights, and as such, the partition was more complex and problematic. However, even in the latter cases of re-marriage and neolocal residence in the same village, such partitions were seen to be less serious and were dealt with in a different way than those exemplified by the Norkhang house above. Hence, a youngest husband's marital discontentment had several solutions, and indeed those that did not involve fragmentation of land were preferred. A very easy solution was to re-marry as a *makpa*, thus moving into his new wife's home and eventually taking over his father-in-law's estate. This solution did not only keep the land intact but also potentially developed a network for labour exchange, in which he continued to help his natal house. The youngest husband's separation from a marriage was not marked ritually, nor was it sanctioned morally; it was mainly seen to be loss of labour, as well as emotional loss of parting with a close relation. The acceptance of a youngest son's wish to move was connected to the expectations of his contribution to the household as a common economic endeavour, and to the house as the basic social unit of belonging, expectations that were fundamentally different compared to the eldest son. While the significant domestic group, the house, remained unmarked by the youngest husband's departure, it deteriorated significantly upon the eldest husband's establishment of a new household.

Summing up, much has been written on fraternal solidarity among Tibetan-speaking peoples in the Himalayas and elsewhere, reflecting an old concern of kinship theories.[10] Through local procreation theory, a group of brothers was seen to be if not identical then very similar in bodily substances. Consubstantial similarity produces expectations of fraternal solidarity and good relations, and these expectations were important when considering fraternal polyandry. Yet, fraternal solidarity does not exclude a hierarchical organisation. Dominant masculinity ideals also emphasise collaboration among brothers, and it forms a category of subjectivity that defines the premises for authoritative agency (as Makley phrases it, 2007: 32) and decision making. Throughout childhood, the hierarchy of relative age is internalised. The hegemonic masculinity of male collaboration informs this process of naturalisation of power and the doxic status of an age hierarchy. A younger brother remains in a position with limited influence in his natal house throughout his life. At the same time, this subordinate position gives him more freedom to choose whether to remain as part of the polyandrous marriage throughout his life, or to move out. The socio-symbolic unity of the house is internal and external in the sense that members perceive themselves to constitute parts of a whole and others perceive the house to be one social

Figure 3.1. In an ideal polyandrous constellation, one husband would work the land, one would herd the animals and one would bring cash income to their household. The *dzo*, the cross-breed of yak and cow, were used for farm work, including male tasks such as ploughing and threshing. © Heidi Fjeld

Figure 3.2. All households in Sharlung had goats and sheep, and some had *dzo* and cows. The animals had been redistributed from the communes to the individual households as part of the Household Responsibility System, in 1981, and the numbers had increased over the decades. © Heidi Fjeld

Figure 3.3. The eldest brother and husband is expected to become the household head (*sayön*), responsible for the running of the household, including making sure that the ritual obligations are fulfilled. © Heidi Fjeld

unit. Like the right hand encompasses the left and comes to stand for the whole body in Hertz's old article, the eldest encompasses his young co-husbands and comes to stand for the house.

While age and authority can be clearly defined and easily translated into roles, in the following chapter we will see that gender is more ambiguous. In different life phases, younger husbands, as younger wives, have limited influence in their households. Yet, the pathways of women and younger husbands are divergent, and in the next chapter, we turn to women's roles in polyandrous houses and continue to explore the question of being central or peripheral to the order of things.

Notes

1. Several theorists have taken a similar stand on the association of the unity of a sibling group with the prevalence of fraternal polyandry before Levine (see Mandelbaum 1938; Radcliffe-Brown 1941: 7; and to a certain extent, Prince Peter 1963). However, Levine explores fraternal solidarity from an empirical rather than a theorical point of view.
2. In other cases of adultery, people say that it most often occurs between a married man and his wife's sister(s). This is also not an uncommon perception among exiled Tibetans (Tsomo Svenningsen, personal communication, Oslo, 2004). In Sharlung, a sister of a deceased wife is also a preferred second marriage partner, for reasons more related to expected concerns for her sister's children.
3. Similarly, co-wives in polygynous marriages are ranked according to relative wedding order, most often corresponding to age (although young age tends to be an advantage in terms of influence and ability to build alliances with the husband).
4. The concept of hegemonic masculinity has been broadly critiqued (as reviewed by Connell and Messerschmidt 2005). More recent turns in masculinity studies, informed by post-structural sensitivity to plural experiences and discursive productions of gender, have moreover questioned the very concept of 'masculinity', among other things for essentialising the complexity of male lives but also for giving a false flair of unity to this complexity (MacInnes 1998; Whitehead 2002).
5. See, for instance, Goldstein (1978b), Schuler (1987), Levine and Silk (1997); Haddix (2001).
6. The case featured in this section was also discussed in Fjeld 2008a.
7. The two have five sons and three daughters, of which the two youngest sons are still in junior middle school in Panam and primary school in Sharlung and not considered as potential partners in marriage. One daughter was sent as a *nama* to two brothers in a neighbouring valley, while the fifteen-year-old daughter still lived at home together with the eldest sister, who was an ordained nun in the local nunnery.
8. Agreeing on the transfer of a *nama* is often a long negotiation over compensation for the loss that her household will suffer when she moves out. The receiving household first has to bring gifts to her household members (very often clothes), and *khatak*. Some ten to thirty days later (depending on the astrology), the *langchang* is arranged, in which the girl is informed and led to her new house. On this occasion, her natal household members receive more gifts, and most importantly, her mother is given a new woollen *chuba*, an apron and blouse as the '*uri pangden*' (*uri*: breastfeed, *pang*: the area on the belly

where the baby sits while breastfeeding). In addition, the *nama*-receiving household should bring at least two bags of *tsampa* and/or barley (unroasted), a *sha khok*; a newly slaughtered sheep where the wool and the head are kept and the stomach is filled with wool. These gifts are standardised, and the negotiations rather concern the amount of *tsampa* and barley, extra meat and wool, as well as extra demands from the girl's household leader.
 9. Samdrup, personal communication 2002.
10. Fürer-Haimendorf (1964); Prince Peter (1963); Levine (1988); and Radcliffe-Brown (1941).

Chapter 4

FEMALE ROLES

Polyandry is not reversed polygyny. It is a marriage between a group of men and one woman, rather than one woman and several men. As with polygyny, it is initiated by the men's family, and the cultural logic of polyandry is based on a wish to secure the perpetuation of the patrilocal residence group. Although not female-initiated, men and women had a shared preference for polyandry in Sharlung. At the same time, polyandry was recognised as a complex form of marriage that requires careful manoeuvring, not only within the conjugal group but also within the larger household, where most, but clearly not all, members have strong filial ties. The *nama* has a special role – a responsibility – in making the polyandrous marriage work. This chapter explores women's perceptions of polyandry and their concerns, considerations and efforts to establish and maintain a good marriage. This is not a small task, as the frame within which they manoeuvred their marital and household relations is a gender model that identifies women as inferior to men, and a social organisation where women are ideologically peripheral to the order of things.

Social organisation in Panam is patrifocal, reflected particularly in male inheritance rights, post-marital patrilocal residence and patrilineal kinship ideology. We have seen that the eldest husband is at the centre of the marriage arrangement, encompassing his co-husbands as *pala* and later as *sayön* (household leader) and representing the house both socially and symbolically. Such a distribution of centrality was also evident in the organisation of married life and in the allocation of work and the execution of authority more broadly. We can also approach women's positions in polyandry through the notion of centrality, not in the sense of being either central or peripheral but rather as moving between more or less central positions – positions that change over the course of married life.

Both men and women talked about polyandry as a form of organisation where women are structurally subordinate and symbolically peripheral. In Panam, this was expressed both in the aim to perpetuate the house (which ideally corresponds with a patrilineage) and in the value of maximising male labour in the household. Men were simply seen to be more important. Women's roles were comparable to the youngest husband(s) in large polyandrous marriages – as being subordinate to the eldest brothers and father(s). Indeed, the *nama* was *initially* also structurally peripheral and subordinate to her husbands, including the younger ones. However, with time she gains authority over others in a trajectory that is not open for her younger husbands. As such, gender models can only partially explain intra-household gender relations and women's roles in polyandry. An analytical approach that goes beyond gender alone is concurrent with what Levine described in her article on differential childcare in three Nyinba communities, where she argued that what at first glance seemed to be a son preference should rather be interpreted as the discrimination against not daughters as such but 'against any less desirable child' (1987a: 281). In other words, daughters and sons with several older brothers were less central to the perpetuation of the corporate household, and their degree of centrality was thus defined by their roles. At the same time, hierarchical gender models clearly informed marital and household relations both as ideas and practices. Levine also found that although the rationale of differential childcare goes beyond gender alone, in practice a significant percentage of the neglected children in her ethnography were girls. The same point can be made regarding *nama*s and their positions in Panam; gender alone cannot explain their often subordinate position, yet in practice gender models inform their ability to enact and negotiate their roles and relations, also compared to younger husbands. Women in Tibet are – broadly speaking – structurally subordinate and must, in significantly different ways than younger men, depend upon personal skills and interpersonal relations to gain a secure and stable position within a marriage and a house. Also, women's work obligations are heavy and extensive, particularly in a context where continuous periods of pregnancies and childbirths are common. As such, it is fair to say that the burden of women is heavier than that of men. Women are also more vulnerable in the cases of norm violations, such as divorce, children born out of wedlock, or infertility. At the same time, as *nama* a woman has the potential to consolidate a very strong and powerful position in the course of a lifetime, and this potential is, I argue, greater in a polyandrous marriage.

Being a Woman/Being a *Nama*

Compared with women elsewhere in South Asia, 'Tibetan women', particularly nomads, have often been depicted as more independent, less shy or timid, more outspoken and in general more active in participating in public spheres.[1] Yet, as Charlene Makley (1997) has noted, the category 'Tibetan women' is essentialising and blurs the differences and nuances of geographic regions, class and relations to production, and it would serve our purposes better to focus on women's experiences as 'subjects in their lives' in the larger social context of which they are part (ibid.: 18). In the introduction to the ground-breaking anthology *Women in Tibet*, Janet Gyatso and Hanna Havnevik (2005) delineated two generalised findings on women's experiences in Tibet: first, that individual women have achieved prominence in Tibetan societies throughout history, also in the areas traditionally dominated by men, and second, that 'enduring androcentrism and misogynistic gender tropes' are readily observable in Tibetan communities, but that these tend to vary according to geography and social status/class (Gyatso and Havnevik 2005: 9). Indeed, we know of outstanding women from Tibetan history, although they are most often only mentioned in passing and are described as exceptions. In the history of Tibetan medicine, for instance, there are cases of skilled daughters of medical houses (*mendrong*) being trained as physicians by their father or uncle (also in cases where they had brothers). In the history of war, there were woman warriors fighting and leading battalions in eastern Tibet (McGranahan 2010).[2] At the same time – also in Tibetan medicine and on the battleground – 'women', and female bodies in particular, were associated with pollution and thus danger, weakness and lower birth.

Androcentric and misogynistic gender tropes inform how women and men talk about women and can be summed up in the general assumption that being born a woman is less fortunate than being born a man.[3] In Panam, people explained this simple fact with the worldview of karma, merit and reincarnation, in which a woman can pray to be reborn as a man. When talking with women about gender (in)equality, I often got the impression that they pitied themselves for being born a woman, thinking that it comes with obvious disadvantages, such as a weaker body, childbirth, more sickness, as well as an emotional mind. Hamsa Rajan describes similar observations about internalisation of female subordination in her study of domestic violence among Tibetans on the north-eastern edge of the Tibetan plateau (2014, 2018a, 2018b). Although I did not see signs of domestic violence in Panam, Rajan's findings are relevant in terms of how women interpret their subjective experiences. Rajan found that 'The husband, often seen as the disciplinarian and head of household, was viewed as having the right to punish and silence his wife when "necessary",' and that 'hitting was often considered not particularly heinous, but rather relatively mundane and normal', a view that women, also those who had been victimised, agreed with (2018a: 5). When explaining why a woman can expect to have a harder life than a man, Tibetan language itself is often engaged as evidence. Indeed, a common word for 'woman', *kyéme*, translates as 'low birth' (*skyes* is birth and *dman* is low or inferior).⁴ Also the alternative, more neutral term for women, *bümé* (*bud med*), can easily be confused with *bumé* (*bu med*), meaning 'not boy', indicating that women are negated men, or that the female is a deviation, or inversion, of the standard male. Although these terms had different meanings in the past – *dman*, used in *kyéme*, was simply a feminine ending, and *med*, used in *bümé*, was an archaic feminine form – they have come to convey inferiority and negation today.⁵ Gyatso and Havnevik also noted that androcentrism and misogynistic expressions are explained in the truism 'that to be a woman is to have bad karma, low status and poor abilities' (2005: 9). There are numerous Tibetan proverbs describing women as being of lower birth and subordinate to men. For instance, one well-known saying describes the value of monks over nuns: 'If one wants a teacher, one makes a son a monk, and if one wants a servant, one makes a daughter a nun'.⁶ Yet, gender models of Tibetan Buddhism are contradictory. While clearly misogynist, there is also 'the deification of a female principle in Buddhism', as Gyatso has summed up (2003: 89). In practice, however, this deification did not come to the fore in my interaction with people in Panam, rather, ideas of women being inferior and subordinate to men were readily expressed both by men and women.

In explaining the poor abilities and hard life of women, people in Sharlung often referred to the disadvantages of having a female body. This body was generically understood to be inferior to the male body, perceptions that are in line with Tibetan medical texts as well. The main medical treatises – the Four Tantras (*Gyüzhi*) – clearly explain that the female body is the result of 'less merit' and is a weaker body (Fjeld and Hofer 2011: 194). One passage in the *Gyüzhi* notes: 'since she is of lower birth, the female (*bud med*) body has extra illnesses' (g.Yu-thog 1984: 393, cited in Fjeld and Hofer 2011: 194), referring to the thirty-two illnesses that only affect female bodies.⁷ This weakness and associated suffering also connects to childbirth, a painful and high-risk event with a potentially deadly outcome. In addition to being weak, the female body is also inherently polluted, epitomised by menstruation blood. The possibility of spilling menstrual blood on the ground is the explanation often given as to why women are prohibited from entering certain temples, such as protector temples of monasteries. Carole McGranahan, in an article on gender and Tibetan historical narratives, describes some of the ways that the notion of polluted female bodies informed Tibetan soldiers' practices (in the Chushi Gangdrug movement); women could not be soldiers due to pollution, bullets dipped in menstruation blood were perceived to be more deadly and soldiers were not allowed to have sex on the evening before or the day of the battle. Underlying these practices was the fear that female pollution could 'weaken one's protective amulets or even eliminate its powers' (2010: 772). These characteristics of the female body include particular sufferings of the mind as well. Dan Martin cites an early commentator named Kunga, writing a message to the future generations of women, saying: 'Women's bodies are vessels of pain, and women's minds are vessels of suffering' (2005: 78). Analysing medical texts and illustrations, Rae Dachille-Hay has shown that also in those the representation of female bodies indicates an emotional vulnerability of women (2011). The weakness of the female body and mind was emphasised by my interlocutors as well; as one older woman explained: 'Women cry so easily because we cannot control our minds. With these strong emotions, we cannot make good decisions because we are too attached to everything: to our children, to our natal home'.

When asked, women in Sharlung described themselves as being of lower value and less skilful than men; however, they seemed to accept this as a matter of course. I could not find any emerging feminists in the villages of Panam, which resonates with Rajan's research from the north-east as well, where 'feminist consciousness is extremely rare' (2018b: 291).[8] This lack of engagement with female hardships did not reflect disinterest, but rather I got the sense that women did not conceptualise and interpret their experiences through being part of the group of 'women' (*kyéme*). Rather, kinship categories – female roles, that is, being a wife or a daughter, or an ordained nun – were the basic reference point when considering lived experiences. Living a life as a *nama* – having moved away from home, performing *nama* work, having *nama* duties, being pregnant and giving birth, building and managing close relations within a new house – formed shared experiences of relevance when women talked about 'gender issues'. My questions about the relations between women and men were often answered in the context of intra-marriage and intra-household relations. The life trajectories of a *nama* and a resident unmarried daughter, for example, were described as fundamentally different, pointing also to the importance of exploring female roles – women as subjects in their lives – rather than 'women' as *one* category.

When talking with *nama*s about female lives, they were most concerned with the process of relocation after marriage, and the difference between being married or not. Being sent to a new household, often in a new village where they did not have established connections, was for most the core of their narratives of hardship. Marriage form, and number of husbands, on the other hand, did not often come up as a worry. Many women spoke about *makpa* marriages as a significantly different situation. Although a wife of a *makpa* also has a hard life due to a heavy workload and childbirths, they do not have to suffer leaving their natal home. Similarly, women in monogamous, neolocal

Figure 4.1. Women's workload is both broad-ranging and heavy, both in the field and within the house. Here women are winnowing using the tractor as a fan. © Heidi Fjeld

Figure 4.2. A nun washing clothes in the river. Ordination does not exclude domestic work for women. © Heidi Fjeld

khatukpa ('love') marriages did not experience the emotionally strenuous move into a new household. Common to all categories of women, though, was the expectation that their lives would be filled with heavy workloads and bodily suffering, and be harder compared to the lives of men.

Women's Preference for Polyandry

Gender (in)equality was also less of an issue in discussions about marriage forms. Plural marriage is seen to be neither more nor less exploitative of women. When considering the alternatives, '*zasum* is better', women repeatedly told me. Their preference for polyandry was based first on the prospect of being able to better maintain the land, and second on a sense of safety. Women were drawn to the possibility of having an easier transition into a new household after the wedding and the positive implications of having multiple husbands in a household – several fathers to the children and stronger allies when dealing with the often delicate relationship with parents-in-law. Yet, polyandry was recognised to involve a way of life that is not compatible with all women, nor all men. For this reason, women were often consulted when parents were considering a polyandrous marriage offer, and refusing to marry more than one husband was accepted without much

Figure 4.3. Nuns from the local nunnery practising playing *gyaling*, a woodwind oboe-like instrument used for rituals. © Heidi Fjeld

argument. Sonam, a *nama* of three husbands in Sharlung, was born into a wealthy and influential house in a village outside Gyantse city. She was one of the women I spent most time with in the village. She grew up on a farm with three fathers and one mother, as well as her paternal grandparents. Her eldest father (*pala*) was also the village leader. At the age of seventeen, her *pala* started to receive inquiries about marriage, and he conveyed some of the offers to her. She explained:

> *Pala* said that he wanted to ask me about my opinion on the offer that had been made because it involved living in the city. A leader in Gyantse had asked for me to marry his son. They were very rich. But when my father said this, I became scared because I did not know about life there, and I did not know how to live in the city, with a leader. So, I said that I did not want to marry him. *Pala* accepted this. ... Later he came with a new offer, this time from Sharlung. This was much better for me, and I agreed to go here.

As Sonam had not mentioned the fact that moving to Sharlung had involved plural marriage, I asked her if she had preferences in terms of numbers of husbands. She said:

> Most important for me was to live in a village, so that I could live the way I knew. I can only do farm work, not much else. So, for me it doesn't matter about the number of husbands. Even though moving to Gyantse would be easy – with wealth and only one husband – I could not live there.

Sonam preferred a polyandrous marriage in a village even when given the alternative of a monogamous marriage in a city. This is a choice that my Lhasa friends found perplexing. To Sonam, polyandry meant a good and manageable life. The two of us often engaged in wishful thinking, trying to formulate the unimaginable, she was also very curious about my life as a mother. One of her amusing ideas was to send me as a *nama* to three brothers she knew in her home village. She would laugh so hard when thinking about the looks on their faces when this blue-eyed woman with a daughter and very limited spinning skills appeared during the wedding ceremony. In line with these conversations, I asked her if given the choice she would choose to live with only one of her three husbands. She replied:

> Why? We would be so poor! Who wants that? It is very difficult to live one-to-one (*réré*) here, also for the *nama*. Being a *nama* is much work here because we do agricultural work, domestic work, milk the animals, feed the babies and many other things. Then we have to take care of the husbands, and their parents. When we are more people it is less work – so *zasum* is good. The most important thing is to reduce the work because it is too much. But I think it is easier for the *nama* with one husband because it is only one husband to take

care of, and not many to take care of. But if the marriage fails and some are unhappy, it is always blamed on the *nama*, right? She has to do good *kora khor*. If she cannot do this, then the husbands will be unhappy and maybe they will divide.

Sonam's reflections illustrate well the ideas about marriage alternatives that I often heard in Sharlung; her concerns were about livelihood, the amount and character of work, rather than the number of husbands. She also recognised the increased emotional strain associated with more than one husband to care for but concluded that the benefits outweighed the negatives. Larger households have an obvious economic advantage, which was intensified with the economic development policies of the 2000s encouraging off-farm activities, and women were very well aware of this. In general, the expectations were that a polyandrous life would involve less hardship than a monogamous life. This was an assumption shared by most of my interlocutors in Sharlung. As the grandmother (*achi*) in Takrab said: 'Sometimes a boy makes a girl like him (*gabo chewa*) and then – *khatukpa* (sic!). This happens, but it is a pity because they will have much hardship in life.' In other words, falling in love can happen, but it is unfortunate. This concern about degrees of hardship is thus not associated with marriage arrangement – whether it is initiated by the couple or the parents – but rather with residence implications. Following *khatukpa* marriages, the couple establishes a household on their own, a situation that is vulnerable both economically and socially, with a small farm and limited possibilities for help.

Moving households as a newly-wed woman is a precarious transition that brings worry and vulnerability, also in Tibet. The relation between the in-marrying daughter-in-law and the resident mother-in-law is one of potential conflict, often expressed in work expectations, demands and sometimes exploitation. In the initial phase of marriage, the *nama*'s work abilities and also her personality is under scrutiny, and this period lasts until she has children. Several proverbs address this point. Rajan quotes this saying: 'Don't say a bag is not heavy when you've only just started carrying it; don't say your daughter-in-law is good when she has only just arrived [to your household]' (2014: 146), while Geoff Childs quotes this Tibetan saying from Nubri in Nepal: 'However ferocious a warrior may be, a friend of valor he shall need. However pretty a wife may be, a son on her lap she will need' (2004: 106). Chökyi, the *nama* in the Longchen house and a young mother of two, said this about arriving into a new house:

> It is the same for every *nama*. In the beginning, we don't like to leave from our parents. When we come to a new place, we don't know anybody. We are afraid that we will not work well enough and maybe the household leader will be angry and treat us badly. It is difficult and many cry.

Explicitly comparing polyandry with other marriage forms, women in Sharlung explained that with multiple husbands this transition could be less onerous. The potential conflict of this initial period is with the parents-in-law, and the *nama*'s support and alliance then primarily lies with her husband, and hence, multiple husbands can strengthen her position in relation to the older generation. With the support of one or more husbands, the recently arrived wife can feel less vulnerable and more protected against extreme workloads, neglect or maltreatment.[9]

Yet, relational maturation is a complex process when multiple husbands are involved. The *nama* has only formal and not yet emotional relations to her husband(s), and this develops with time. Chökyi, talking about her own entry into marriage with three husbands, continued:

> After some time in the new house, I liked my husbands. First, I became close to *genshö*. It is natural because he is oldest. He was very nice to me, always looking after me. He also helped me to fetch water many times. I liked him from the beginning. But I also tried to pay attention to the two others because my mother had told me before the wedding that it is very important to be just and treat the husbands in a fair/impartial (*drangpo*) way. It was only a short time after the wedding that I felt good with *genshö*. Then it was easier to like the others also. *Achung* was young, much younger than me, but he is very kind. So, I never said anything bad to him. *Ajok* was also nice, but he was shyer. Also, he was often herding and not so often there.

I asked her about the other people in the house and her relation to them during the first period after the wedding.

> In the beginning, I was very shy with them, and also afraid, especially with the *sayön* (household leader). Longchen is a big house, so it is a lot of work for the *nama*. I tried to work hard so that mother (-in-law) should not complain. . . . I was also afraid of Ani (nun). She is almost my age, but still I did not dare to approach her. I thought that she was not so nice also, because she did not help me with work. . . . In the beginning, I spoke with *genshö* for the most, and then if I needed something from the elders, he asked his parents for me. Then, later, we had very good relations. They are nice people and always treated me well. Sometimes now I argue with Ani, but not so seriously.

Other women I spoke with gave a similar account of their initial period in a new household, in that they focused on working hard and establishing good relations with their husbands. It was a clear pattern that the newly arrived *nama* associated herself with the eldest husband, as Chökyi said, 'because it is normal'. However, it is a newly-arrived *nama*'s overall concern to establish affectionate relations with all husbands as soon as possible. Conjugal relations are a *nama*'s introduction to a household and form the basis of her status and support in the village. These relations develop throughout the life course and are essential, especially when negotiating work and roles with the mother-in-law and the often-present unmarried sister-in-law (such as Ani in Chökyi's case). Returning a *nama* was not unheard of in Sharlung and occurred for the most part when there had been disagreements between parents-in-law and the *nama*. In these situations, she would depend upon her husband(s) for support. In one case that had happened two months before our first arrival in Sharlung, a *nama* had been sent back to her parents four months into the marriage. The relations between her and the two husbands had not yet developed to be very affectionate, and thus when her parents-in-law complained about what they perceived to be her lack of willingness and ability to work, the husbands did not take her side in the conflict. She returned to her natal house with a compensation of 200 *jin* (100 litres) of *chang*.[10]

Having multiple husbands can also act as social security for women – a safety net. As a young woman called Tsering told us:

> My grandfather died when he was young, and my grandmother had to feed my mother and her siblings alone. It was a very difficult life. Because she had no land, she had to take work as a carrier for big traders. Once a year she went with them to India, carrying their things for a small salary. Every time, she was gone for maybe six months. Then my mother was left alone with her siblings, and they worked with their maternal uncle (*ashang*). My mother has told me about this difficult time, and she said that there was no protection for them. I am thinking that this is different now with *zasum*, so the children have more than one father. Many things can happen; one can become sick and maybe die, and then it is easier for the wife to get help with the children.

Rural development policies since the 1980s have encouraged a diversified household economy, leading men to leave the farm. Even with predominantly subsistence farming before 2000, men left to herd the animals, and although trade was no longer a major work opportunity, they departed for whatever labour opportunities appeared. Pilgrimage also contributed to men's mobility away from the wife and children. With the economic development policies since the 2000s, off-farm activities have become an increasingly attractive source of income, leading more and more men (and later also women) to 'go for income' and be away from the house for longer periods of the year.[11] These historical and contemporary drivers to diversify the economy and encourage the mobility of household members has reconfirmed the notion that polyandry serves as a safety net for women. As Tsering continued: 'A *nama* is vulnerable and is easily put in a difficult situation if something happens to her (one) husband.' From a local perspective, going for income is not without risk. Leaving the village for longer periods also exposes young people to different lifestyles, challenging village and household loyalty, identity and their sense of belonging. Therefore, it was primarily the eldest husbands that were sent to work off the farm, as they were expected to have the strongest attachment and commitment both their wife and to their household. In our conversations, women also expressed their concern that one of the husbands would stop returning; indeed, this has happened many times in Sharlung, but often with the youngest husbands, as described in the previous chapter. The safety net of polyandry thus also works in the case of divorce and division.

Being Sexually Active with Several Husbands

Polyandry was also recognised as being a demanding form of marriage. Women were very much aware of the responsibility that lies on the *nama*s to make sure all marital partners were content. Central to this sense of responsibility was the importance of establishing a *kora khor* system that would be fair to all. Some divorces in Sharlung had stemmed from a woman's lack of will, or ability, to do *kora khor* in a way accepted by the husbands (and parents-in-law). As Chökyi said: 'Not everybody is able to do *kora khor*. It depends on your personality.'

The fact that a woman has several sexual partners was a topic discussed with some embarrassment (*ngotsa*), also among married women themselves.[12] Although fully accepted as a marriage form, I noticed a self-consciousness among women that polyandry is unusual. This was particularly reflected in giggles and laughs when we asked about sex. One of our afternoons sitting in the open space of the living quarters, Mingzom (my daughter's nanny) and I asked Lobsang Drolma about affection and sexual practices. It was a quiet afternoon. Nobody else was in the house – Tashi-la had gone to visit relatives; her eldest husband had not yet returned from Ngari, Orgyen and Wangchuk were outside working, and Ani-la was in Gyantse to help relatives there. Although Tibetan women are often not particularly shy when talking about sex, it is taboo in the presence of male relatives, and so we were careful with the timing of these conversations. Lobsang Drolma had told us that Namgyal Tsering, her eldest husband, was on his way home after five months in Ngari. Talking about him, she was smiling more broadly than usual. I asked her if she was looking forward to seeing him again, and she laughed and confirmed that she was very excited. It seemed to me that she had a different expression when talking about Namgyal Tsering, compared to her two other younger husbands, so I asked if she had an especially close relation with him. Lobsang Drolma explained: 'No, no, I love all three just the same. This is the most important for a *nama* – to treat all equally.' Mingzom, interrupting her, said that it must be very difficult to love three men at the same time. 'I cannot do that!' she exclaimed, giggling. Lobsang Drolma replied: 'It is not so difficult for me. It is true. But Namgyal Tsering is different because he is the eldest, and most important to the family.'

During most of our stays, we had lived with Lobsang Drolma and her two younger husbands. Trying to observe expressions of affection between them, I had only noted a few differences, such as a bit more distance between her and Wangchuk, the middle one (*ajok*). Orgyen, the youngest husband, was often in the house playing and taking care of their children and also occasionally helping Lobsang Drolma with preparing dinner. This caring masculinity seemed to have little effect on her. While his relation to the children was very affectionate, his interaction with Lobsang Drolma was less so. At first, I took this lack of affection between the three as an expression of what is normative and accepted regarding intimacy – you are not supposed to show affection in public. However, after the return of Namgyal Tsering, Lobsang Drolma's behaviour changed. When he was around, she paid close attention to his doings and sayings, flirting and giggling at his small jokes. Her eyes followed him, and she was often physically close to him, touching his leg while laughing and gently hitting him when he teased her. Having been away for a long time, upon his return Namgyal Tsering was very busy visiting friends, and he regularly came home late, often rather intoxicated. Lobsang Drolma often waited for him to return, serving him *chang* before the end of the evening, something I did not see her do with her other husbands. Her behaviour towards Namgyal Tsering was, I believe, an expression of the special relation between the *nama* and the eldest husband described in the previous chapter. Bringing the conversation back to *kora khor*, Lobsang Drolma continued talking about the return of her eldest husband: 'When he comes home, I stay with him again. Because he has been away for a long time, I stay only with him for a long period. Then, I only visit the others occasionally.'

Mingzom, who is from a village outside Lhasa where polyandry is uncommon, tried to formulate a question between all the laughter: 'Do you have sex very often? Don't you get tired?' Lobsang Drolma started to giggle loudly and moved her index finger back and forth on her cheek as if to indicate that the questions were embarrassing. She never answered the first question; however, concerning the second question, she explained: 'No, no. But the pregnancies make me tired.' Lobsang Drolma was carrying her fourth child at the time and was often nauseous. She continued: 'I get sick a lot. Still I have to work and do *kora khor* in the same way. That is tiring.' I asked her if the *kora khor* is constant or if it changes at some point.

> It is the same most of the time. After a childbirth – then there is no *kora khor* in the first month. But after that it is the same. This is maybe a difference between a *nama* with one, and a *nama* with many husbands. With one hus-

band it is easier to rest if needed. With many husbands it is difficult to change the *kora khor* because maybe some will be upset.

Mingzom, still not convinced about the value of polyandry, continued: 'But – what if you don't like one of your husbands? What can you do?' The issue of a fair distribution of sex and affection is at the core of a successful polyandrous marriage, and, as mentioned, the *nama* is blamed for failures. However, both the eldest husband and the *nama* are credited for the success of a marriage. People gossip about *nama*s and their ability to love all their husbands, and the public interest in larger marriages with a significant age difference between the *nama* and the youngest husbands is particularly strong. Lobsang Drolma continued:

> It is the responsibility of the *nama* to be fair (*drangpo*). Sometimes the *nama* does not love one husband, but she has to try hard to visit him and show affection. And then, affection can change. This happened to the *nama* in the Sharlung House. At first, she did not like the *ajok*. She did not want to visit him often, and he was angry. The other [two] husbands were also upset and told her to treat him well. So, she included him into the *kora khor*. She told me that in the beginning she thought it was horrible, but after some time she was used to it, and now she likes him.

Independent of marital form, sex is considered an important part of marriage and of utmost importance to the formation of bonds between the partners.[13] Although many women did have a special relation with their eldest husband, it is in the interest of not only the marriage and the household as a whole but also of the woman herself to develop good relations with all husbands. Stronger relations with more people enable the *nama* to negotiate more individual autonomy – that is, to participate in decisions about how she uses her time, about distribution of work, and when to leave the village for events such as pilgrimage or visiting her relatives.

Gender Roles across the Life Course: The Struggle for Female Headship

The experience of being a *nama* changes with time – that is, with stages of life – and is shaped by marital form, household composition and interpersonal relations. In addition to the patri-orientation, the cumulative effect of patrifiliation results in houses consisting mostly of individuals who are agnates. However, a *nama* in a polyandrous marriage has the potential to become very influential and, importantly, gain a strong position vis-à-vis a mother- and sister-in-law. In this process, building strong relations with her husbands is essential. Yangzom, a woman in her late 40s, explained the roles of a *nama* in this way:

> The *nama* is very important in a marriage, and especially in *zasum*. She is responsible for her husbands' happiness, for working hard so that the mother-in-law likes her, and for listening to and working hard for the household leader. If she is a bad *nama*, she is blamed for the failure of the marriage, and then she is treated badly also. If she is a good *nama*, everybody in the house will treat her well. People see her as a good person because the marriage is good. Then, when her oldest husband becomes the household leader, her power is very strong, not only over the women in the household but also the men. Then, she has good relations with all her husbands, and her sons support her, and nobody can treat her badly.

The presence of large sibling groups within one household complicates the power balance between those who gained their membership by other sources than filiation, mostly only the in-marrying wife. One of the demographic implications of high polyandry rates is a surplus of unmarried women in the community, as I described earlier. Parents acknowledged the potential conflicts between a resident unmarried daughter and an in-marrying wife, but still, these household constellations were common.[14] Unmarried daughters in the household reduce the work burden of the *nama* and enable women to participate with agricultural labour to a larger degree. Also, parents see an unmarried daughter, lay or ordained, as a caretaker for their old age.[15]

The *nama* primarily forms alliances with men, and most importantly her husbands, and only secondary with other women in the household. This is similar to what Levine noted from Nyinba communities (1988). Often intra-house female relations can remain strained throughout a lifetime. It is not an easy task for a young *nama* to integrate in a potentially impenetrable group of parents and siblings, and although the set trajectory of a *nama* is to become the female household head, this is complicated in the cases of an un-unmarried sister-in-law living in the house. The following example serves to illustrate *namas*' possible struggle for influence in the midst of cumulative patrifiliation, pointing to the significance, but also limitations, of wife-husband(s) relations in intra-household dynamics.

The main negotiation between the *nama* and her unmarried sister-in-law was the distribution of authority over women's work. This was formalised in the status as *nangma*, female household head. While the male household leader (*sayön*) administers the male tasks of the household, the female head is responsible for the distribution of domestic tasks or what is seen to be women's work, such as cooking, taking care of the children, washing clothes, keeping the agricultural produce, weaving as well as doing some agricultural work (such as weeding). The female household headship (*nangma*) was ideally transferred from mother-in-law to daughter-in-law in the same gradual way as with the male household leader. The exact point of transfer was therefore undefined – depending on the health and interest of the *nama* and her relation to the *sayön* – and varied from a few years after the first children were born to much later in life and often following the death of the mother-in-law. In Sharlung, the *nangma* was usually the oldest woman in the house (i.e. the mother-in-law), and the norm was to hold back the power transfer until the younger woman's children were no longer dependent upon her, or until the elder woman's health was deteriorating in such a way that she was no longer capable of performing her tasks. However, there were some exceptions to this slow transfer, most commonly following an untimely death. In those cases, if the eldest son is suddenly taking over as the household leader, he might argue for the transfer of the *nangma* status from his mother to his wife as well, given that ideally the male and female household heads are married. Depending on the nature of the relation between mother and daughter-in-law, this occasionally led to conflict, which may not be resolved before one of the women passes away. In Sharlung, there were cases of power struggles involving unmarried daughters of the house (of two generations) that had resulted in a draining of real power from the *nangma* position and a transfer of 'de-facto' headship to an unmarried daughter of the house. This had left the *nama*s in difficult situations, often involving loneliness and also sometimes neglect and maltreatment.

One well-known case of such conflict was the long and complicated history of the Darkhang house, where two generations of women had been involved in power struggles – with different results. Darkhang was one of the older houses in Sharlung, but due to a series of unfortunate events, in addition to the local political history, in the 2000s it was a poor house. When we entered the story, the household consisted of a man and his wife (Yangdröl), his unmarried sister (Pema), their two sons, a daughter-in-law (Nyima Tsering) and their three small children, as well as their two unmarried daughters (Tsomo and Loyang, of which the latter was a nun). Pema, the unmarried woman of the older generation, had been ordained in the local nunnery in the past but had been forced to disrobe in 1959. Pema had therefore moved back into her natal home, where her brother lived with his family. She remained unmarried throughout her life and was still called Ani, referring both to her former status as a nun and her kin relation as 'father's sister' to the children of the house. Darkhang was a female-dominated household in terms of internal organisation and power distribution, reflecting the presence of unmarried daughters with strong personalities, especially in the older generation.

The *nama* of Pema's generation, Yangdröl, was entitled to receive the female headship from her mother-in-law. This, however, both did and did not happen. In practice, Pema and her mother had been sharing the leadership tasks, distributing the women's work and controlling the agricultural produce, and little, if any, of that influence was transferred to Yangdröl during the mother-in-law's lifetime. Following the passing of the mother-in-law, Yangdröl took the formal title of *nangma*, but this was not reflected in practice. By that time, Pema had – through years of cooperation with her mother – established herself as figure of authority within the household. When Yangdröl, on the other hand, tried to execute her given powers by taking charge of the cooking and serving, she was simply disregarded, not only by Pema but also by her husband and their children. As one of her sons said, 'Ama [Yangdröl] was not as strong as Ani [Pema].' Yangdröl had tried to enact the *nangma* title, but after a while she realised that all household members related primarily to Pema as the female head, including her husband and her children. Gradually, after that, Yangdröl said, she accepted her subordinate and unfortunate, position.

When Yangdröl's two sons reached mature age, they married a young woman called Nyima Tsering. She was only two years older than the youngest daughter in the house, Tsomo, and a little younger than Loyang, the nun. The first years of this marriage were amicable. Yangdröl spent much time by herself at that time, walking the fields and sitting around the hearth engaging in religious activities. Thus, the new *nama* Nyima Tsering worked mostly with Pema from the beginning. The two developed a good relation, but it was still too early to share leadership of any kind. Nyima Tsering's children were small and still depended on her, and she was only at the beginning of consolidating her position from an outsider to an insider. After some years, Nyima Tsering explained, she started to notice a deterioration in her relation to Tsomo, her sister-in-law; Tsomo worked more closely with Pema than before and at the same time she felt that Tsomo was rude and refused to help her with chores. Aware of Yangdröl's sad experience, Nyima Tsering worried that her sister-in-law would actively work to marginalise her in similar ways. Thus, Nyima Tsering decided to confront Tsomo. The conflict escalated, and it took several years before it was resolved. In the process, the other house members had to side with either her or Tsomo.

Most people sided with Nyima Tsering, despite her original position as an outsider, which I believe is an indication of the expected gender roles and life course development, on the one hand, and personal attributes and abilities to make alliances, on the other. When Nyima Tsering confronted Tsomo, she already had three sons. Her relationships with her two husbands, her father-in-law and Pema were solid. The first two critical phases of her marriage – pre-pregnancy and before having several children, including a son – had passed, and therefore she was confident to bring up the problem with Tsomo. The conflict was solved by sending Tsomo to work in another household – that is, not depriving her of membership in her natal house but creating a distance between her and Nyima Tsering. Through this, Nyima Tsering was recognised as the future *nangma* of Darkhang house, and she continued after this to consolidate a central and influential position.

In this house-based organisation, the formal, and expected, trajectory of an in-married wife is to transition from a peripheral role in the initial phases, during which she could easily be replaced, to a more solid attachment with the birth of children, to a more central role in moving towards taking over as female head of the household. The expected trajectory of a resident unmarried daughter, on the other hand, is to remain peripheral – an assistant – serving the household. Indeed, as Schuler showed in detail in *The Other Side of Polyandry* (1987, from Chumik in northern Nepal), unmarried women were characterised as peripheral to the social structure and organisation in a community of normative polyandry. This was also the case in Panam. However, as Childs, Goldstein and Wangdui have shown from other Panam villages, people's attitudes towards daughters are changing. As parents prefer to 'receive care from one's own daughter rather than a daughter-in-law who is viewed with some trepidation' (2011: 20), they found that to an increasing degree parents were investing in daughters so that they will remain as care contributors in their old age.[16] Despite these changes in which unmarried daughters have gained more social value and have thus indirectly become an incentive for continued arrangement of polyandry, their roles were still peripheral to the social organisation of normative polyandry. This is a peripheral position that they share – in some ways – with the youngest husbands in large (more than three husbands) polyandrous marriages, which can serve to remind us of the limits of a gender focus alone when discussing plural marriages. As Levine argued in terms of 'the less desirable child' in the corporate household being vulnerable to neglect or differential childcare in Nyinba communities, the social categories of 'young *nama*' and 'youngest husband' shared a precarious position in larger polyandrous marriages.

Yet, gender and gender models are not irrelevant. Underlying many of the concerns expressed by *nama*s above are implications of a post-marital residence pattern. For a *nama*, it was the initial phases of a marriage, after leaving home and settling in her husbands' household, and being an outsider in a well-established group that was talked about as the most difficult.[17] *Makpa*s share this position of outsider, in leaving their natal home and settling into a well-established group. Yet, there are fundamental differences between *makpa*s and *nama*s, and these reflect not only organisational factors (through which the *makpa* will become the household leader and eventually embody the centre of the house) but also gender factors (that women, their bodies and their work are of lower value, less important and fundamentally more peripheral to the order of things). In Sharlung, this gender hierarchy was naturalised and not contested.

Unidirectional Gender Manipulations

Despite a naturalised hierarchy, gender categories and classification were somewhat open to manipulation and transgression. Yet, as two very different examples will illustrate, such manipulation has the effect of reproducing and reconfirming an established gender model. The first example is about cross-dressing and female transgressions of gender expectations, and the second is about incidents of sex-change during childbirth.

When we met her, Phuntsok was fifty years old and lived in her natal house, Lhokhang, together with her elder sister and her family. Her appearance was like that of a local man, and she was unmarried. In rural areas such as Panam, bodies were clearly gendered through clothes, shoes, jewellery and hairstyles. In the 2000s, most people, and especially the women, wore traditional clothes. They wore dresses (*chuba*) with aprons indicating married status and kept their hair long, often in braids with colourful thread. When women wore traditional boots (*lham*), which was not very common, these had patterns and colours defined as being 'for women'. Phuntsok, by contrast, wore woollen trousers, a jacket and male-patterned boots, and her hair was cut short. Upon meeting her for the first time, it was not obvious to me that she was born a woman. She smoked cigarettes, and her bodily movements appeared more masculine. Her male appearance concurred with the work she was conducting; she was responsible for the male chores in the Lhokhang house, as she operated the draft animals and she ploughed and harrowed. Through these responsibilities, she also cooperated with other men in the village, providing labour assistance to male chores. In her spare time, Phuntsok was also making boots; a clearly defined male task. In order words, she lived as a man. Among her co-villagers, this performance was unproblematic, and I never heard any condescending or stigmatising attitudes towards her; in fact, her gender identity and performance was not a topic of much interest or concern.

Phuntsok's biography is interesting, as it illustrates gender transition, also to her co-villagers, who, they told me, had no previous experience with women acting as men, or men acting as women. Phuntsok's parents had six daughters and no sons; therefore, when the daughters became of marriageable age, they decided to invite a *makpa* (adopted bridegroom) for one of them. Four daughters were sent as *nama*s to other villages, and Phuntsok remained in the house. When I asked why she never married, she laughed and explained that she was never interested in living a married life and that her parents accepted this.

Talking about her life history, Phuntsok explained that she had dressed like a man for as long as she could remember, something that others also confirmed. When she was about 12 years old, Phuntsok announced to the rest of her family that from then on she would do the male chores of the household. She explained her decision with two main points: she had no brothers, and her father was physically weak from illness, hence there was a need for male labour. She cut her hair short and started to wear trousers. From a very young age, Phuntsok had assisted her father and learned all the skills from him, including ploughing and harrowing, considered the heaviest work and prohibited to women (I will return to this prohibition below). Throughout her adult life, she had, villagers said, 'been like a man' (*pumo bu trawa*). Her work history was identical to most men in Sharlung: when she was younger she helped herding smaller animals; in her adult life, she was responsible for the draft animals; later in life, as her hair turned grey, she was involved in less tiring, but still male, activities, such as making boots. Her sewing skills were well-known, and many customers came from the surrounding villages to use her services.[18] Throughout Central Tibet, women are restricted from ploughing and harrowing because of their innate ability to bring pollution to the fields; hence, it would be a moral wrongdoing (*dikpa*).[19] Phuntsok was the only person born as a woman who ploughed and harrowed in the area around Sharlung, showing that gender manipulation and transgression was possible. Cross-dressing can enable women to perform male tasks, something that has been reported from other areas of the Tibetan ethnographic region. Watkins, working with Tibetan-speaking Nyeshang in Manang, northern Nepal, found that some women disregarded gendered work restrictions simply by dressing in men's clothing whenever ploughing their fields (1996: 49). McGranahan has written about Chime Drolma, a woman born in the late nineteenth century in Kham, who was a 'female leader in a male dress' that fought the Chinese nationalists and communists in the 1930s, not only as a warrior but also as a leader of warriors (2010: 787–88). She is described as 'an exceptional female ... whose action were designed to protect her people, land, and country, and who chose to dress as a man to accomplish her goals' (ibid.: 789). Cross-dressing is clearly a means to cross gendered boundaries and evade restrictions, also in Phuntsok's case, yet the direction of transgression points to a gendered order of things in which a woman performing as a man is made sense of as an act of upward mobility.

Phuntsok's male appearance does not alter people's classification of her as a woman; she is merely 'like a man'. Tibetan grammar and name traditions help with the blurring of gendered identity: the name Phuntsok is gender neutral (as many Tibetan personal names), and the personal pronoun *khong* is used to denote both 'she' and 'he'. Takrab *achi* pointed out that 'Phuntsok is not a man: she (*mo*) is a woman. But a special woman. Like a man.' Phuntsok's transgression from female to male appearance is best understood, I argue, to be an expansion of the gender categories of man and woman, on the one hand, a challenge of the gendered division of labour, on the other; yet it does not produce new gender categories (such as a third gender) but rather reconfirms the established 'man' and 'woman'.[20]

In the excellent article 'One Plus One Makes Three' (2003), Janet Gyatso discusses a third sex category that is mentioned in Indian and Tibetan medical texts, called *maning*. Phuntsok is not *maning* or intersex, nothing of the kind was ever suggested in Sharlung. However, what Gyatso indicates as a 'mucosity' of sex categories can help us understand the expression 'just like a man'. Gyatso describes an analysis made by Zurkarwa Lodro Gyalbo, one of the most influential medical commentators of the sixteenth century. He suggested that there might be a deviance between a fixed sex and what he termed a mind-continuum (*semgyü*, similar to personality). By separating sex and mind, he points to their different character in terms of permanence and argues that while the latter can change during a lifetime, the first cannot. Zurkarwa Lodro Gyalbo concluded that 'there can be a woman who possesses a man's mind-continuum, but that does not automatically mean that she has actually become a man' (cited in Gyatso 2003: 106). One way to understand Phuntsok's gendered being is as someone who 'possesses a man's mind-continuum' (*semgyü*), enacted through cross-dressing, appearance and labour, while at the same time being classified as female.

If gender categories are open to manipulation, and their boundaries are not strictly defined, we could perhaps expect to see in Tibet an egalitarianism in which gender identity is one of individual choice of both men and women involved, and where men, as well as women, engage in transgressing the borders of sex and gender. This is, however, clearly not the case. Gender manipulation is not only very rare in Central Tibet, but it is unidirectional; women aspire to be, and perform as, men, and not the other way around. Within the logic of Tibetan gender models and the local world of rural Tsang, the opposite is absurd. There were, however, according to Lhasa friends, a group of male cross-dressers performing in one of the popular *nangma* (nightclubs) there at the beginning of the 2000s. Their appearance as women was filled with great amusement, and my friends interpreted their performance as commercial entertainment rather than an expression of 'mucous' personal gender identities. Apart from the *nangma* drag performers, I have not found examples of men cross-dressing as women, or living as women, in Central Tibet.[21] I asked people in Sharlung if they had heard about a reverse process, where a man lived and performed as a woman; however, I could not get an answer to this, because, I believe, of what they thought was the absurdity of the question.[22]

The second example to illustrate the unidirectionality of gender manipulation is a phenomenon called *lunglok*. *Lunglok* is a widely shared idea in Central Tibet of a baby changing sex in the process of childbirth – that is, from the moment of being inside the womb to the moment of appearing to those helping with the delivery (see also Levine 1987a: 290). *Lunglok* is not uncommon, and it is seen as a result of harm (*nöpa*) caused by ghosts or bad spirits (*döndré*) during the course of the delivery.²³ *Nöpa* from a *döndré*, or from other sources, is a common threat during childbirth, and women sought protection from lamas or other local religious experts during pregnancy to try to resist these external harmful forces. According to Lobsang Drolma, who had experienced *lunglok* twice, a *döndré* can cause three degrees of harm during childbirth: the first and most serious is the death of both mother and child; the second is the death of the mother or the child; and the third is the sex change of the child. *Lunglok* is seen to be a physical process, involving a substitution of genital organs, which can be partly observed by the person helping with the delivery. The mother, on the other hand, will not be able to see the actual transformation, simply due to bodily constraints. However, there are some general indications of *lunglok* that also the mother might observe, the most important being that blood appears before the baby, and often that this happens two times. During the birth of Lobsang Drolma's youngest daughter, both Tashi-la and Orgyen (her youngest husband) were present, and they both claimed to have seen the baby's penis disintegrate (*mépa jé* – dissolving into nothing).²⁴ Both cases of *lunglok* were talked about as unfortunate events.

I have not been able to find examples of a reverse process – that is, a baby changing from a girl to a boy during the delivery. When asking this in Panam and Lhasa, the question was held to be as absurd as the question about men living as women. As Lobsang Drolma said: 'I don't think it is possible to change from girl to boy, I have never heard about this. Maybe if you are very lucky! But *nöpa* cannot bring that.' *Lunglok* is caused by harm – by forces producing unwanted results – while the change from a girl to a boy would be a positive and fortunate event. In other words, *lunglok* is a process of downward gender mobility, as compared to what would be the upward mobility of a girl changing into a boy. Both these processes reflect gender norms involving a hierarchy in which women are subordinate to men and seen to be of lower value.

Woman as Initially Peripheral and Processually Influential to the Order of Things

Gender hierarches do not (in)form all categories of women in the same way. Gender ideologies are also contextual and contradictory, as we know from the many studies on the multiplicity of gender discourses conducted across the world. In Central Tibet, these discourses play out very differently in urban and rural areas, among younger and older generations, among highly educated Tibetans, among monastics and cadres. In Panam, gender norms were clearly connected to roles and to the life course, and particularly to the status of being married or unmarried, and if married, being a mother, and if a mother, being of age. Gendered roles are not very flexible, yet gender manipulation is possible, such as in the case of Phuntsok. McGranahan notes that because 'a sexed, gendered body is a very real means of grounding lived experience for Tibetan individuals . . . [e]mbracing masculinity as a personal style is thus to launch a critique of cultural norms' (2010: 789). And yet, if Phuntsok's act of transgressing female gender expectations is a critique, its reception is muted. Many times her co-villagers pointed out to me that her being 'like a man' is unproblematic, uninteresting – a topic unworthy of discussion. McGranahan notes in the same paper, thinking about exceptional women who are stronger than men, that 'Transgressing the expected order of things is remarkable, but not necessarily to be remarked upon' (ibid.: 789). In a similar way, avoiding focus on Phuntsok's exceptional gender performance enables the normative gender categories to remain unchallenged and unchanged.

Normative polyandry produces a higher number of unmarried women compared to normative monogamy or polygyny, and so-called 'surplus women' remain peripheral to the house-based social organisation and its cultural rationale. In the past, many of these unmarried women, lay or ordained, lived very precarious lives, often in poverty and reliant on personal relations for sustenance. Yet, compared to *nama*s, unmarried women also have more freedom to make their own lives. The roles of daughters are changing, and this freedom also manifested in new ways in Panam, leading women out of the village and to more independent lives (see also Childs, Goldstein and Wangdui 2011 and 2012). Nicola Schneider, in her work with nuns in eastern Tibet, found that the idea of marriage and married life was one of the motivations for seeking ordination in a nunnery (2013). A life as an unmarried woman, lay or monastic, is a life on the periphery of the social and cultural order of things in rural areas; unmarried women are not central to the reproduction of the corporate household and not central to the upholding of religious expertise (although attitudes towards nuns are changing). A married woman, on the other hand, moves from a peripheral to a more central position within the house throughout her life course. *Nama*s in polyandrous marriages talk about the potential influence and centrality of their position. Such potential is greater for women married to more than one husband, with whom they build close, supportive and collaborative relations. For *nama*s in polyandrous houses – often houses of relative wealth – they might also enact that centrality in inter-house relations and village affairs.

Discussing gendered values among Lio in Indonesia, Howell (1996) made the point that we should be careful not to privilege sexual difference over other more relevant forms of differences and concluded that 'Having escaped from a previous gender blindness, we must not now become blinded by gender' (1996: 267). This well-made point is significant also to the case of gender and polyandry. If we look beyond gender and compare the social category of 'young *nama*' with that of 'youngest husband', they do share some experiences; both are initially peripheral to the house as a social unit. Yet, the initial process of establishing a secure position in the household differs – while the peripheral husbands are ascribed their positions, in-married wives achieve theirs by their own personal abilities to form alliances and affectionate bonds. A *nama*, as a woman who has moved patrilocally after marriage, is also more vulnerable to maltreatment and abuse as Rajan describes from north-east Tibet (2014), especially in the initial period, as compared to younger husbands. At the same time, in-married women are expected to establish a leading position within the house; to become the female household head. Comparing across gender boundaries, the youngest husband and the unmarried woman are in the most precarious positions, as the expectation of their roles is to remain peripheral through their lifetime. For women marrying into a polyandrous house, this marriage form can provide a stronger sense of safety, enable economic vitality and, despite involving a demanding and complex form of relationality, more broadly, a less strenuous life.

Notes

1. See Bell (1928: 129ff.); Ekvall (1968); Stein (1972); Havnevik (1989). While there are very few studies of Tibetan lay women (with the exception of some chapters in Gyatso and Havnevik (2005); Fjeld and Hofer (2011) and Hofer (2015) on outstanding women in Tibetan Medicine; Rajan (2018a) on domestic violence in north-eastern Tibet), there has been a growing body of literature dealing with monastic women during the last decades, such as Havnevik (1989, 1999), Gyatso (1989, 1998, 2003), Gutschow (2004), Diemberger (2007), Schneider (2011, 2013) and Jacoby (2014), and also, female ritual practitioners and experts, Schrempf and Schneider (2015).
2. See Fjeld and Hofer (2011) for more on female *amchis* in the history of Tibetan medicine, and McGranahan (2010) on women warriors and gender and history more broadly.
3. These perceptions of women are found across the Tibetan plateau; for instance, to the south of Ü-Tsang, Childs notes from Nubri valley in Nepal that: 'Women are considered to be more intelligent than men, yet less able to control their passions and hence less suited for the life of contemplation' (2004: 62), while in the northeast, Makley, writing from Amdo, notes that: 'Tibetans across the community (men and women) tended to argue that the male body was the result of greater stores of merit (Tib. *bsod nams*) from past lifetimes and that this underlay men's ability to transcend bodily limitations and to succeed in pursuits of the mind. Meanwhile, the female body was considered to be a lower rebirth (Tib. *skye dman*), more hampered than male bodies by physiological processes and thus suited to household labor' (Makley 2003: 601).

4. After strong pressure from Tibetan Women's Association in India, the exiled government in Dharamsala suggested a new spelling for 'woman', *kyéme*, where *kye* is still spelled *skye* (birth) but where *me* is spelled *sman*, meaning medicine, thus giving *kyéme* a new etymology meaning birth medicine (Tsomo Svenningsen, personal communication, Oslo, 2006). Rumour has it that it was a Western ordained Tibetan Buddhist nun in Dharamsala that initiated this rewriting. I cannot confirm this. Women Hofer and I talked to in Lhasa have asked their husbands and family to avoid the term *kyeme*, replacing it with *Aji* (*A ca*), meaning both wife and woman. We have also been told that the Dalai Lama avoids using *kyeme* (Fjeld and Hofer 2011).
5. I am grateful to the reviewer who pointed out the historical meanings of these two terms.
6. See Lopez (1998: 211). Another example is from Kim Gutschow, writing about nuns Zanskar in Ladakh, who found that in Tibetan proverbs women are said to be seven lifetimes behind men and that women must accumulate the merit of seven additional lifetimes before they can be reborn as men (2004: 16). She further points out that there is a rather dubious logic to such a system, for if it always takes seven more rebirths, how can a woman ever be reborn as a man?
7. Gyatso and Havnevik speculate that these thirty-two illnesses might reflect the negative counterpart of the thirty-two marks of the Buddha that women cannot have (2005).
8. Rajan nuances this statement and holds that 'local forms of feminist consciousness' do circulate among Tibetan women but often in artistic expressions, such as poems (2018b: 291). Moreover, among some Tibetan Buddhist nuns, and especially in exile, there are feminist initiatives that debate also the situation of women in rural Central Tibet (see, for instance, tibetanfeministcollective.org).
9. Rajan, writing from an area with stronger patri-orientation and where women are more exposed to domestic violence, also notes that 'At times, husbands help to shield their wives from the worst of their sisters-in-law's or mother-in-law's abuse' (2014: 147). She also found that heavy burdens of work, scolding or maltreatment from the mother-in-law to the daughter-in-law were not seen to be acceptable. For more on acceptable and non-acceptable reasons for beatings of a wife in north-eastern Tibet, see also Rajan 2018a.
10. Being a returned *nama* is not uncomplicated. Re-marriage is possible, and indeed most common, according to my interlocutors; however, she cannot expect to settle in a high-ranking house. A re-marrying woman contradicts marriage patterns by being sent to a household that is lower-ranked than her natal group. Hypergamy is thus the result of moral disruptions. Re-marrying women are looked down upon and termed second-hand, or 'used' (*chelmo*). However, after the re-marriage has been arranged, the *nama* seems to be treated well. For the husbands, on the contrary, a new marriage would not lead to a decline in status.
11. See Goldstein, Childs and Wangdui (2008) for more on 'going for income' from Panam villages.
12. When talking about issues related to sex, there is always a significant amount of giggling involved. However, I do believe that we managed to talk about these issues in a substantial way (see also the previous chapter on the varying practices of *kora khor* systems). Mingzom, my daughter's nanny, was very curious about the sexual aspects of polyandry, and with her straightforward personality, she started many discussions with the women of Sharlung, and particularly Lobsang Drolma in our house. These conversations were, however, characterised by many questions and only brief answers.
13. See also Levine (1988) for the importance placed on sex in polyandry among Nyinba.

14. These patterns have been changing with the development of job opportunities since 2005, in which it is becoming common to send daughters for income outside the village.
15. See also Childs, Goldstein and Wangdui (2011) for more on changing roles of daughters in Panam.
16. That is, economic and social investment in externally-residing daughters, such as education and financial aid to set up an independent livelihood, in the hope that they will remain close to their natal house (Childs, Goldstein and Wangdui 2011).
17. See Rajan (2014) on the differences of women's experiences of abuse depending on the post-marriage residence patterns, in the north-eastern edge part of Tibet.
18. Making shoes is defined as men's work, and in Sharlung no woman except for Phuntsok knew how to produce these traditional boots, although women spin the wool and make the frieze that is used as the main material for the boots (and clothes).
19. Despite the fact that women's restriction from ploughing in Himalayan societies has been mentioned in much of the ethnographic literature (Levine 1988; Watkins 1996; Vinding 1998; Gutschow 2004), explanations are limited. Carrasco, for instance, simply states that women occasionally can plough (1959: 48), but he does not suggest circumstances for such occasions. One exception is Vinding, who claims that no ethnic groups or castes in Nepal allow women to plough and suggests that ploughing is sinful because it involves killing worms (1998: 211, 32n). Gutschow, writing from Zangskar in northern India, links the prohibition to the defilement of the female body and its ability to pollute the fields (2004: 69–70), an explanation similar to those I found in Panam. She refers to a local proverb that gives an indication of the rigidity of the gender restriction against ploughing (and in Zangskar, weaving): 'If women were to weave or plow, the mountains would fall down' (ibid.: 69).
20. Nepal and India recognise a third gender for those who do not identify as male or female; however, this is not a strong notion in Tibetan communities.
21. More recently, Tenzin Mariko, a transwoman from Bir now living in Dharamsala, has become a public activist for trans-rights in Tibetan communities, challenging these unidirectional gender transitions.
22. In neighbouring areas to Tibet, such as Mongolia and Nepal, there are known ritualised inversions where men act as women, and women act as men (Lindskog 2000). These inversions are commonly termed 'reversed rituals' (social order is reversed in bounded ritual contexts). I was not able to find examples of such reversing practices in Sharlung.
23. In early Buddhist texts, the sex of a person is described as something that can change within one life, as well as between lives. In the Vinaya, rather than being the result of spirit attacks these changes are referred to as being karmic in nature. Apparently, the Buddha himself accepted sex change, both from woman to man, and from man to woman, as is described in the Vinaya to have happened with a monk and a nun. Further, in the Dhammapada commentary, sex change is not seen to limit the spiritual potential of the person (Harvey 2000: ch. 10).
24. It is interesting to note that the word used to describe the change from a penis to a vagina, *mépa jé*, does not imply a transformation of something to something else but, rather, something dissolving into nothing.

Chapter 5

THE HOUSE AS RITUAL SPACE

Every morning, just after ten, I could hear *Achi* (the grandmother) whispering chants. When the sun started to warm up the air, and people were already busy with the chores of the day, she lit the bowl of incense (*sang*) and slowly said her *Om mani padme hum* prayers. With repeated whispers and the juniper smell of burning *sang*, she walked through the spaces of the house. Starting in the room of the hearth, she encircled the water reservoir and spread the incense into all four corners. She left the first room and carefully blew the *sang* towards the stone hearth (*tsala*), where the barley beer (*chang*) would later be boiling. Approaching our room, *Achi* greeted me smilingly while she continued to murmur her prayers and let the *sang* spread itself out into the corners, focusing on the sitting and sleeping place and around the door. She continued into the neighbouring 'prosperity room' (*yangkhang*) and dispersed the pleasant smell around the grain and the shrine of the house protector (*namo*). Following this, she entered the shrine room (*chökhang*), making sure the *sang* still burned and the smoke spread out into the air. After this round, *Achi* carefully climbed the ladder to the roof and let the smoke transport itself with the wind. Coming down again, she smiled and said: 'Now, the house is clean (*khangpa tsangma sö tsar*).'

The house building (*khang*) is the site for both everyday and extraordinary events of life; it is where the closest relations are produced and reproduced, among married partners, siblings, parents and children, and others living their lives together. Houses are also homes providing (for most) a sense of belonging, not only for humans but also for the many nonhumans who share these spaces, and much work – such as *Achi*'s daily offerings and cleansing – goes into making and maintaining houses as a space that mediates coexistence and allows for prosperity, amicable relations and a sense of safety. As shown in the many examples in the anthology *About the House*, 'the house and the body are intimately linked', the house being an extension of the body, and extra layer of the skin, that both 'reveals and displays' and 'hides and protects' what is inside (Carsten and Hugh-Jones 2005: 2). Bodily practices are also central to the making and maintaining of the boundaries of the house, such as *Achi*'s daily careful movements. *Achi*'s house is a potentially bounded space that, with proper action, can provide her and her co-residents with not only cover from the harsh environment but a sense of belonging and also a representation of ontological order and ritual protection.

The following observations of physical houses stem from the beginning of the 2000s, before the government launched the programme called Comfortable House Project (CHP). From 2006 and onwards, the CHP provided loans and subsidies to encourage (or coerce, and something in between) farmers and nomads to renovate or (re)build their houses. Whole villages were also resettled (Robin 2009; Yeh 2013). People who visited Panam after 2012 told me that 'almost all houses' in Sharlung had been renovated or rebuilt, albeit to different degrees. One of the semi-pasatoralist villages higher up in the township had been relocated closer to a road, to an area with better access to grass and water. The households in Sharlung received between 2000 and 10,000 RMB in subsidies, depending on their economic status, and secured the rest of the funding themselves, mostly through loans.[1] As one person said: 'They just accepted it.' Although there were policy guidelines of CHP that encouraged things like moving animals out from the ground floor, in Sharlung people rebuilt 'the same houses, with the animals and grass inside'.[2] This is only anecdotal information, and for sure, the renovation and rebuilding processes have produced changes to both the exterior and interior of the houses in Sharlung (as Yeh 2013 details). However, according to the information that I have the main architectural structures seem to have been maintained.

Farmers' houses in Tsang are by no means randomly organised; they are deeply meaningful and orderly places. In studies of vernacular architecture, houses have often been compared to books 'in which the order of [the] world is recorded' (Schulte Nordholt cited in Waterson 1997: xvii). Moreover, houses can be, in Bourdieu's terms, an embodiment of cultural messages – messages that are internalised by its residents. Children read the house 'book' with their bodies, he wrote in his work on Berber houses, 'in and through the movements and displacements which make the space within which they are enacted as much as they are made by it' (Bourdieu 1997: 90). Through daily, embodied practices, *Achi* and her co-residents (re)produce the Takrab house as an ordered space, reflecting the world (*jikten*) itself and their place within it. The house is a microcosm, placing the humans and nonhumans in an ontological order and facilitating proper and friendly relations between them. Ordering the house, and acting accordingly, enables ritual efficacy. This efficacy is existential in a state of ontologically continuity, where humans, animals, sprits, demons and deities, and corporeal, semi- and non-corporeal beings and forces share the world. The concept of *jikten* encompasses a wider mode of understanding human and nonhuman engagement with the world, as they are entangled and enmeshed in what can be called extended sociality – that is, a sociality that extends 'beyond immediate relations between human consociates' (Sillander and Remme 2018: 3). Much ritual activity in Tibetan communities is conducted to tame the local deities and to maintain proper relations between humans and nonhumans, and the house is a crucial space in which an extended sociality unfolds, is explained, and is controlled.

The house as a tamed, controlled ritual space was an important element in Sharlung, reflected in the villagers' emphasis on strengthening their domestic unit, the *khyimtsang*, and this points to the very constitutional nature of the domestic, not only as an economic entity but also as an ontological, symbolic and ritual space. The social dynamics of polyandry are centripetal – they move towards the centre – seen in the efforts involved to maintain people, material and immaterial wealth within the already established social institution of the house. The inward-focused, centripetal effects of polyandry concur with ontological values that are spatially represented in vernacular architecture. The following investigates the efforts involved in creating and reproducing the house as a ritually efficacious space in which the extended sociality between humans and nonhumans can enfold, and where protection can be secured, increasing fertility and growth on the one hand, and reducing harm, misfortune and pollution on the other.

A Fortress-Like Exterior

In the preface to the newly reprinted *Man and his House in the Himalaya*, Toffin writes that 'Beyond their physical contours, the dwellings and settlements of the Himalayan range embody a number of social and religious implicit meanings' (2016 [1991]: i).[3] Across the Tibetan ethnographic region there is a set of core principles that are utilised to varying degrees, forming comparative structures of lay architecture.[4] Traditionally, in the rural areas, there were two main types of dwellings for lay people: mud-brick and stone houses for farmers and black tents for nomads (although nomads often also had access to houses). While these dwellings clearly are very different, in symbolic terms their interiors are organised in similar ways.

Tsang farmers' houses are very well adapted to the arid, mineral natural environment of the Tibetan plateau, where wood is scarce and material alternatives are meagre. Yet, vernacular architecture is not simply 'some ill-defined adaptation to the environment'; as Humphrey has pointed out, the structures and forms also 'have purpose and intention' (1988: 17). The houses in Sharlung were for the most part two-storey rectangular buildings made of stones, dried mud bricks and wood. They were surrounded by a courtyard enclosed by a mud-brick wall, conveying a sense of enclosure and containment. The houses varied in magnitude and architectural elaboration, with the number and size of windows, the use of white paint and general amount of decorative and protective work increasing with the contemporary economic situation and social historical position. However, across class and other hierarchies, there was a shared architectural ideal readily apparent in Sharlung, similar to Central Tibet and other places in the high Himalayas. Houses provide individuals with, as Maréchaux noted from the Indian Himalayas, a 'profound sense of security' (1991: 224): physically they protect against fierce winds and cold climate, and ritually, they protect against misfortune, harm and pollution.

Approaching a house in Sharlung, we would meet mud-brick walls framing the gates (*chigo*, outside door) and marking the boundaries to the inside; only those living threre or those with established relations should enter the *chigo* without invitation. During fieldwork we spent much time outside such gates shouting a polite '*lo*' to make our presence known. The courtyards varied in size and function, but they sheltered the draft animals such as cows, *dzo* and horses when they were not grazing in the mountains or in the cleared fields, and the young calves, lambs and kids in the periods when they needed extra care. Also, the much-feared watchdogs spent their lives chained in the courtyard. Depending on size, people used the courtyards for additional needs, such as drying dung, or they cultivated potatoes and turnips on small plots of land. Tractors and mechanical equipment was also stored there.

The economic situation of a household clearly affects the material structures of a house. The Sobnub house can serve as an illustration of a typical architecture for those with limited means, although they were not the poorest in the village. The house had been built some twenty years earlier and had two storeys; the ground floor hosted two cows and the family lived on the first floor. The house itself was small (some 70 square meters of which only two rooms had a complete roof), and the courtyard on the southern side was barely large enough for the tractor parked there. Both the stone fence and the walls of the house were without paint, as they could not afford the white lime used by many others in the village. The Dagpo house can serve as an opposite example. When we arrived in Sharlung and told people that we were interested in learning about local culture and history, we were often advised to visit Dagpo. The Dagpo estate covered an area of some 200 square meters, and the courtyard was exceptionally large. A former *genpo* house, Dagpo illustrates the building style of those with financial means and the fine traditional architecture of Tsang farmhouses. The Dagpo house had been rebuilt four years before our visit, after a flood had damaged the previous structure. The ruins of the former, smaller house were still visible. The new house was a two-storey rectangular building laid out on a north-south axis; the entrance faced the east. Slightly widening towards the ground, the massive walls gave the house a bottom-heavy look, with only small window openings. The house was painted white, and the large windows on the first floor, placed on the southern and eastern side and framed by black paint to attract the warmth of the sun, dominated the house. The outer wall encircled the courtyard; the house was imposing and gave the impression of restricted access. The economic situation at that time was not, however, the only defining factor for the architectural structures in Sharlung. There were several large, old houses inhabited by poor households that were nevertheless architectural ideals. These were often ritually powerful houses, with immaterial wealth – that is, ritual and protective objects and forces, and long biographies. Common to all houses was the form of enclosure, particularly visible in the affluent and old houses yet also part of the smaller, often incomplete, houses. Stein's note back in the 1970s, that 'even the dwelling-houses are fortress-like' (1972: 120), indicates a strong continuity of vernacular architecture.

The Interior House as Cosmological Space

House construction and maintenance in Central Tibet is clearly linked to cosmology; it is the place within which cosmology unfolds. Much in the same way that has been shown from across the Tibetan ethnographic region (Toffin 2016 [1991]),[5] the material and immaterial structures of Sharlung houses reflect the vertical tripartite ordering (*sa sum*) of the phenomenal world (*jikten*). The vertical axis that organises the house interior is a reflection of a verticality found in the ontological order exterior to the boundaries of the house. As pointed out by Dollfus, the notion of height and elevation are highly esteemed in the Tibetan world in general, and he links this notion to the creation of a hierarchy of space and man, where the high is pure and the low is impure and to be despised (1996). In addition to interior design, the value of verticality is also found in perceptions of the body, of nature and popular celebrations of geography, and in time (Humphrey 1995; Ramble 1996, 1999).

Pervasive in Tibetan thinking about the world, the tripartite ontology consists of an upper domain (*tok*), mountains and passes inhabited by powerful tantric deities residing in sacred mountains (*néri*), as well as local deities such as *yul lha* and *gyelpo*; a middle domain (*bar*) inhabited by humans, animals, minor deities (such as *sadak* and *tsen*) and demons (*döndré* and *dü*) as well as jealous (dead or alive) women (*söndréma*); and lastly, the domain below (*ok*), inhabited by serpentine deities (*lu*). This same three-tiered arrangement of space and its inherent cosmological reflection is the most visible order in a house's interior, seen particularly in the localisation of different shrines. It manifests hierarchical cosmological values in a way that is often described as a 'microcosm'.[6] Writing from Ladakh, Martin Mills describes how, in an ideal Tibetan Buddhist house, such three-tiered hierarchical organisation orders cosmology, beings and activities. He writes: 'the dominant activities of the household – production/reproduction; hospitality; offering – were spatially embodied . . . producing marked divisions in the quotidian use of the house as a lived space, organising the social, economic and ritual practices of the household members and their guests' (2003: 156). The three domains are connected through a pillar (or set of (often four) pillars (*ka*) that links the three floors and domains (ibid.: 157).

This spatio-symbolic organisation was apparent also in Panam. As a general pattern, Tibetan farmers' houses are built facing east, indicating the value of cardinal directionality, but more importantly they point to a vertical rationale. Typically, the northern part of the house is designated to the most powerful ritual activities, while social activities take place in the southern part because, as Tashi-la explained regarding the placement of the kitchen (*taptsang*) in Takrab: 'It is bright and the furthest away from the north.' Verticality is also the basic principle of nomad tents, with the rear symbolising the highest part of the tent. In an article on the distribution of 'the black tents' (*dranak*) from Persia to Tibet, Manderscheid (2001) describes the symbolism of the tent's interior. A *dranak*, she explains, is divided into a female (left) side for women, children and female chores and tools, and a male (right) side for men and guests and the implements operated by men. In addition, the rear of the tent 'is the sitting place of honor and the family shrine' (ibid.: 159, as well as the storage room for religious objects and excess butter. Manderscheid does not specify the directional pegging of the Tibetan tents, which has some implications for the understanding of spatial and symbolic organisation. However, as Manderscheid also suggests, these could be placed on a north–south axis like Mongolian tents (Mong. *ger*), where the rear of the tent faces the north and the opening of the tent faces south (Fjeld and Lindskog 2017). According to Jest's descriptions (1991), Dolpo tents are placed somewhat differently, as the entrance faces towards the east. Despite the difference in terms of directionality, both the Mongolian and

Tibetan pastoralist tent share a fundamental organisation based on the value of upper versus lower – that is, a vertical axis. Inherent in this axis is what Huber calls a 'strong vertical gradient from gross at the bottom and more refined or pure above' (1999: 45). Indeed, the rear of the tent is perceived to be the sacred space – it is the highest on the symbolic axis of pure–impure. The rear is the location of the Buddhist shrines. Opposite, the entrance is perceived as 'down', hence the impure place. The up–down rationale is also found in sleeping positions in a tent, where people should keep their head positioned upwards towards the shrine (Jest 1991; Lindskog 2000; Manderscheid 2001). The human body is inherently impure, yet pollution is also distributed from top to bottom.[7] Hence, the perceptions of the body also reflect the value of verticality and the conceptual concurrence of high and pure. The value of verticality is hence represented in a horizontally laid out Tibetan tent, which also reflects the tripartite ordering of the world. The rear of the tent is the upper domain; the right, masculine side is the middle domain, while the lower domain is the left, feminine side. This is reflected, for example, in Dolpo tents, where the rear of the tent is the place of what they call the *phuk lha* (god of ancestors); a dedication to the *tsen* deities is placed on the male side, and an offering to the *lu* is located on the female side (Jest 1991).

Cardinal directions were of guiding importance in Sharlung, too, but there was not a rigid formalism to the layout of the houses. As found in the *dranak*, the spatial organisation of a house is based on a vertical axis of pure: impure :: high: low :: upper: lower. While in Mongolia these pairs of oppositions also correspond to the direction of north: south, this is not the case in the Sharlung houses. As Tashi-la noted above, the main place for socialisation (the *taptsang*) is located to the south – that is, down – due to its maximum distance from the north, indicating that human activities should be separated from the most sacred space. The entrance of the houses, as in the Dolpo tents, most often faced the east and was regarded as 'down'. The furthest point away from the entrance ('down') was in the north ('up'). There were exceptions to this, but I cannot recall having seen an entrance facing the north or west. In the houses I have systematically registered in Sharlung, the main Buddhist shrine room (*chökhang*) and room hosting the house protector were located towards the north. Hence, the axis of upper–lower seems to be more fundamental to the spatio-symbolic organisation of the house than the cardinal directions as such. In the following, I describe the three domains of the Dönkhang in all cases in Sharlung, and this will also show the similarities to previously described Ladakhi houses (Mills 2003).

The Ground Floor

The inner door (*nang-go*) of the house lead to the ground floor, where animals were kept at night. This was the domain of female chores, including as caring for animals and the spirit living there. It was also the dirtiest (*tsokpa*) place in the house. Hay and agricultural tools were stored in the northwest corner, and the middle of the room was the designated space for milking cows, lit by an opening in the roof through which the sun's rays penetrated. The room in the south-east corner provided protection for lambs and goats, though animals were also tethered on both the north and south sides of the space. Internal walls had been built in all corners to provide extra storage spaces.

Ritually and symbolically, the shrine of the *lu* – the *lukhang* – is the most important object on the ground floor. The *lukhang* was placed high up on the northern wall under the ceiling. The *lu* (also called *lumo*, female *lu*) is a well-known serpentine spirit in the Tibetan world. They often live beneath the surface of streams and rivers as well as in trees. Relations with the *lu* influence growth in women and animals, and in Sharlung, as many other places, the *lumo* were closely associated with milk and fertility. The women of the house (usually the *nama*) were responsible for quotidian offerings to the *lumo*. Tashi-la pointed out that it should be the *nama* that makes the offerings to the *lumo* because, he said: 'She [*nama*] needs milk.' When I asked Lobsang Drolma about how and when she makes the offerings in the Takrab house, she explained:

> I have to go on auspicious days. We look in the [astrological] calendar and find the Palden days. On some of the Palden days I make offerings three times. Sometimes I have to wait for a long period. I have to put different things into the container (*pumba*); I put three sorts of agricultural produce (*shing*), a few *lungta*, and grain blessed in the monastery, and some flowers from the fields. *Lumo* likes flowers, and we try to find *tsanga metok*, as she prefers those. These things should always be there. Then I take *pangbö* [a small plant that grows high in the mountains], dry it and crumble it into small pieces and put it into the container. In one side I put the *pangbö*, and in the other side I put *tsampa* and sugar and make fire. Then I make the offering.

There were two types of *lu* residing in Sharlung: one had a kind personality and positively contributed to milk production, and another was easily angered and lived mostly underground, outside, and if upset would cause illness to people and animals. A *lu* can obstruct the flow of blood in the veins (*tsa*), causing great pain, and *lu* attacks are often recognised by swollen limbs and skin rashes that make the arms and legs resemble snakeskin. They can also make the eyes of sheep and goats grow out of proportion and, in severe cases, fall out. An attack is usually a result of someone having

Figure 5.1. A *lukhang*, the main shrine on the ground floor. © Heidi Fjeld

disturbed an unknown *lu* in their dwelling place, and *lu* disease (*luné*) is cured primarily by making offerings and, in serious cases, by building a new shrine; with the help of a spirit medium (*lhapa*) the *lu* is invited to accept it as its new home.[8]

Newer houses in Sharlung did not usually host a *lu*, while some of the houses with long biographies could have up to four *lumo*s on the ground floor. Humans will inevitably come into contact with one or several *lu*; they are connected through shared land. By building *lukhang* and inviting them into the house, the *lu* are enmeshed into a network of relations with the people of the household, particularly the women, who feed and care for them. The ground floor clearly corresponds to the lower ontological domain in hosting the spirits of this lowest (*ok*) domain and being the residence for animals. The production activities of the ground floor are closely interconnected with – yet separate from – the reproduction and hospitality of the middle domain on the first floor.[9]

The First Floor

The wooden ladder located close to the inner door (*nang-go*), lead to the living quarters of the first floor – the place of both the middle (*bar*) and upper ontological domains. In Dönkhang, the first floor was an open, uncovered space surrounded by rooms on all sides. The first floor is the domain of humans, but it was also shared with a few small animals (chickens and occasionally sick young animals) as well as minor deities. The activities of this domain are concerned with reproduction, both in biological and social terms, enacted as socialisation and hospitality. As most of the farmers' houses did not have a second floor (apart from the roof), the first floor also included the upper (*tok*), and third, domain. The first floor was therefore symbolically arranged into upper and lower parts; hence vertical principles are applied horizontally in ways that resemble the black tents.

In the case of the Dönkhang house, the first floor included the kitchen-cum-living room (*taptsang*), sleeping quarters and a room for produce (*norkhang/yangkhang*). The *taptsang* is the place of the hearth and the social heart of the house. It is where the women prepare food and where meals are shared and guests entertained. The kitchen also contained the water reservoir (with the water deity, *chu lha*), and it was where important documents were kept, such as records of mutual aid received and given, as well as the leather pouch (*yangkhuk*) used to store the auspicious objects of the house.[10] The *taptsang* was also the bedroom for the eldest generation, for unmarried members of the house, and the children that are no longer nursing – that is, for those who are no longer or not yet in the reproductive phase of life. In most of the relatively affluent houses, the *taptsang* was a large room with white, auspicious patterns painted on the wall, and it offered seating arrangements for some fifteen people. This room was at the heart of social life in the house and the prime site for socially (re)producing a sense of belonging and practicing hospitality. Just outside the *taptsang* in Dönkhang, in a corner of a small in-between space protected from the wind by a roof and tarpaulin, was the traditional stone stove (called *tsala*) used to boil water and make *chang*, and where the important *taplha* (god of the stove) resides. The *tsala* is crucial in the process of relocating a house, as we shall see later.

In addition to the *taptsang*, there were five other rooms on the first floor in Dönkhang. On the southern side was a small bedroom usually used by the *nama* and her eldest husband when he was home, and babies still nursing. There was also an empty, uncompleted room the same side that still needed a roof. Two bedrooms were located on the eastern side, and these were used interchangeably by the two younger husbands. The toilets were on the western side. The first floor was a place for offerings; indeed, it was the abode of several deities of different categories. The minor deities, such as the *taplha* (hearth) and *chu lha* (water), resided close to the kitchen on the southern side and were cared for by women. The north-eastern end (*norkhang*) stored all that was important – the material (*nor*) wealth of the house as well as the immaterial wealth (*yang*). The room consisted of two parts; the first was the

Figure 5.2. A *namo* on the first floor. © Heidi Fjeld

main storage room where the year's production of grain was kept in large, handmade woollen bags; the second part also stored grain but hosted the *namo* (also referred to as *norlha*), who resided in a shrine high up on the wall in the north-eastern corner, overlooking the produce. The shrine was made up of twigs (*wu shing*), and the offerings to the *namo* mainly consisted of *chang*, *tsampa*, wheat, salt, hay, as well as dried meat called *yang sha*, meant to enhance the *yang* (prosperity) and *nor*. The female head of the house was usually responsible for providing these offerings, although occasionally a younger *nama* could do it. Offerings to the *namo* should be done on Saturdays or on a day advised by the spirit medium; in this case, it would occur at a different time to the other regular offerings inside the house. Access to this room was restricted, and non-members refrained from entering. The inner part of the room could be used as a bedroom but for house members only. The bedrooms, kitchen and the *norkhang* were shared by humans and nonhumans engaged in social and moral economies of production and reproduction and constituted the middle ontological domain (*bar*) in a microcosmic reflection. However, on the first floor there was another very important room that complicated this microcosmos model.

The northern end was also the location of the *chökhang* – the shrine room – hosting Buddhist devotional items and protective forces (texts, blessed objects, photos and paintings) as well as being the place for ritual activities conducted by ordained monks. The room contained a large shrine on the back wall of the room – that is, furthest away from the entrance – and had a place for people to sit and read. The activities that took place in the *chökhang* were restricted; it was where monks or ordained household members slept when needed. In exceptional cases, other people held to be morally virtuous stayed there.[11] The restrictions on the use of the *chökhang* maintained the room physically but just as important kept it ritually clean and at a distance from lay people's bodies. As *Achi* in Takrab said: 'People are dirty. And their behaviour brings *drip tsok* (pollution).' Sexual activities were strongly prohibited in the *chökhang*, as well as washing, cooking, spilling dirty water and spitting, again reflecting degrees of pollution. This room was distinct from the rest on the first floor as it symbolically represented the third, upper (*tok*) ontological domain – that is, the domain of the highest deities. Being located in the north – symbolically the highest point – and furthest away from the human social activities represented by the *taptsang* in the southern corner, it reflected the vertical axis of pure/impure, sharing design concerns and features with black nomadic tents.

The Roof

The roof in Dönkhang was accessible via a permanent wooden ladder on the first floor and was open to all house members. The corners of the roof were typically marked by small offering. In the north-east corner, there was an elaborate collection of twigs (*wu shing*) and white flags and prayer flags, surrounded by white round stones, a yak horn and empty bottles,[12] marking it as a particularly auspicious place. Two *wu shing* with flags were also placed above the entrance to the house, halfway between the southern and eastern point of the roof. In the south-east corner was additional *wu shing*, and large white stones with hay underneath. There was often a cumulative increase of hay and stones around the roof towards the northern side. In the west, close to the north-west corner, there were three stones; one bigger stone marked the actual north-west corner, while eight stones were spread along the northern side of the roof. The ritual importance of the north, and particularly the north-east was clearly expressed.

More important than the hay, stones and other material markings was the *lha khang* (the 'house for deities'), located in the middle of the northern part of the roof. This was a small square temple built with mud bricks and dirt and decorated with various offerings. It resembled the residence of the *yul lha* or other local *lha*. The *lha khang* shared features with human houses; it had its front towards the east, and a small square opening framed with black paint, resembling a window. Inside this opening was the incense (*sang*) burning. Pierced through the middle of the small house construction was a wooden stick (resembling the house pillar, *ka*) surrounded by three *wu shing* with white flags and/or five-coloured prayer flags. The roof of the *lha khang* was decorated in similar way to a human house; with stones and hay in the four corners, a yak horn and a *khatak* (white ceremonial scarf) on the northern side. The *lha khang* was painted white with a red line. The white colour indicated that it is the house of a *tsen*, explained to be a deceased lay relative. Other houses had a red-painted roof, indicating the presence of *gyelpo*; a deceased ordained relative. According to Takrab *Achi*, in their case they built their *lha khang* at the same time as the house itself because the *tsen* had insisted (through a spirit medium) that he would follow them into the new building. 'He has lived with us for a long time now. We wanted him to have a house so that he would not be angry.' The *gyelpo* and the *tsen* are deities of the middle domain (*bar*); however, they were often talked about with respect.[13] These nonhuman beings are powerful and needed regular offerings to be kept happy. They were also meant to reside away from humans (hence, away from the first floor).

In Sharlung, as most houses had only two floors and their financial means were limited, mapping a cosmological representation in the interior space

Figure 5.3. Offering to the *tsen* on the roof. © Heidi Fjeld

was done in a pragmatic way. While the ground floor (what Mills (2003) calls the basement) corresponds to the lower ontological domain, the first floor (Mills' central floor) corresponds to the middle and upper domains, laid out practically (horizontally). In an ideal house, the ontological tripartite is clearly reflected in the interior space, placing humans and nonhumans and their associated activities in proper relation to each other. The upper domain is inhabited by the most powerful Buddhist and local deities, who receive offerings and protect the house as a whole. The middle domain is the place for humans and (smaller) animals and is shared with the household protector (the *namo*) and other minor deities, who support biological and social reproduction and protect the wealth of the house. The lower domain is the home of serpentine spirits, who reside in the *lukhang* and influence fertility and, with that, production. None of the houses I mapped in Panam corresponded exactly to this ideal. However, when I asked about the interior arrangements of a house, the residents were quick to offer explanations for major or minor deviations from this ideal, conveying the principle of downward verticality. How are relationships enacted and maintained within these houses, and what is at stake in the efforts to keep the three domains of the house distinct and apart?

Enabling Relations through Separation

Moving through the Panam valley, as elsewhere on the Tibetan plateau, the land is marked by Buddhist elements. Devotional architecture, such as monasteries and temples, stupas and cairns, as well as colourful flags spreading prayers with the wind, remind villagers and visitors of the tamed nature of the land and its potential dangers. A well-known conversion myth, first described in the twelfth-century Mani Kambum text, and still popular, tells the story of how pre-Buddhist Tibet was inhabited by a plethora of malevolent spirits and chthonic beings before being brought under Buddhist control through the subjugation of a demoness. In this myth, the vast Tibetan land was seen in the form of a supine body of a demoness (*sinmo*), lying on her back, wild and ferocious. In order to place this land under Buddhist jurisdiction, the *sinmo* was tamed through the placing of Buddhist temples on thirteen crucial points; her hands and feet, elbows and knees, hips and shoulders, and lastly, her heart; pinning her down, taming her, and hence taming Tibet (Gyatso 1989). The Jokhang temple in Lhasa, standing firmly on her heart, and the most important pilgrimage site in Tibet, is a reminder of this taming. This sense of residing in, and thus sharing, a land of powerful, vengeful and dangerous forces that need to be handled, controlled and tamed is central to being-in-the-world across the Tibetan ethnographic region.

While monasteries and *trulku* lineages provide an advanced and, according to themselves, the only truly efficacious protection against the forces and deities of the world in everyday life, Tibetan farmers are enmeshed in extended socialities with nonhuman beings in ways that demand action and organisation in their daily life.

The central notion of interdependence or interconnectedness (*temdrel*) in Tibetan Buddhist ontology refers to the idea that 'everything is constituted by the coming together of multiple causes and conditions; everything is dependent for its existence upon something else' (Gyatso 1998: 179). Interconnection is reflected in many Tibetan conceptions of the natural world; *nö chü*, for instance, meaning 'container-content' points to the interconnection between the world and its many inhabitants (Samuel 1993: 159). Moreover, in the Tibetan cosmological notion of the 'phenomenal world' (*jikten*), entities and beings – bodies and materiality – are fundamentally made up of the same five elements, thus humans, animals, spirits and deities share the same qualities, capacities and abilities, which is similar to what we know from Mongolia, where humans, spirits, streams, lakes and mountains share a vital life force (*la*), a notion of lifespan (*tsé*) and also genders, personality and sociality (Fjeld and Lindskog 2017). For instance, while the *lu* are hot tempered and easily upset, the *dü* are plainly malevolent, and the mountain deities are kindred through marriage or ancestry. These types of beings are 'embedded within the wider landscape in which a person is born' (Mills 2003: xviii), and hence are part of social events, with the small and large offerings made to them, visits and circumambulation, and the maintenance of a continuous relation to them within villages and individual homes. Given there are potentially vengeful spirits and deities, much ritual activity among Tibetan farmers is focused on protection from these forces and other sources of potential harm. The house, with its specific architecture and its interior spatio-symbolic organisation, enables these relations to be productive and, in some ways, controlled, as it separates the domains of different being.

In her classic monograph *Society and Cosmos*, about Chewong of Peninsular Malaysia, who have become known for their elaborate cosmology and close relations with nonhuman beings, Howell (1984) developed the notion of connection through separation. One of her conclusions is that for many Chewong ideas and practices there is an underlying principle of keeping prescribed things apart, to avoid incorrect mixing. She calls this 'the principle of separation' and finds that this implies a paradox of Chewong rationality, namely that 'the essential unity suggested to exist between nature and supernature; between humans and superhumans, which moulds all actors into one extended society, can only be maintained through a continued process of adhering to the principle of separation' (Howell 1984: 4). In a comparative analysis of Mongolian and Tibetan ontologies and human–nonhuman relations, Lindskog and I

Figure 5.4. Numerous *lu* reside in Sharlung, and the land and water are marked by the offerings made to them. © Heidi Fjeld

took inspiration from this principle of 'keeping prescribed things apart' to explore the interdependence of the ontological principles of 'connectedness' and 'separation' underlying the organisation of domestic space in Tibet and the land itself in Mongolia (Fjeld and Lindskog 2017). Both Tibetans and Mongolians make a clear distinction between human and nonhuman realms, yet in a shared territory 'a "cosmological collapse" is inevitable' (Da Col 2012b: 75). Such collapse has harmful consequences that should be limited. In order to do that, Tibetan farmers engaged in continuous (re)production of bounded units and enclosed space to enable proper actions that ensured growth, fertility and reproduction (i.e. of animals, children and produce, and hence of the household). The house is the most important bounded space in the daily life of lay Tibetans. The three domains of the house, as units kept apart, enable proper behaviour, and through the separation of one domain from the other, unavoidable transgressions can be controlled with less risk involved. Constituting a whole, these domains form the entity within which the villagers work to 'keep', or contain, all that is valuable. One way to conceptualise the forces that enable growth and fertility of all that is valuable is '*yang*' (corresponding to the Mongolian *hishig*). An 'energy' that, Da Col (2012b: 76) writes, is 'prone to leak, liable to flee, to be stolen, or to be parasitized upon', and thus needs to be guarded. Just as the leather pouch (*yangkhuk*) hung from the pillar in the house contains *yang* from valuable sources, the house itself is made into a bounded entity that enable *yang*, and other valuables, to be kept inside, and kept apart from unfortunate connections.

Da Col has introduced the term 'cosmoeconomics' to account for these specific 'economies of fortune': 'the conception . . . that efficacious actions, economic activities and political success are underpinned and supplemented by the storage and maintenance of a vital yet volatile field of energies' (2012a: 175). Constituting the potential for growth, in a broad sense, in Central Tibet these 'energies' (*yang*) are gathered, pinned down and stored through ritual and daily practices in the house. The cultural meaning of the Sharlung houses could also be seen within this framework.

Bounded Efficacious Space

As a bounded space, the house is also a tamed place and a place of ritual efficacy. Asserting 'human mastery over the natural environment' through ritual work (Gardner 2006: 283) is central to Tibetan communities more broadly and to tantric rituals in particular. Through 'site rituals' (*sa chok*), deities of the soil are called forth, tamed and placed in Buddhist service, enabling humans – that is, Buddhists – to be 'masters' (*dak*) inside that particular closed ritual space. There are numerous annual rituals of subjugation through which religious experts reassert that local spirits and forces remain loyal to Buddhist powers and hence re-establish a tamed, sacred place (Ortner 1978; Mills 2003). Similarly, the house must also be repeatedly and continuously reproduced as an enclosed protecting space – as a microcosmic whole. Daily cleansings, lifecycle rituals and annual rituals expelling bad forces and impurities reproduce the boundaries of the house. This, and the continuous remaking of the interior tripartite spatial arrangement through proper conduct and caretaking, (re)establishes humans, animals and other beings in their interrelated and correct place. Keeping prescribed things apart forms relations that affect fertility/growth (*sa chü*), wealth (*nor*) and fortune (*yang*) on the one hand, and harm (*nöpa*), pollution (*drip*) and misfortune (*kyen ngen*) on the other – that is, it enables the house to be a place of ritual efficacy and keeps what is valuable inside and what is unfortunate at bay.

When boundaries are crucial, openings are potentially dangerous, and just as the openings of the body are associated with ambivalence and are carefully protected, so are openings of the house. In most Tibetan houses, we can find strategies for protecting the physical openings of both the outer (*chigo*) and the inner door (*nang-go*). Talismans empowered by a local religious expert often protect the inner doors, while sigils, in the form of scorpions or auspicious signs such as the eternal dot (drawn by the villagers themselves), are often placed on the outer door. The inner door talisman in Sharlung is called *nöpa kak* ('harm stopper') and is empowered by a *lha* through the *lhaba* (the medium) and is often a collection of various auspicious objects. These are blessed and donated by the local medium as a response to a particular problem in a house. Hence, not all houses had a talisman, although most did. In Takrab, the *nöpa kak* contained pieces of Tibetan calendars, a *khatak*, animal feet and small animal bodies, eggs and yak hair. I asked *Achi* about the history of the *nöpa kak*. She explained:

> We've had it for many years. It was also in the old house. After we built this new house, we had some problems with the animals. Many got sick. Also, our daughter got sick. So, we asked the Chunup *lhapa* (spirit medium) what to do. We thought that it was an angry *lumo*. But the *lhapa* said that we had to bring the *nöpa kak* from the old house to stop *dön* (external harmful forces, often translated as evil spirits) and 'jealous women' (*sindrê*). They were causing the harm to come (*nöpa yong*).

The material objects comprising the inner door talisman had been collected over many years. Initially, it was for protection against one particular ghost, to which the *lhapa* responded by attaching a blessed *khatak* above the door. In the years that followed, the *lhapa* recommended continued protection of the entrance and provided additional blessed objects. The *nöpa kak* as other material protections, physically hinder the entrance to a house, hence rather than removing bad spirits, these blessed objects subdue or tame these beings so that they no longer wish to harm the house and its residents.

Moving Protectors, Re-establishing the House

Houses are not static entities; they have doors that open for human and non-human beings and agents on a daily basis, and thus their ability to protect needs to be maintained. A physical house is not protective in itself; it must be established as a bounded, tamed space and filled with protective forces. This becomes clear in the building, and relocation, of houses, where important ritual objects, and nonhuman beings, must carefully be transferred into the new space. The house protector (*namo*) is connected to the house both as a physical space and as a social unit. The *namo* has often lived in the same house for years, and people said she is often unwilling to move. In addition, these protectors often had strong personalities and were easily angered, hence her transfer was a delicate event. In the following, I describe in some detail the process of moving into a new house.

After a new house has been built – that is, after the roof has been successfully put into place and properly celebrated (with what is called *tokchang*) – the transfer can begin. Moving involves people and animals, practical and ritual objects and also spirits and deities. In the process, the new house is transformed from a physical structure (*khang*) to a socio-symbolic house (*khyimtsang*) and is re-established as a ritually efficacious place. The first step is to fill the new house with objects that symbolically represent household activities. Tashi-la explained:

> The first thing we have to do is bring the *dojung* (a mortar). *Dojung* has a similar sound to the *pecha* – the '*dojur*' (the *tengyur*) – so when we bring the *dojung* into the house it brings prosperity (*yang*). So, it is most important to move the *dojung* first. After that, we move the *tsala* (the stone stove).

Transferring the *dojung* and the *tsala* practically and symbolically initiates the process of relocating the hearth, which unites the household. The second step is for the people to move, a process that often took three days. The third step involves the transfer of nonhuman beings of the house and, most importantly, the house protector (*namo*), which completes the relocation of the house.

The *namo* of the Takrab house was perceived to be very powerful. She protected not only the individual members but also the house as a whole and was associated with its material fortune (*nor*) and prosperity (*yang*). The *namo* had several names that, for the most part, referred to motherhood, such as *Ama namo-la*, 'honourable mother protector'. Lobsang Drolma explained: 'She is the mother of the house (*kyimtsang kyi ama*). *Namo* is very powerful, and she is easily upset. We have to treat her carefully and give her the offerings she needs; otherwise she might be angry and bring harm (*nöpa*).' The spirit medium (*lhapa*) had helped to convey to them the personality and preferences of the *namo*. During the yearly trip to the *lhapa* in the neighbouring township, Tashi-la had asked the *namo* how they could best maintain her contentment and make sure she would continue to protect them. The *namo* communicates through the *lhapa*, and as Tashi-la explained: 'She easily gets angry. When we come to the *lhapa*, she is angry and says that "I don't get anything from you, just a little *tsampa* and just a little *sang*." So, she says that we should make more offerings.'

The transfer of the *namo* was highly ritualised and structured by prescribed rules. Although monks should preferably lead the process, no Buddhist texts were recited or in any ways consulted in the event. Tashi-la pointed to the importance of creating the best possible setting for the transfer of the *namo*, again pointing to the hot temper of these beings and explaining that the timing was crucial. I asked if they consulted an astrological calculation, but he waved his hand in refute of that.

> A transfer should only happen when it is dark, maybe after ten in the evening. Quietness is very important. It should not be windy, and there should not be any sounds. This is very difficult, especially because of the many dogs that bark continuously. So, we need much help to calm the dogs during the time of transfer.

I asked who participates in the transfer.

> Only two people should participate because it should be quiet. One of them should be a woman that lives there. The second could be anyone, really; it is not important. But it is most important that the two persons are clean. They must wash their bodies and hair and wear clean or, preferably, new clothes.

The symbolic connection between the house and the body is again notable, as the state of the body should reflect the state of the house; clean and preferable new. The issue of dirt or pollution was also important in terms of providing a good environment for the transfer. Others in the village told me that the second person to participate in a move should not be randomly chosen but should preferably be a monk from Sachung gompa, as 'they are not dirty (*tsokpa*)'. Common to several of the local deities in Sharlung is the fact that they are easily upset by uncleanliness, and this was also true for the *namo*. Tashi-la continued:

> The two participants are needed in order to carry the two items: one basket with food and offerings that the *namo* likes, and one large bowl of incense.

Figure 5.5. After the harvest, the house is cleansed by monks performing *Sharnyig dütok*, an exorcising ritual common throughout Tibet. In the ritual, the negative forces – leading to illness and general misfortune – are driven out of the house, in the form of effigies called *nédak* (the owner of illness) and his protector *ngarmi* (strong person) that are carried out and left in the fields, one towards the west and one towards the east.
© Heidi Fjeld

> The basket should contain *chang*, tea, cookies, dried fruit and *ja mar thuk* (tea, butter and soup) and then be covered by a new apron. Then, twigs with colourful ribbons attached (*dadar*), representing the five elements, are put into the basket. *Namo-la* likes these things. Therefore we show these to her so she can follow the smells she likes. It is always difficult to know whether *namo-la* wants to leave or not.

I asked Tashi-La if he goes to the *lhapa* beforehand to consult the *namo* about moving.

> No. No. If we ask her, she will say no. So we bring the baskets to lure the *namo* out of the old house. The two people whisper, 'please come, please come' (*pe ro nang, pe ro nang*) and start to walk slowly towards the new house. They find the shortest way and do not stop along the way. When they approach the new house, they continue to whisper and hope that the *namo* has arrived.

After the *namo* was transferred, the house was regarded as safe – that is, a ritually effective bounded space.[14] With this, the rest of the nonhuman beings of

Figure 5.6. A harm stopper (*nöpa kak*), placed on the inner door of a house.
© Heidi Fjeld

the house could also be moved. Except for the *lumo* residing on the ground floor, the other numina of the house did not need ritualised transfer.[15] As Tashi-la said: 'The *tsen, gyelpo, chu lha, taplha* and the others will come.'

The Protective House

Moving a house can be ritually planned to make sure protective forces are in place. With their protected openings, proper domains and orderly relations inside, houses are effective protective spaces that enable safety and enhance prosperity. Maintaining a household in a house is inherently risky: it involves incorporating new members and seeing others leave; bringing material and immaterial substances in and out; and inviting guests to come and go – that is, household activities open the house's interior to the exterior, with all the precariousness implied.

Engaging with this precarity is an embodied, ongoing activity in which all household members risk letting bad influences in and good forces out. While staying in Sharlung, we often visited blacksmiths, butchers and other households that were considered low-ranked and associated with pollution (*drip*). After some time, I noticed that upon our return to the Takrab house after these visits, the smell of incense was stronger than usual, especially around the inner door opening and sometimes also close to my body. The houses of blacksmiths and other skilled workers are considered to be places where the risk of being affected by *drip* was high, and I realised that our visits there had raised some concerns. My body – moving in and out of these houses – could bring *drip* into Takrab. Stopping household members' movements outside the house was of course neither desirable nor possible; rather, safety measures were taken upon return, such as the simple and subtle act of burning *sang* after visits to blacksmith houses.

Ontologically, humans and nonhumans are guests, conceptualised as tenants, and they are embedded in fragile relations of exchange with the lord of the earth (*sadak*). In this extended sociality, with (potentially polluted) humans, (benevolent or malicious) spirits and powerful (and potentially wrathful) gods, the house serves as a protective place. By establishing the house as a bounded ritual space, inside–outside relations can be controlled and exchanges can be managed by protecting the openings, by daily and periodic offerings and by the maintenance of a yearly ritual cycle. At the same time, production and reproduction is made possible and potentially prosperous. By engaging in proper social and ritual relations and activities with humans and nonhumans, the house is reinforced as a place that not only protects the individual and the group but is a microcosm of the cosmological order and thereby defines humans' proper ontological place in it.

These cosmological and ontological aspects of houses are important, not only because they constitute the immediate world for the people living there but also because they are symbolically interconnected to the architectural ideals of inaccessible and protective fortresses and to the value of the house as a physical, social and ritual space.

Returning to the house as a social institution, in the final chapter we move out of the house and into the village and to the complex networks of which individuals and houses are part. Friendships and forms of relatedness connect different people in ways that inform and express established and evolving social hierarchies. This finally brings me to the skilled workers – that is, artisans and others identified as being of lower rank – and the dynamics of economic and social mobility in these farming communities in Central Tibet.

Notes

1. See Yeh (2013) for an interesting analysis of how the CHP contributed to significant shifts in citizen-state relations in TAR, transforming farmers to consuming subjects.
2. The poor one-storey houses were rebuilt into two storeys, allowing the animals inside. They were built in line with traditional architecture.
3. This book received new interest after the massive earthquake that hit Nepal in 2015; not only did it take many human lives but also destroyed the traditional architecture.
4. See Tucci (1961); Khosla (1975); Paul (1976); Chayet (1988) for descriptions of sacred architecture. For lay architecture, see the already mentioned Toffin 2016 [1991], Corlin (1980), *The Lhasa Atlas* by Larsen and Sinding-Larsen (2001) and the impressive *The Lhasa House* by the late André Alexander (2019), as well as Pommaret-Imaeda's brief description of Ladakhi construction techniques (1980), Diemberger and Schicklgruber's preliminary notes on Khumbo architecture (1988) and Harrison and Ramble's work on houses in southern Mustang (1998).
5. See also Phylactou (1989); Samuel (1993); Mills (2003).
6. Phylactou (1989); Jest (1991); Ramble (1996).
7. In Tibet, numerous proverbs and rules for proper behaviour illustrate the dirt of the foot sole and the lower part of the body. One saying I was told concerns the need to prevent children from crawling under somebody's knees or feet: 'When being stepped over, the body will not grow.'
8. In severe cases where this method is found ineffective, villagers consult the *ngakpa* in Gangkar, who is known for his effective healing by blowing on the affected areas.
9. Only in exceptional cases do people live on the ground floor. Some nuns who refused to live as householders after the closing of the nunnery in 1960, for instance, chose to stay on the ground floor. By doing this, they marked their disinterest in the activities of the first floor, associated with production and reproduction, and established a semi-monastic environment on the ground floor.
10. The most important records are known as *kyiduk* lists, which include a record of help received and provided for happy events (*karto*) and unhappy events (*nakto*). I will return to these in the next chapter.

11. As mentioned in the Preface, Samdrup was offered the *chökhang* to sleep in during our stay in the Takrab house.
12. Yak horns, symbolising *yang*, are commonly used as offerings. They can be presented either with or without the skull. In the latter case, the inside is filled with *né*, *tsampa* and rice. According to the *pala* in Dönkhang, yak horns placed on the roof are offerings to the *lha*, while the horns on the ground floor are to the *lu*. Regarding the bottles, they were placed there simply because they liked them. I do not know what they might represent beyond that, but due to limited access to bottles (of beer, for the most part), they might have been a general offering of something seen to be valuable.
13. Samuel, citing Cornu (1990), writes that *tsen* are 'red spirits who live in the rocks. They are all male and are the spirits of past monks who have rejected their vows'. About *gyelbo*, he writes: 'The *gyelpo* or "king-spirits" are said to be the spirits of evil kings or of high lamas who have failed their vows.' (1993: 162).
14. A new shrine for the *namo* was not necessarily built immediately; it could be better to wait until the spring because, as she was very fond of spring flowers the presence of these would be an incentive for her enjoy and settle in the new house.
15. An angry *lumo* might cause hindrances to the people and animals that have moved. Hence, a *lhapa* is often consulted concerning the possible transfer of a resident *lumo* and, according to Tashi-la, most *lumo* shrines are brought to a newly built house. Further, in some cases, malevolent *lumo* take up residence in a newly built house. Then, the *lhapa* can lure them to a different place, most often a beautiful place; for instance, a flowery meadow. However, this often turns out to be a complicated process of much repetition. A benevolent *lumo* will normally follow easily to a new house. On some occasions, of which the background is still unclear to me, she will also have to be lured with items of preference. Then, the process resembles that of transferring the *namo*, with the significant difference that the *lumo* is presented with milk rather than *chang*, and that the cow that produces most milk carries the basket with food and *dadar*.

Chapter 6

MORAL NETWORKS AND ENDURING HIERARCHIES

Within the context of what was predominantly a subsistence economy in the beginning of the 2000s, Panam farmers were part of extensive and complex networks that they could turn to for practical assistance in preparing and harvesting the land, house building, travels and more. They also needed help to perform other vital activities, such as the performance of the yearly cycle of household rituals and life cycle events – rituals that are both labour intensive and costly. These relationships shaped emerging social hierarchies and were themselves shaped by enduring hereditary divisions. Although people, of course, establish individual relations within the community, crucial moral networks of mutual assistance and social control were fundamentally based on house membership. These relations might be individually contracted, but once formalised into relations defined as networks of mutuality, the points of connection changed from individuals to houses. Hence, houses cooperate with houses – as corporate bodies – and within these relations individuals assist individuals based on their house membership. Participation in these extended networks was of vital importance, and the loss of access to these upon exclusion from a house was yet another incentive for the younger generation to remain within their natal home. The dynamics of inter-house relations also informed the local rationale of polyandry and the desire to keep sons together in one house.

The centripetality and orientation towards containment in the social organisation in Panam is striking. Polyandry keeps brothers, land and material and immaterial resources together. Economically, new income is invested into the household, and domestic rituals and architecture aim to contain that which is driven inwards, to the core of the house. This centripetal sensibility brings me to the parallel dynamics of independence and interdependence, autonomy and collaboration, noted in other Tibetan communities as well.[1] So far, this book has primarily dealt with the autonomy of the individual houses, and we now turn to the interdependence between these. While collaboration and networks are extensive, they are not socially neutral; they involve different forms of mutuality, of reciprocity, and thus, morality. Looking first at the networks of which individual houses are part, and secondly at how social dynamics play into the formations and limitations of these, I want to bring houses and kinship into a broader sociocultural context of classification and hierarchies. Houses as social institutions are most visible in the interactions (and lack thereof) with others, and a closer look at inter-house connections can bring otherwise muted social exclusion mechanisms to the fore.[2]

Issues of classification and hierarchy – namely, hereditary social divisions and what can be called caste-like dynamics – address an aspect that is often left out in ethnographies from Tibet.[3] These dynamics are based on notions of pollution and involve restrictions on certain forms of relationality and village cooperation between the farmers and those classified as being part of a hereditary low-ranked group. In the case of Panam, this low rank was called *menrik* ('low kind'), *mi tsokpa* ('unclean people') and sometimes *rik ngen* ('bad kind'). The groups identified as *menrik* were blacksmiths, butchers, funeral workers (called *baru* in local vernacular) and beggars. Investigating issues of low *rik* is a delicate matter in Tibetan communities, also in Panam.[4] Also in conversations with people from a blacksmith or butcher background, getting direct access to their experiences of exclusion, stigmatisation and discrimination and to their perceptions of pollution, is complicated by the taboo of openly recognising another person's low *rik*. When I asked questions about hereditary rank I often received superficial answers, such as 'it used to be like that, but now we are all the same'. Villagers of other than *menrik* background were also reluctant to talk about social exclusion and pollution – these issues were handled with a sense of idiosyncrasy. Given these challenges, I found that exploring the extent and limitations of individual and house relationality and participation in village networks provides an alternative, indirect way to unpack these enduring, and in new ways emerging, social hierarchies.

Mutual Networks of Care

Tibetan communities are known for their intricate and elaborate mutual aid networks.[5] The exchange networks serve different purposes, the moral obligations involved vary, and the temporal and spatial entanglements also differ.

However, these networks are well developed and clearly outlined, and, most importantly, they operate on the principle of mutuality.

In farming villages, the various relations of exchange are activated in different spheres of life: some for agricultural production, some for travel assistance, some for house building, and some for life cycle rituals. In Sharlung, villagers talked about assistance and mutuality as something that had been an established practice for a very long time. People took part in social networks of friends (*drokpo*), relatives (*pun*), of houses (*ganyé, kyiduk ngalak*), co-villagers and people from the region (*yul chik*). Associated with these relations are various obligations and expectations; however, common to all is a sense of closeness that can be contextually activated. Some of these relations were individual, others were house-based. The house-based and long-term relations entailed a morality of obligation, while individual relations largely involved a morality of expectation. In addition to these long-term social relations, people were involved in labour exchange (*lérok*) and wage labour (*milak*); these were contracted between individuals and households and were not house-based. Morality and reciprocity informed the social distribution of (restrictions to) participation in the various networks, and the issue of temporality, of open and closed relations, came to be of particular concern in interactions across the boundaries of *rik*.

Ganyé – *the Near and Dear*

Ganyé is a contraction of *dga' po* and *nye bo*, meaning 'likeable' and 'close'.[6] The term denotes both a close and dear associate and the particular ego-centric network that these associates constitute. *Ganyé* relations are formed on the basis of house membership – that is, a set of *ganyé* follow upon inclusion into a house and the same set remain within the house after exclusion (upon partition or death). Individuals might establish new *ganyé*, but these relations must then be consolidated within their respective houses. Thus, if a person moves out and becomes a member of another house, he/she loses all original *ganyé* and gains a new network – that is, the *ganyé* of the new house. The establishment of a new household also involves developing new *ganyé* relations. The term itself cannot be modified – close or distant *ganyé* is not possible – and it is a permanent relation that does not decrease or increase in quality or strength, although it has to be activated in the necessary situations and contexts.

Based on interviews with farmers from Tsang living in India in the 1970s, Aziz (continuing Beatrice Miller's work from 1956) provided a detailed analysis of *ganyé* relations as found amongst her informants. She argued that *ganyé* networks were of crucial significance for cohesion and reciprocation, not only in the exiled community of study but also in their place of origin in Tsang. Aziz described *ganyé* as a moral system that had a 'particular nature, distinct from the moral systems that guide other social behaviour, e.g. family ties, economic choices, and piety' (1978b: 48). It was a wide social network, a set of people (often known to each other) forming an unbounded category with no corporate aspects in terms of common goals or functions (hence, they should not be defined as a 'group').

In Sharlung, everyone I asked reported to have a number of *ganyé* relations, although the extent of these networks varied greatly. There was a clear association between polyandrous houses of some size and large sets of *ganyé*. When I asked the leader of Norchen, one of the former *trelpa* houses in Sharlung, to name their *ganyé* in the village, he replied: 'We have many, many *ganyé*. Norchen is old and has a long history of *ganyé*. It is the same for all the *khyimtsang* – there are many *ganyé* now.' This was also the case for smaller households transitioning to named houses, such as the Wangchö. This house had expanded after the Household Responsibility System reform, through a combination of economic strategies and a beneficial constellation of people. Jampa, the household leader, narrated a success story; he had been a *yokpo* in the Lungko house before the Democratic Reforms but had since then taken up political positions in the village, built a large house to live in, chosen a marriage form that secured the transfer of intact land, and sent his children to school for them to later take up leading positions around the valley.[7] In this process, Wangchö had become one of the wealthiest houses in the village, and during our stay in Sharlung, many people tried to develop *ganyé* relations with them because, as one villager said, with an expression that they were stating the obvious: 'they are important people.' The size of the *ganyé* network is indeed an indication not only of the history of a house but also of its contemporary socio-economic position and rank.

The Public Handling of Achi's Passing

Aziz argued that one of the core obligations of *ganyé* relations is information exchange – that is, securing the flow of relevant information from the community to the individual (or his/her house), and the other way around. This is a moral obligation and concerns both the reputation of the individual and his or her proper participation in the community. Similar concerns were also important to *ganyé* relations in Sharlung. In addition, *ganyé* helped to protect an individual against emotionally painful situations. In a way, *ganyé* was like oil in the social machinery, smoothing interactions from individual to community levels.

A concern with avoiding emotionally difficult situations became clear upon my return to Sharlung for my last stay. When I arrived in Lhasa, only two days passed before I received the tragic news about the passing of the *achi* in the Takrab house. It was Samdrup who told me. Rinzin, a man in his thirties from the village, had taken upon himself the task to inform us, and he had done so at some cost. As Sharlung was without phone coverage at that time, Rinzin had hitchhiked to the county seat and made the call to Samdrup from there. Why did Rinzin find it important to inform us about *achi*'s death before we arrived in Sharlung? There is obviously an emotional side to this, as Rinzin knew that we both felt connected to her and would appreciate knowing as soon as possible that she had passed away. However, what is more interesting in this context are the implications that Rinzin's doings had for my arrival (that year without Samdrup) in Sharlung some months after her passing.

Hearing the news of *Achi's* passing in advance enabled me to prepare properly to enter the mourning Takrab house. Upon my arrival in Sharlung, I presented an envelope with a monetary gift and a *khatak* to the house while uttering my condolences, as expected by a visitor to a house in that situation. I knew I should be careful not to mention *Achi*, and I avoided both the otherwise common small talk about the health condition of all family members and talk about our previous experiences together. As is well known in many societies across the world – described as early as 1922 by Frazer – in Tibet it is considered improper to mention a person who recently passed away. This taboo is not so much because of ritual repercussions, but rather an emotional concern that it will remind those left behind of their loss and their sorrow – it brings sadness. The main mourning phase of a house lasts for one year, and throughout this period a range of taboos need to be observed, and failing to do this would have been emotionally painful and embarrassing, not only for the residents of the house but also for me, the visitor.[8]

In a conversation about the different networks in the village, I asked Rinzin about the circumstances of his phone call to Lhasa and whether Tashi-la had asked him to inform us. He strongly denied that Tashi-la had any role in this. On the contrary, he said, 'I don't think he knows that I called you. He was mourning then; he could not think about other things. I called because it is my obligation. We are *ganyé*, right. That is what we have to do.' By making that phone call on his own initiative, Rinzin – the Takrab house's *ganyé* – contributed to a socially controlled and emotionally smooth return of an outsider into the house.

Involving the corporate houses, *ganyé* relations are defined by long-term obligations to assist in particular contexts and with particular concerns. This obligation is based on the morality of mutuality; more so than with kin relations but in a less direct and strict sense than other mutual aid networks.

Kyiduk ngalak – *in Happy and Sad Times*

As with *ganyé*, *kyiduk* is an institution of some pride among Tibetans. Today, *kyiduk* has come to be understood as (welfare) 'associations' of people of the same origin but residing elsewhere, such as the Sherpa and Mustang Kyiduk in the US and Mugum Kyiduk in Kathmandu and Amdo, Kyirong or Gyarong Kyiduk among exiled Tibetans in India. Also, people sharing experiences and challenges forms associations, such as the New Arrivals Kyiduk in Dharamsala (Swank 2014).[9] In Sharlung, *kyiduk* and *ganyé* coexisted, and although they occasionally overlapped, they were distinct in terms of history, function and meaning. Both networks are based upon mutuality, but *ganyé* leaned towards the social and emotional, and *kyiduk* towards the material and was administered by written records.

In their work, both Miller and Aziz described reciprocation (*ngalak*) as fundamental to the *ganyé* bond. Aziz wrote that local concepts of reciprocation are connected to *ganyé* as *ganyé ngalak*; this is a specific form of mutual return where the mutuality lies in the obligation to return in equal kind, be it the provision of grain or labour assistance or anything else (1978b). In Sharlung, *ngalak* was central to local networks of cooperation but connected to *kyiduk*, often also termed *kyibö ngalak*, rather than *ganyé* (as described by Aziz). *Kyiduk* is a contraction of the words *skyid po*, meaning 'happy', and *sdug cag*, meaning 'bad'. *Ngalak* is a combination of *snga*, which indicates a previous action, and *lag pa*, meaning 'hand'. Hence, *kyiduk ngalak* can be understood as 'the return of a hand in good and bad times'– that is, mutual assistance. The functions of the *kyiduk ngalak* networks vary throughout the Tibet ethnographic region, but in Panam these were networks of associated houses that were obliged to provide help during life cycle rituals. As an old man in the Samchang house explained: '*Kyibö ngalak* come for wedding celebrations and funerals. These are very costly events – too expensive for one family. So people bring *chang*, grain, butter and food. And money of course.' *Kyiduk* brings material support.

Similar to what Aziz pointed out concerning *ganyé* reciprocation, in Sharlung *kyiduk ngalak* was a reciprocal relation in which each house was obliged to return exactly the same as received and registered. When house A receives butter from house B for a wedding, house A must provide butter for the next wedding in house B. Each house kept a record of these exchanges on a paper roll or notebook that they stored in the *taptsang* and that they consulted when needed. The record of happy events – primarily weddings – was tied with a white thread or a *khatak* and called *karto* (the white list), while the record for bad events – that is, funerals – was knotted with black thread and called *nakto* (black list). Due to the relatively seldom occasions that *kyiduk* were mobilised, correct reciprocation depended upon consultations to these lists. In his essay *The Gift*, Mauss pointed out that in gift exchanges an increase in the counter-prestations is fundamental to the continuation of an exchange relationship; one cannot simply reproduce the original transaction between two parties (1990 [1950]). The dynamics of exchange are found exactly in the reinforcement of an increased return; while Aziz noted that returns of the same kind 'hold the relationship equal' (1978b: 60), it is also the increase in the amount of the return that holds the relation open. The question of openness of exchange relations is a core issue when unpacking inter-*rik* relations in Sharlung, as we shall see later in this chapter.

Kyiduk ngalak is financially demanding, and many of the poorer households did not have the means to establish and maintain such relations. When talking with the elderly woman in Magnub about the wedding of their two adopted children, described in Chapter 2, she explained: 'There was a small celebration. We are poor and had little to offer.' 'How about *kyiduk* – did somebody come with offerings for the wedding?' I asked. She continued:

> No. *Kyiduk* did not come. Only some relatives (*pun*) came. Tsering's (her adopted son) father came from (his natal village); some came from Dagpo (her adopted daughter's natal house). That's all. There was a celebration for two days, and we had enough food for those few who came. They brought a little *chang* and some tea, but not much. *Kyiduk is ngalak*, isn't it? But we are so few people, and too poor, so we cannot help others. . . . People know who made offerings, so they know that we have not given anything. . . . It is the same with *bangsöl* (baby cleansing); only a few relatives came. Sedön's mother brought new clothes for her and the baby, that's all.

Life cycle events are usually large-scale celebrations that last from three to seven days, and most of the village houses send at least one representative to participate. As with *ganyé*, a large set of *kyiduk* was considered a sign of high rank, and much village talk concerned the scale of the celebrations in the different houses. Not being able to contribute to these celebrations not only reflected badly upon a poor house, such as Magnub, it also reduced the help they could expect to receive for their own ritual arrangements. Limited *kyiduk* networks thus complicate and slow down a potential social mobility process.

Ganyé and *kyiduk*, as relations of moral obligation, do not exclude the importance of kin relations. Relatives outside the house – that is, patrilateral kin (*pa pün*) and matrilaternal kin (*ma pün*) – were also close associates who might provide material or immaterial assistance. In an article on corruption in Mongolia, David Sneath points out that although many material transfers are reciprocal – that is, they precondition a direct or indirect return – many are not. He takes food supply from pastoralists to their relatives living in the city as an example of a substantial material transmission so common and expected that 'they can be seen as materialisations of the social relations themselves' (2006: 96). Sneath suggests that such materialisations of social relations, or rather social statuses, could be termed 'enactions' and should be held separate from 'acts of material transfer – transactions' (ibid.: 90). Enactions and transactions could be seen as two ends of a moral continuum, in which hospitality and sharing are placed at one end, and instrumental, conditional and impersonal transfers are placed at the other. Sneath's point is that rather than employing a reciprocity model, we need to focus on the concept of obligations in social relations when analysing material flows. This separation of enactions from transactions can help in understand differing moral networks and social relations in Panam as well. Relatives and close friends are expected to help each other; material transfers should be seen as enactions of established social relations, of being kin or friends. Material and immaterial transfers in *ganyé* and *kyiduk ngalak* networks were also enactions of social statuses in the sense that these flows of values were materialisations of defined (*ganyé* or *kyiduk*) relations. However, these entail different expectations and obligations, and various degrees of reciprocal commitment. 'Kin (*pün*) are like good friends,' people often told me. *Pün* differ from *ganyé* or *kyiduk* because a *pün* relation is characterised by a (strong) expectation of receiving help and being able to return it but with no obligation to do so. In other words, the relation itself is not based upon a moral obligation of reciprocity. Separating expectations from obligations can further develop the analytical potential of enactions as different from transactions. Although many *ganyé* and *kyiduk*, or friends, are relatives as well, they are not necessarily so. While relatives were perceived to be close, this form of relatedness did not define particular rights and duties. By contrast, *ganyé* and *kyiduk* did. There was a significant distinction drawn between material flows as enactions of social relations, such as *ganyé* and *kyiduk* on the one hand, and labour exchange (*lérok*) and material transactions such as wage labour (*milak*) on the other. This distinction corresponds, as we shall see, to social hierarchies based on *rik* and is reflected in social relations across *rik* boundaries.

Both Miller and Aziz described *kyiduk* as a corporation conceived in economic and business terms only, and Aziz in particular argued that *kyiduk* and *ganyé* are two sets of relations never to be associated (1978b: 70). The main difference between these two sets, she held, is the lack of social and emotional elements in *kyiduk* relations, on the one side, and the corporateness of its members, on the other. People also separated *ganyé* and *kyiduk* in terms of emotional involvement in Sharlung. However, contrary to Miller's and Aziz's descriptions, I found no evidence for *kyiduk* being a corporate group. On the contrary, it seems that establishing *kyiduk* was an ongoing process between many houses, and that, similar to the *ganyé* set, these relations were egocentric (the ego then being the house).

While villagers of all social backgrounds in Sharlung have had, although very limited, a set of *ganyé* for as long as they can remember, the *kyiduk ngalak* was a more recent establishment for many people. This increase in the distribution, and emphasis, of formalised mutual aid networks could be seen in a broader context of social and economic changes in the rural areas. The celebration and marking of life cycle rituals, such as weddings, birth celebrating rituals and funerals, had taken on a more elaborate form since the 1980s, and stronger participation and assistance from various associates had therefore become more important. Further, in a social organisation of strong autonomous corporate households, the establishment and continuation of formalised, long-term mutual aid networks not only facilitates significant village cooperation but also produces new relations of dependency and contributes to the reproduction of old social hierarchies.

New Relations of Dependency

Who, and for whom, were *ganyé* and *kyiduk* in Sharlung and the neighbouring villages? Investigating the networks of the various houses, three patterns stand out. First, there was a correlation between the social standing of a house and the size of its networks; second, there was a new social distribution of dependency between the houses; and third, the low-ranked, traditional skilled workers did not participate in these mutual aid networks. Before 1950, *trelpa*, and particularly *genbo*, were associated with extended networks of *ganyé* and *kyiduk*. During my time in Sharlung, a large *ganyé* set indicated social influence and high esteem, much in the same way as described by Aziz (1978b), and the villagers were involved in ongoing processes of establishing new relations and reconfirming old ones. In these processes, social status and rank were negotiated and new constellations of networks established.

The various Chinese reforms and interventions have, as we know, dramatically altered Tibetans villagers' relations to land, and since the 1980s, access to fields has been based on equal distribution. The Household Responsibility System with its redistribution of land and provision of autonomy for households also changed the fundamental criteria for social classification and differentiation in local village organisation. This reform provided people of all social backgrounds with new opportunities, enabling many to embark on a process of social and economic mobility, in ways that have blurred the traditional social hierarchies and also brought new ones into being. These coexisting social hierarchies reflect two underlying and contested criteria for rank among the lay population in Central Tibet; namely, economic status and hereditary background (*rik*).

While the local response to the Household Responsibility System has led the majority of villagers in Sharlung to establish a larger corporate household, with polyandry and a *trelpa*-like structure of the house, it has not been possible for all villagers to take part in these socio-economic transformations.[10] Instead, poorer households have instigated dependency relations with larger houses. The relations have taken the form of patron–clientship, where the two parts share a flow of values based upon personal connections and a sense of reciprocity.

Patronage and Dependency

Patron–client relations are not new to Tibetan village organisation. As already described, pre-1950 agrarian communities in Central Tibet were based upon a hierarchy where some claimed the taxes, some extracted the taxes from the estates, and some farmed the land. The latter were to a large extent dependent upon landlords – the patrons – as a source of regular income as well as help with more extraordinary events.[11] After 1980, dependency relations took a new form.

According to Goldstein and his colleagues' studies in Panam at the end of the 1990s, most people expressed that they were better off than they had been in the past, yet 31 per cent of the participants in their studies were defined as poor – that is, unable to feed themselves by their own fields or income (2003: 769). In the household survey that I did in Sharlung in 2002, sixteen – out of 44 – households relied on external help for food to sustain themselves throughout the year. Of these, nine considered themselves and were considered by others to be trapped in a chronically poor and dire situation, while the remaining seven were periodically poor (their situation strongly depended on the result of each harvest). One of the main strategies that the chronically poor households used to sustain themselves was to establish relations with more affluent houses in the village.

The relations between Sobnub and Takrab can serve as an example. Sobnub, the small, unpainted house briefly described in the previous chapter, is the neighbour to Takrab towards the east. The house consists of Wangmo, her old mother, her husband Palden, who married in as a *makpa*, and their three children, who were at the time aged four, seven and ten. During the land division in 1980, it was only Wangmo and her mother who lived together, and, because Palden did not inherit land to bring as a *makpa*, the Sonub house only had fields for two persons. This was clearly too little to feed three adults and three children; they were amongst the poorest in the village, and every year they had to rely on help to have sufficient grain.[12] Moreover, they depended on help to be able to cover the expenses of the mandatory schooling of the children, and they did not have the means for extra activities, such as inviting religious expertise in times of need.

During my stays in the Takrab house, I noticed the regular presence of people from Sobnub. However, they were not treated as guests in the sense of being seated in the *taptsang* and served *chang* or tea, or entertained in other ways. Rather, they seemed busily engaged in practical issues. Wangmo and Palden, as well as their two eldest children, provided Takrab with different forms of labour. Most often, they helped with agricultural chores and Palden also worked as a repairman. Further, Palden assisted Tashi-la on his travels, either by driving the tractor or simply by keeping him company. He also conducted religious offerings on behalf of the Takrab, if for various reasons they could not travel. In daily life, their daughter often helped the women in Takrab to fetch water, make wool, clear the courtyard and boil *chang*.[13] When I asked Palden and Wangmo about their friendship with Takrab, Wangmo explained it this way:

> Tashi-la is a very good man, very helpful. If we have difficult times, we can ask him, and he never says no. When my mother was ill, he gave some money so we could go to the hospital and buy medicine. And he gave some money to buy our son's school uniform. This was very expensive. It was indeed. We have good relations . . . Our fields are not so many, you know. So, many years we do not have enough barley. Now, we can buy barley cheaper from the government, but it is not so cheap. It really isn't. So, when we need barley, Tashi-la gives us. Takrab has quite a lot of barley, so he is able to offer some to us. But then, he cannot sell it, you know.

I asked him whether Takrab was their *jindak*, or patron. 'Yes, yes, *jindak*, it is. He is very generous. We can ask for help.' 'But when you stay in the house, it seems that you also help them,' I continued. Palden answered: 'No, no, we don't do much. Sometimes I travel together with Tashi-la, or sometimes I do something with the animals, but really – it is not so much.' This humbleness also points to the one-directional flow of support in the *jindak*–client relation. When I talked to Tashi-la about their relation to Sobnub, he explained it in a different way:

> Sobnub are our helpers (*rokpa*). They help with many, many things. Sometimes I don't know what they do (he laughs). They just do it! . . . I can't say no when they come. It is like that. They come because we have good relations. But when they come, it is often also very useful. Like last week, Palden went with Orgyen (the youngest son) to look after the *dzo* grazing. This was good for Orgyen.

Looking back at discussions on theories of patronage and brokerage in anthropology in the 1970s, Paine argued that the most salient place to search for 'the diacritica of the roles of the patron and the client, respectively, [is] *within patron–client transactions*' (1971: 10, original italics). By doing so, he suggested, we can establish a point of departure that enables us to see beyond the asymmetrical, and thus unequal, power relations associated with dependency. Paine's point was that patron–client relations must be investigated empirically in order to determine the social dynamics of various elements within these transactions: mutuality, reciprocity, as well as power relations and particularly the definitional power of the flow of values. What constituted these transactions between Takrab–Sobnub? The relation of the flow of values and resources was simple; Sobnub provided help in a general way, while Takrab provided grain and occasionally money when needed. It was, however, Tashi-la, as the patron, who made the decisions on the amount of financial help to provide, although he was informed by a moral obligation to be generous. Palden and Wangmo had no rights, or position, to challenge his authority, but at the same time, they could, and did, increase their participation in Takrab activities, which intensified the moral obligation of Tashi-la to be generous and, hence, influenced the amount he gave them. As Tashi-la said above, 'I can't say no when they come. It is like that.' And their relation was produced and reproduced by the manipulation of personal relationships of reciprocity. Throughout daily life, Palden provided his help and friendship to Takrab members by simply initiating his own participation in Takrab activities, indicating a more nuanced power dynamic in which the inferior part can instigate a flow of values and resources and also maintain this flow. At the same time, this complementary aspect should not blur the significance of the definitional power that Tashi-la, as the patron, had.

These relations of dependency and autonomy were not absolute nor static. The establishment of these valuable relations was a constant concern for many leaders of poor households. There were ongoing processes to initiate, negotiate, terminate, expand on and renew relations of material and labour transfers, within which people of most social categories had some power to influence the nature of these relations. As with the other poor households in Sharlung, Sobnub initiated their position as a 'helper' to Takrab by offering their labour during the harvest time. The harvest was thus a time when social divisions became apparent, not only in terms of the economic differences seen in the amount of harvested produce but also in the distribution of labour and the clustering of helpers in the fields of the (potential) patrons.

Although most of the poorest houses in Sharlung had *lérok* relations with more affluent houses, some did not. Chakpa, for instance, had not been able to instigate and consolidate such relations and depended upon occasional support from the village or township leaders, or relatives, friends and neighbours. Chakpa was a small house located in the eastern part of the village, not far from the Lungko and Nyikar houses, with whom they were related. The house consisted of Pempa, his wife and two young children, and his mother's sister, a nun who moved in with them after the closing of the nunnery in 1959. His wife explained why Chakpa did not have *jindak* relations with other houses in the village:

> Sometimes we ask for help from our neighbours, but they are not so wealthy. We don't have good relations with our relatives. You know, Pempa is the illegitimate child (*nyelu*) of Lungko *achung* (the youngest husband). He never supported them, and now we have bad relations. So, they are wealthy, but we don't have good connection.

I asked whether they could approach some of the more affluent houses that were located at the other end of the village, and she continued:

> Yes, yes, we can, but it is difficult. Ani-la's health is not so good. She cannot work or look after the children. So, I have to watch the children, and Pempa is often away working with the tractor (for income). So, who shall we send as helpers? If you want good relations and maybe to receive help later, you have to offer much help. Perhaps you have to come every day in the first year, or offer to help often. We are too few people to be able to do that.

Chakpa's problems reflect the underlying importance of having some defined connections before establishing dependency relations that involve long-term moralities of reciprocity and mutuality. In Sharlung, these were usually connections of relatedness, of friendship, or of being neighbours. Yet, I think a favourable household composition (more than connections) determined whether helpers could be sent to potential patrons (and stay for a sufficient amount of time) and hence enact the role of a client. The advantage of polyandry is again evident, as a large household not only enables a group to diversify their economy but also, in cases of poverty and precarious agricultural production, to send individuals to establish valuable relations on behalf of the house.

Beyond indicating patron–client relations, the organisation of the harvest also exposes fundamental and enduring social hierarchies of a different kind. Looking closer at the participation of various helpers in the fields of the relatively affluent houses, it was striking that none of them were from the traditional skilled workers households – that is, they were not blacksmiths (*chak zowa*), butchers (*shenba*) or funeral workers (*baru*).[14]

Enduring Social Exclusions

A complementary power perspective might be taken to indicate an underlying relativism in terms of authority and influence, but that is not my intention. While a client positionality does provide considerable possibilities to instigate, continue and terminate a relation to a patron, the patrons have the important power to define the flow of values in the relation. As such, there is a form of power complementarity in the relation, but within a defined hierarchical model, much in the same way as with gender relations within and beyond marriage. More rigid power structures were apparent in the exclusion of certain people from the mutual aid networks, and particularly from *ganyé* and *kyiduk* relations; namely, those identified as being of a low or unclean 'kind' (*menrik*). The lack of long-term and continuous transfers across *rik* boundaries points both to the distinction between social and ritual rank and, on a more general level, to the intrinsic material aspects of social relations. Also, it illustrates the relevance of the differences – the particular moralities – between transactions and enactions.

Low-ranked groups in Panam were blacksmiths (*chak zowa* or *gara*),[15] butchers (*shenba*), funeral workers (*baru*) and, in a distinct category of their own, beggars (*longkhen*). Pre-1950, members of these groups performed services – skilled work – for the villagers across the valley and were not involved in agriculture.[16] They were, and continue to be, defined and internally ranked by notions of ritual pollution (*drip*) and termed the 'lower kind' (*menrik*). *Drip* has a double connection to *menrik*; their work is seen to be polluting, and their physical body (particularly the bones, hence the patrilineage) is inherently polluted. Hence, they share many experiences with low caste and Dalits among Hindus to the south. Similar to what we know about caste identity from India and Nepal, *menrik* status in Tibet is not determined merely by occupation but social status is hereditary, handed down from parents to children (Ramble 2019: 154). The first three decades of the Chinese annexation of Tibet had a major impact on the status of the low ranked.[17] First, as part of the emancipation ideologies, they (particularly the blacksmiths) were given political positions by the new regime; second, they were included in the collective communes and farmed the land together with the other villagers; and third, the decollectivisation reform also provided them with land and animals on equal terms with the rest of their communities. Hence, since the 1980s, the former skilled workers have been performing the same agricultural work as their co-villagers; in the case of *baru* and butchers this has been in combination with their traditional skilled work. This opens the questions of mutual aid networks again because with fields to farm these former skilled workers share the need for labour assistance.[18]

Politico-economic settings – that is, relations to land and control of political power – have often been described as the foundation of social differentiation and position in Tibetan society pre-1950 (see Carrasco 1959; Stein 1972). In one of the very few papers dealing explicitly with hereditary social divisions in pre-1950 Central Tibet, Ugen Gombo strongly argued for an important correlation between what he called 'caste' and the socio-economic position of a person. He wrote that: 'even vertical ritual (status) stratification in the Tibetan context can be seen as ultimately determined by socio-economic status' (1983: 50). Following Ugen Gombo's argument, we could expect that the implementation of the Household Responsibility System led to a significant alteration in status and esteem for the lower stratum in Tibet, as the reform provided equal shares of land to all households, including the traditional skilled workers. Along the same lines, others have argued that the low rank of the skilled workers was likely an implication of what would be the different nature of their work, and hence, the formation of and participation in different work exchange networks. Because the skilled workers traditionally were not engaged in agriculture, they were excluded from the significant mutual aid networks of the farmers.[19] How the change of livelihood has influenced the position of the former skilled workers in Tibetan villages after the Chinese invasion then becomes an interesting question. Contrary to what Gombo's argument suggests, the experiences of blacksmiths and butchers in Panam show that although access to land has led to a greater degree of equality in terms of socio-economic position, it has not led to a significant alteration of 'ritual stratification'.[20]

Economy is certainly crucial to social status and rank in rural Tibet, and this recognition of economic success also applies to the traditional skilled workers. One of the *baru* houses in Sachung and one of the butcher houses in Bargang, for example, were amongst the most affluent in the valley, and this was positively recognised by others in the villages.[21] Yet, economic success did not transform, or encompass, rank based on an 'unclean' *rik*, and participation in village life remained restricted for those identified as *menrik*. The endogamy of the low-ranked groups in Tibet is well known in the literature describing the pre-1950s,[22] and in Panam such restrictions on inter-*rik* marriage were strong. In Bargang, for instance, the affluent butcher house mentioned had tried to invite a *nama* from a non-butcher household; however, they did not succeed. When talking with commoners in Sharlung, it was unthinkable for them to establish affinal ties with *menrik* houses. Sexual contact with someone of *menrik* background was a moral offence that might also lead to serious pollution and illness, and *rik* was the first issue to be investigated in the search for a marriage partner.

The lack of inter-*rik* marriages, also among the affluent former butcher and blacksmith households, did not surprise me. However, I was expecting that with the transition of livelihood to farming former skilled workers would participate in the various village networks, but this was not the case.

Individual Friendships: Inter-*rik* Relations

The villages in Kyiling township are small, both in layout and in population, and not surprisingly, people find friends, amongst their peers, depending upon age, gender and also social differentiation. While socio-economic position of one's house was of little importance when establishing friends, *rik* was. This part of Panam had a reputation in Lhasa for being a place with many lower ranked people; as noted in the Preface, Sachung village was said to be the home of many blacksmiths, and the neighouring Bargang village to host many butchers. When I asked commoners about their relation to people of blacksmith, butcher or *baru* backgrounds, I often got a quick reply that it was 'good'. They *could*, they said, have had close relations, but for reasons unclear to them, they simply did not. At the same time, some of the former skilled workers still performed their traditional occupations (especially the butchers and *baru*, who earned a significant income from this), and the villagers happily used these services. These services were paid for; they were transactions rather than enactions, if we follow Sneath's distinction.

During fieldwork, I spent as much time as possible in (former) blacksmith households, particularly in Sachung village. Asking about their family history, in the beginning they would tell me that their relations with the local community were no different than those between their co-villagers. Yet, with time and conversations passing, I learned that the relations of blacksmiths, *baru* and butchers to their neighbours and co-villagers were both limited in extent and restricted in kind, and the cause of a sense of exclusion. The main obstacle for inter-*rik* relations was the pollution (*drip* or *driptsok*) perceived to be carried by those of low rank and the associated fear of contamination. While the effects of *drip* can be controlled by observation of taboos in social life (particularly of touching mouths and bodily substances) and proper post-contact physical and ritual cleansing, most commoners felt it was too much effort and therefore social interaction with people of *menrik* background was rare.

In the three villages in Kyiling that I visited most, I only came across one person who had the habit of visiting a *menrik* house simply to socialise. Rinzin told me that he was friends with a man from a *baru* household in Sachung. Rinzin and Lhakpa were *changdrok* or beer friends; they enjoyed each other's company. This friendship, although being close per definition, came with some restrictions, and these were related to the potential transfer of pollution (*drip*) from Lhakpa (and his house) to Rinzin (and his house).

Therefore, they took measures to avoid this such as never sharing cups, no matter how drunk they would get, which is otherwise common among friends. Moreover, Rinzin did not sleep in Lhakpa's house, because he would then have had to use their bed covers through which *drip* might be transferred. In addition, to avoid pollution, Rinzin explained that he cleaned Lhakpa's cup in a particular way; by turning it upside down and putting it aside in a place in the shade for two to five days. This was done because 'nobody likes to touch a warm *rik tsokpa* cup', and because the pollution is less potent when cooled, he explained. Also, a cup turned upside down signals to the children in the house that they should avoid it. This was an important point for Rinzin because, he said, 'children are more open for *drip* than adults'. After two to five days, he washed the cup in a thorough manner, preferably with soap and always without sharing the water with other cups or utensils. When the washing was completed, he put the cup outside for it to dry completely in the sun. After it was dried, the family used the cup again as any other utensil. Rinzin pointed out that he had never been affected by *drip* from his friend, precisely because he had taken these precautions and done the necessary cleansing procedures.

Had Rinzin not taken the cleansing precautions he described, he would have risked being contaminated by pollution. This pollution is of a ritual kind, and while in Lhasa people tend to separate *drip* (pollution) from *tsokpa* (dirt), in Panam the two terms were used interchangeably, and even combined into *driptsok*. *Drip* is potentially everywhere, not only among the traditional skilled workers, and there are, in fact, much more serious forms of pollution elsewhere.[23] Even so, if one is affected by pollution from a person of low *rik*, it could result in physical illness, such as a sore throat, blisters and spots, or a swollen tongue, or in severe cases (usually caused by sexual contact) it could hinder a person's rebirth. These perceptions vary to a great extent, but the belief in physical illness caused by *drip* is widespread, also outside Central Tibet.[24]

Other villagers talked about Rinzin and Lhakpa's relation as a curious friendship that could best be explained in terms of an exceptional personality. Lhakpa, being from an affluent *baru* house, was seen as a good person, despite his family background.[25] The connection implied here between *rik* and personality is found in the very constitution of a person – in the substances of the body. As described in Chapter 2, *rik* is inherent in the father's sperm and materialises as the child's bones (*rü*), which are the template of the body and as such constitute a strong influence, not only on the child's physical traits but also on their personality. Levine argued that the concept of *rü* denotes not only the physical bones and a group of people sharing the same bones (*rüpa*) but also the 'ranked hereditary social strata' (Levine 1981: 56). The interchangeability of *rü* and *rik* indicates the essential character that hereditary social status has in Tibetan kinship, as the *rik* is the bones that constitute the body and the mind. Being of a 'bad' (*ngen*) *rik*, blacksmiths, butchers and *baru* are perceived to be more likely to act immorally (Fjeld 2005, 2008; Ramble 2019). These notions of moral inferiority also influenced *menrik* participation, or the lack thereof, in the local networks based on mutuality and obligations, such as the *ganyé*. Friendship across *rik* boundaries was possible by observing prescribed taboos; however, friendship was an individual relation that did not involve their respective houses. While friends expect loyalty and assistance from each other, they were not obliged to provide this. Contrary to these 'loose' expectations of individual help, *ganyé* relations were formalised relations between houses in which the moral obligation to assist was fundamental and unbreakable. Within the context of formalised mutual aid, *menrik* remained on the symbolic outskirts of rural village organisation.

Menrik, Mutuality and Reciprocity

When talking with interlocutors about *menrik* and their participation in mutual aid networks, people often said similar things as the Darkhang *achi*: 'They could have been our *ganyé*, that is not a problem.' However, I did not find any examples of commoners who had mutual aid relations, *ganyé* or *kyiduk*, with *menrik*.[26]

Despite the great potential for change over the last four decades, not only endogamy but also exclusion from inter-house mutual aid networks have maintained two distinct social categories in Panam: commoners and those of low rank (*menrik*). These two categories are fundamental in the sense that they cannot be negotiated or modified – that is, all houses are clearly classified as 'unclean' or not. Not including those classified as 'unclean' in exchange networks was seen as pragmatic, as a way to avoid practical problems, such as the distribution of food and drink during the help-receiving and help-providing events. To be able to get help, a house must provide quality food to those who come. Because of the strict observance of not sharing cups, or food, with *menrik*, it would be necessary to prepare two different servings. The help-receiving house would have to provide an extra cook (of *menrik* background) to make separate food for the low-ranked guests because, as one old woman put it: 'nobody wants to share food with *mi tsokpa* (unclean people).' These practical requirements, many said, would increase the economic burden on the help-receiving house. However, people of low *rik* were obliged to, and participated in public work (*chilé*) in the village, and the food practicalities during those events were easily solved (primarily by bringing their own food). The fear of engaging in somewhat close inter-*rik* relations is more complex that observing the taboo of not sharing cups and cutlery. We might understand this reluctance through looking at the moralities involved in notions of reciprocity. Mauss made the general point that a (material or immaterial) gift must be returned, and if it is not done immediately, if there is a delayed return, the receiver finds himself (or his group) in a vaguely defined debt situation that they must reciprocate in some way at some time (1990 [1950]). A relation of ongoing gift exchange is an *open* relation. The lack of reciprocal relations of mutuality between commoners and *menrik* is also, I argue, an unwillingness among commoners to engage in relations with delayed return– that is, a reluctance to establish and maintain open relations with people of low *rik*.

Being outside the reciprocal spheres in which commoners interact, people of blacksmith and *baru* background exchanged labour and aid among themselves. Several of the *baru* families descended from one of the blacksmith houses generations back, and these kin relations were easily activated in times of need. The butchers, on the other hand, invited relatives from further away when they needed help, which they claimed was only very seldom; having established large households, they had sufficient labour resources among themselves.[27] Relatives who came to help in the butcher houses in rituals brought gifts and food, but their participation was not classified as *kyiduk ngalak* and their gifts not recorded.

When talking with members of blacksmith or *baru* houses about inter-*rik* relations, they also spoke hypothetically and told me that *could* have had a larger set of *ganyé* or *kyiduk* but that they simply did not. They also did not have mutual aid networks with butcher houses. The explanation they gave was similar to that of commoners – that is, the practicalities of food preparations and sharing. Just as a commoner avoided the 'mixing of mouths' with *menrik*, there was a hierarchisation within the category of *menrik* as well, and this implied restrictions on sharing cups amongst the blacksmiths, butchers, *baru* and beggars, and none of them share cutlery if not related by kin.[28] The mutual aid networks of the lower ranked, then, consisted to a large degree of relatives.

Some of the *menrik* households were large and relatively wealthy, having received land during the decollectivisation reforms, and having arranged polyandrous marriages and continued to provide skilled services for payment (slaughtering animals and arranging funerals, primarily). Hence, they had many fields to harvest and houses to build, and when these more affluent *menrik* houses asked for labour assistance, they did so within the frames of what was called *milak*, a commercial exchange relation where the worker is paid immediately after the service has been completed. As the *nama* of Dochang, a blacksmith house in Sachung, explained:

We have many fields, but not enough people. So often we have to ask for help. We ask different people; it doesn't matter because it is *milak*. Usually we have to pay ten yuan per person per day. Sometimes we pay more if they bring their own *dzo*. Other people can ask their relatives (*pün*) when they need help, but we do not have good relations (with the relatives). So, I send one daughter to Tromo (a neighbouring village) to make salary, and then we can pay *milak* when we need help.

Baru, butcher or blacksmith services were paid for in money (or in kind).[29] When I asked Rinzin whether the work of the smiths or the butchers could be seen as labour exchange (*lérok*), he explained:

If you need something from a blacksmith, let's say new shoes for your horse, you go to ask him to make it for you. When he has made the shoes, and put them on your horse, you pay him his salary. After that, there is nothing more to say. This is *milak*; it is not *lérok*.

Milak, then, was a commercial relation that involved immediate exchange of labour and salary. Contrary to *lérok*, *ganyé* and *kyiduk ngalak*, *milak* did not carry an obligation of a postponed return and was completed upon payment. *Milak* was not an enaction of particular social relations; rather, it was a terminated material transaction. As such, *milak* could be seen as what Bloch and Parry, in their Introduction to 'Money and the Morality of Exchange', described as a 'cycle of short-term exchange which is the legitimate domain of the individual – often acquisitive – activity' (Bloch and Parry 1989: 2). They defined two related but distinct transactional orders that coexist and that people could transgress in any given society. These transactional orders are 'on the one hand transactions concerned with the reproduction of social and cosmic order; on the other, a "sphere" of short-term transactions concerned with the arena of individual competition' (ibid.: 24). Their main concern was the flow of money within these two transactional orders and the processes of conversion between the two. They argued that with these conversions there is in all economies an ideological space for individual acquisition where this type of activity is 'consigned to a separate sphere which is ideologically articulated with, and subordinated to, a sphere of activity concerned with the cycle of long-term reproduction' (ibid.: 26). The individual, short-term acquisition must be subordinated to the transactions concerned with reproduction of social and cosmic order because it is rendered irrelevant in a long-term perspective. In the case of reciprocal relations across *rik* boundaries, the point is not the flow of money or objects in the transaction but rather the inherent moralities of these spheres – that is, the expectations and obligations of the two transactional orders. Returning to Sneath's distinction between material transactions and social enactions, the 'cycle of long-term reproduction' could perhaps more accurately be termed an enaction of social relations, rather than a 'transactional order.' In Panam, labour exchange relations between commoners and the traditional skilled workers took the form of short-term transactions between individuals, and not houses. As such, the corporate groups to which the individuals belong were not defined as part of a social relation of some closeness; rather, the material transaction was short-term and implied no obligations or expectations beyond the immediate payment. This is a contrast to practices among the commoners, who consolidated *lérok*, *ganyé* and *kyiduk* as reciprocal group networks that, ideally, last over generations. As such, these relations would 'reproduce social order', in the words of Bloch and Parry. Labour exchange and mutual aid are hence moral networks in which the material (and immaterial) flow of values must be seen as enactments of the established social statuses of being a *rokpa*, a *ganyé*, or a *kyiduk ngalak* partner from one house to another.

Enacting the Individual and Short-Term Relation

The lack of long-term house-based relations between commoners and traditional skilled workers was also evident in the exceptional cases where *menrik* participated in a ritual in a non-*menrik* house. I heard about only one event in the recent past where a person of *menrik* background had attended a wedding, funeral or birth celebrating ritual (*bangsöl*). This event had its origin in the friendship of Rinzin and Lhakpa described above. When Rinzin's daughter was born, Lhakpa attended her *bangsöl*, as did Rinzin's other friends, neighbours, relatives and *kyiduk ngalak* relations. During the celebration, there were only a few restrictions on Lhakpa's participation, and they all involved the avoidance of mixing of mouths. For example, while other guests put a small piece of butter into the mouth of the child, Lhakpa offered the butter to one of the parents, who then gave it to the baby, to avoid touching the baby's mouth directly. When I later asked Rinzin about Lhakpa's participation in this ritual event, he explained: 'He came as my *changdrok* (drinking buddy), that's all. I had not really invited him. I did not mind that he came. We just had to be careful.' 'But when Lhakpa made offerings to the baby of Menshö [Rinzin's house], did he not also start *kyiduk*?' I continued.

> No, no. It is no like that. Lhakpa is only my friend (*rokpa*). He has no connection to Menshö, and we do not have that to Drachen (Lhakpa's house). No, no. That would not be possible. It is not possible to have that kind of long relationship with *baru*. They cannot have long relations with us also – it is the same.

The temporality involved in their relation and the emphasis Rinzin put particularly on the prolongation of time, is important. Mauss argued convincingly that a gift is an opening of a continuous relation within which the parties stand in a defined position with each other throughout the time of the material or immaterial exchange – a time that might stretch over several generations, depending upon the gift return. In a Maussian perspective, the gift that is transmitted is essential to sociality, and an emphasis on such transmission is fruitful as it highlights the gift's ability to materialise a social relation. Karen Sykes notes that, to Mauss, '[the] gift makes the ideal relationship a material fact because giving and receiving gifts creates and changes human relationships. The gift also makes the relation substantial' (2005: 60–61). Essentially, the flow of what Mauss calls prestations and counter-prestations substantiates the relation – it produces social obligations and long-term bonds between the receiver and the giver. Material transfers, such as food, drink and gifts but also labour, can create relationships between commoners and *menrik* that can be changed to long-term, close and amicable relations. Independent of whether or not values are exchanged or given as a result of obligations, reciprocal relations are open before the value has been returned, and it is the inherent morality of this openness that complicated commoner house relations with *menrik* houses. The result is an enduring social hierarchy and an exclusion of people based on a status inherited from parents to children, sharing some resemblance with caste dynamics in South Asia. However, this does not mean that persons of low-rank were not involved in amicable individual relations, or that *menrik* houses did not have networks of assistance to help with farm work and life cycle rituals. Rather, relations across *rik* boundaries were either individual or, if involving the house, short-term exchanges that were indisputably closed when the transaction was completed.

Exclusion and Unity

The processes involved in the exclusion from long-term exchange relations identify and express the difference that makes the difference, to use Bateson's well-known phrase. At the same time, exclusion of some brings others together. As Howell pointed out in an article on exchange amongst Lio in Flores Indonesia, reciprocal relations not only perpetuate opposition but also unite members into a higher unity. She describes how among Lio both inter-house and inter-village exchanges negate internal differences by joining them in a common pursuit. She reminds us of Mauss' point that the 'unity of the whole is indeed more real than each of the parts' (1989: 435). Such double implication of reciprocal relations resonates with inter-house networks in Panam. The process of establishing relations of dependency between poorer and more affluent houses – by the exchange of labour for care and security – perpetuated opposition and manifested power relations that, although being contextually complementary, defined one part as inferior to the other. These negotiations formed emerging social divisions and hierarchies. At the same time, these long-term exchange relations were social manifestations wherein the involved parties constituted a unity in a moral whole. This shared morality was based upon mutuality and open relations, a form of relationality that could only be easily shared by people of the same kind (*rik*), reminding us of the ranked nature of houses as social institutions and the unequal distribution of positions and possibilities in processes of social and cultural change.

Notes

1. Robert Desjarlais has pointed to the continuous tension between the two cultural values of autonomy and interdependency among Yolmo in Nepal and argues that these frictions seem to 'derive from sociocultural dynamics common to Tibeto-Burman peoples of the Himalaya region' (1992: 47). Ortner, on the other hand, argues that while Sherpa religious principles value closure and autonomy, social bonds such as those expressed in mutual aid relations value openness (1978: 56). Related, Goldstein has also pointed to the balance of centralisation and decentralisation in the political and village organisation of traditional Tibet (1971b).
2. As noted by Lévi-Strauss (1983: 178).
3. The concept of caste implies a relational organisation – that is, there must be more than one group of people for caste to have any meaning. In Tibet, the lowest ranked share fundamental characteristics with the low castes in India, such as ritual pollution leading to restrictions on the sharing of substances; however, we do not find higher ranked grouping that could be termed as castes. The traditional nobility, for instance, share a particular political and economic character, but they are not higher ranked in terms of ritual purity. Therefore, I use hereditary social divisions, the Tibetan term *rik* or 'caste-like', rather than 'caste'.
4. While silversmiths and goldsmiths are also defined as of hereditary low *rik* in Lhasa, this is not the case in Tsang. See Fjeld (2005, 2008b) on caste-like dynamics in Lhasa.
5. See Miller (1956) and Aziz (1978b) for early examples from farming communities and Langelaar (2019) for a recent example. After 1959, some of these networks, particularly *kyiduk*, gained new meaning and agency among exiled Tibetans and in migration processes from the high Himalayan villages in Nepal (Swank 2014; Craig 2020).
6. Miller quoted her informants in Darjeeling and Sikkim and translated the meaning of *ganyé* as 'social friend', 'close friend' or 'neighbourhood friend' (1956: 158). Aziz noted that some of her informants from an exiled community of refugees from Dingri claimed that the origin of the term is not *dga*, as in 'being fond of', but from *tkar*, meaning 'white'. This, Aziz argued, should not be seen as contradictory, as both translations denote 'the bond of closeness' (1978b: 49). In Panam, *ganyé* is pronounced *gani* but often with a weak r, as in *garni*. However, my interlocutors were adamant that *ga* is an abbreviation of *dga bo*.
7. Jampa's children married monogamously (in the 1970s), and while he wanted to arrange polyandry for the next generation, he only had one grandson. Of Jampa's sons, two are

township leaders and one works for the post office in another nearby township. Of these three, only one son is a member of the Wangchö house and thus entitled to its inheritance. The two other sons do, however, contribute economically to their natal house.

8. These include the avoidance of singing and dancing (and hence, celebrating festivals) and larger social gatherings in daily life, as well as limitations on some ritual activities and expansions of others.
9. After the dispersal of Tibetans in exile, *ganyé* relations regained their importance in new contexts. One Tibetan woman who grew up in India told me that when she was planning a trip to New York, her stepfather in India gave her a name of his *gabo nyebo* (as he said) living in New York. He told her that she could contact him and ask for his assistance, because of this man's *ganyé* status (Tsomo Svenningsen, personal communication, Oslo, 2005).
10. Childs and colleagues also noted this pattern of consistent social hierarchies. They found that 'Eighty-five percent of households that are now in the top 25% in landholdings started in the top quarter. In other words, most large households in 1982 remain large today, while most small households remain small' (Childs et al. 2008: 74).
11. For an example of pre-1950 dependency relations, see Bischoff (2013).
12. Subsidised grain from the county government was also available to Sobnub for purchase.
13. This care also extended to us, as guests in the Takrab house. During our stay, Sobnub members took it upon themselves to make sure we had everything we needed. Wangmo would bring us fresh butter and, occasionally, eggs, and their son developed a particular interest in, and sense of responsibility for, entertaining my daughter.
14. I was not able to observe harvest practices in Bargang village, where most of the butchers live. Hence, the ethnographic examples are from Sachung and Sharlung primarily. However, everyone I asked in Sharlung claimed that butchers did not assist non-butchers in the harvest period in Bargang.
15. '*Gara*' is a condescending word for blacksmith that also serves as a generic term to describe *menrik* in general. When addressing people from blacksmith families, the descriptive term 'iron maker' (*chak zowa*) is considered more polite, hence I use this term here.
16. They were also excluded from entering monasteries as monks (Jansen 2018: 50–52).
17. See Ramble (2019) for a discussion about the novel *Phal pa'i khyim tshang gi skyid sdug*, written by Trashi Palden and first published in 1995, in which one of the main characters is a blacksmith man with a rising political career and declining moral standards after the Chinese invasion and during the first period of reforms.
18. The so-called beggars (*longkhen*) are an exception from this pattern; after the land distribution in 1980s, all *longkhen* households, most being travelling musicians, leased out their land and slaughtered, consumed and sold the animals they received. The income from the lease was not enough to sustain themselves, and they have continued to travel, play and beg. In addition, they do not marry polyandrously. Commoners explained the stigmatisation of beggars in terms of what they saw to be economic irrationality and immoral behaviour.
19. Martin Mills, personal communication, Lhasa, 2002.
20. See Fjeld (2008b) for a more detailed analysis of slowly changing hierarchies in Panam.
21. Butchers and blacksmiths were paid in cash or kind for their services, and while there had been a decline in local iron production, leading to less income for the blacksmiths, the services of the butchers were very much still needed and secured a good income for these houses. Moreover, the funeral workers (*baru*) were paid in kind and cash, and in addition, they received the clothes and jewellery that accompany the deceased

to the burial. These items were often sold and provided an extra income for the *baru* houses.

22. See Kawaguchi (1995 [1909]); Passin (1955); Carrasco (1959); Taring (1970); Gombo (1983); Yuthok (1990).
23. See, for instance, Lichter and Epstein (1983); Schicklgruber (1992); Diemberger (1993); Rozario and Samuel (2002), Samuel (2003); Tidwell, Nianggajia and Fjeld (forthcoming).
24. See Fjeld (2005: 47–52) on notions of pollution in Lhasa. See Ramble (2019: 154) for an example of contamination by pollution following sexual contact with artisans in South Mustang.
25. Bad *rik* (*rik ngen*) is commonly associated with bad personality. As an illustration, Ramble notes on author Trashi Palden's description of Lhakdor, the blacksmith protagonist, in his novel: 'Whether by literary design or through alignment with the world view that would have been part of his formative social environment, he conflates Lhakdor's heredity, profession, and personality into a single disagreeable composite' (2019: 155).
26. Investigating hereditary social divisions among Tibetan-speaking communities in Mugu, western Nepal, I found that none of the members in the Mugum Kyiduk in Kathmandu were from blacksmith households either, despite there being a rather substantial number of blacksmith households in Mugum village.
27. The beggars (*longkhen*) did not exchange either labour or any form of aid, as they did not farm and arranged only small-scale, less costly, life cycle rituals.
28. People of various *menrik* backgrounds share the perception that skilled workers (with the exception of their own category) are inherently polluted, and they look down upon the other categories. The reason given by both is the same namely, fear of contamination of *drip*. This is similar to what we know from caste dynamics in South Asia as well.
29. At the beginning of the 2000s, all butcher and all *baru* households were still practising their traditional occupations. The two main *baru* houses in Sachung had divided the township between them, where they conducted the sky-burials of one part each. Butchers have a less ordered service system and are called upon from different areas. Many blacksmiths, on the other hand, have stopped their production. This is mainly due to the increase in both factory-made iron, offered cheaply on the county market, and iron produced by beggars (*longkhen*) in Gangkar village. This has left the traditional blacksmiths without a market.

Conclusion

This historical ethnography of marriage and kinship in Sharlung is a snapshot of Tibetan lives, notions and practices in a farming community at the beginning of the 2000s. It is written in past tense, with a commitment to avoid the timelessness that so easily permeates anthropological texts. Yet, maintaining a temporal sensibility is hard, for the reader and the author, and even in the simple act of putting something into words, we give passing events longer lives. For sure, Sharlung must be a different place now, after eighteen years have passed. A new generation have become adults, women and men have married, and they have formed a range of close relations through which they participate in each other's lives, in the environment of the village and beyond. The Chinese state has again made itself strongly present in the village, not only via new social and economic campaigns but also through an increasingly authoritarian form of governance, in which rural lives, including domestic affairs, are closely monitored, also informing, we can assume, how the villagers shape close relations and networks.

Time also alters perspectives, shifts positions and makes larger arguments smaller and smaller arguments larger. Time allows some nuances to shine and some to blur, but a temporal sensibility also broadens the position from where, and the frame within which, we develop ethnography, as it often comes with more distance. With time, this historical ethnography has also become a case study, describing some examples of the ways that intimate relations, marriage, relatedness and domestic life played out in rural Central Tibet before 2005. Already at the beginning of the 2000s, Ben Jiao (2001) had described the surprising revival of fraternal polyandry in Panam and had explained the many economic advantages of this type of plural marriage in the particular context of village life in the decades that followed the national decollectivisation in the 1980s. These economic advantages remained long after his study ended. Diversification of the local economy and the new possibilities to gain income from outside the farm have again and again confirmed that polyandry, wealth and prosperity are closely intertwined. Large households maintain the potential of a flexible economy in Tibetan communities. The evidence of the benefits of polyandry in Panam is overwhelming, and part of this is the socio-economic effects that polyandry has on the households. Polyandrous households are *vital*; they prosper in people, in material and immaterial wealth, but also in networks, in architecture, in social standing, and they open up possibilities for the future. But they are also sensitive to time passing and they do not always last. When they split, they morph into smaller new monogamous units or, occasionally, other forms of polygamous constellations and start new social trajectories.

Spending time with people in Panam at the beginning of the 2000s, they were eager to talk about the named, corporate polyandrous household as a cultural ideal; as households they had managed to establish, to maintain and to perpetuate over decades and generations, or as a household constellation they hoped to have the good fortune to achieve in the future. During these conversations, drinking tea in so many different farmhouses, I got a sense that these households were somehow precious – they were entangled with social and cultural values of the interior and exterior of the physical houses too, with their social histories, and with their architectural and cosmological manifestations.[1] The embarrassment, even hostility, often associated with polyandry among younger Tibetans in Lhasa did not enter into these conversations; rather, the polyandrous house was a social institution of some pride.

Houses and Beyond

The sociocultural connections and expressions of the farmers' corporate households and the networks connecting them, the widespread discrepancies between patrilineal ideology and actual practice, and the general importance of residence and territory for various forms of belonging among Tibetans, has led me and other anthropologists working in the region to explore 'the house' as an analytic and to think about the potential of seeing Tibet as a 'house society'.[2] This analytical approach also reflects the time passed in the anthropology of kinship and the ambitions of the so-called 'new kinship studies' to see beyond rules, (descent) ideologies and grand models and explore practices and lived lives. A focus on discrepancies between kinship ideologies and practices has proven to be very productive for these purposes. As I have shown in the previous chapters, in Panam, as many places in Central Tibet, people did not talk about the numerous disruptions and discontinuities of patrilineages as something problematic; rather, these were solved in matter-of-fact, culturally acceptable ways that enabled continuation of a household. The patrilineages might be discursively activated to legitimate this continuity, but they were not constitutive of the unit itself.

What is so useful about the house as a heuristic device – as compared to 'the household' – is that it expands the temporal orientation and the frame within which we analyse the domestic unit and brings family, economy, kinship, social hierarchies, architecture, cosmology and religion into conversation. It opens up the analysis of the social and connects household viability – a classic concerns in Tibet and Himalayan studies – to wider cultural processes. The house concept encompasses seemingly contradictory kinship principles – such as descent, residence and alliance, and patrilineal or bilateral organisation, exogamy and endogamy – and enables us to see lineage disruptions not as exceptions but as inherent parts of broader processes of social organisation. This resonates very well with Tibetan kinship. Too many times in the history of anthropology have practices that do not conform to established models been classified as deviances and exceptions. This is particularly evident in studies of kinship and gender, often informed by the persistent interest in patrilineal ideals and ideologies. Tibetan medical history can serve as an example, as Theresia Hofer and I explored in a special issue of *Asian Medicine* (2011) and that Hofer describes in more detail in her beautiful monograph *Medicine and Memory in Tibet* (2018). Lineages (*gyü*) in general, and medical lineages (*men gyi gyü*) in particular, have been (and continue to be) essential for the transmission of medical knowledge and skills, shared both among monastics and, in the lay population, among relatives. A common pattern has been that Tibetan medicine was taught to men, either monks or male heirs. Both the theory of procreation and formation of the body – the flesh and bone – and kinship ideology described in Chapter 2 and the gender models and hierarchies described in Chapter 4 can help explain these patterns. When people put discursive emphasis on the patrilineage and the fact that daughters most often move out from their natal home upon marriage, it is not surprising that there is a strong sense of the continuation of the medical lineage being safer if the knowledge and skills are transmitted to sons. Indeed, when talking with Tibetan lineage doctors, most see training a daughter instead of a son as something unfortunate, reflecting also the gender models described earlier. When looking back in history, though, there are substantial examples of female doctors who were trained by their male relatives; some of these were daughters with no brothers, some were wives of medical doctors and some were trained alongside their brothers

(Tashi Tsering, 2005; Fjeld and Hofer 2011; Hofer 2018). These can easily be described as exceptions in Tibetan medical history, reproducing the idea of patrilineal organisation. However, if we return to the concept of the house, the training of daughters is perhaps not exceptional but an inherent potential in house-based kinship orientations. In some cases, the medical lineages were in fact found in what was called *mendrong*, which directly translates as 'medical house' (*sman* means 'medicine' and *grong* means 'house'), such as the famous Sakya Mendrong and the lesser-known Lhünding Mendrong (Hofer 2018). Membership trajectories into these houses are the same as I described in Chapter 2; filiation, marriage and adoption.[3] Hence, both sons and daughters (as well as *makpa*), and their sons and daughters, are potential apprentices in the medical house. We know that houses consist of material and immaterial wealth, and in the case of medical houses, this includes medical texts, substances and equipment, and knowledge, skills and social reputation and capital. An analytic emphasis on (medical) houses rather than (medical) (patri)lineages enables us to see the examples of female practitioners not merely as exceptions but as a nexus around which an estate of material and immaterial (medical) wealth can accumulate and continue. As such, a house perspective opens for interpretations that allow for a better understanding of daughters, and others in the periphery of normative kinship ideology.

My theoretical excitement for the house concept is not general; it comes from an engagement with a particular place and time: Panam after the decollectivisation of land in 1981. As we have seen, the sociocultural constitution of the corporate household, the *drongpa* or *khyimtsang* – and we can add the aristocratic houses in Lhasa (Travers 2008) – resonates very well with all of Lévi-Strauss's criteria of a house as a 'moral person', and in addition, residence and territory (in)forms belonging and social identity. Moreover, external relations and moral obligations across generations are house-based, the physical houses themselves are socio-symbolic spaces of particular cultural meaning and the houses are ranked – all supporting the argument of Tibet being a *société à maison*. However, such classification carries with it many of the problems from the previous lineage theories. The pursuit of a total model such as that of a 'house society' – a kinship typology like the unilinear paradigm once was – has been exhausted as an analytical approach to kinship for several reasons. These formal typologies are reminiscent of early attempts to sort human societies into large, encompassing categories of kinship systems, such as Morgan's classification of Omaha, Iroquois or Crow systems in the late nineteenth century, which leave little room for nuanced understandings of real-life everyday practices. Moreover, the concept of *société à maison* was introduced by Lévi-Strauss to solve the theoretical puzzle not of lineage organisation but of cognatic kinship, a characteristic different from the earlier descriptions of Tibetan societies. Lastly, broad typologies – such as Omaha or *société à maison* – conceal regional and social differences; they diminish our ability to identify nuances and change, and, as lineage theories did, often leave us with a broad category of 'exceptions' that easily remains analytically blackboxed and thus rendered invisible. The value of a house perspective is rather an encouragement to explore Tibetan domestic lives, marriage, kinship and relatedness, where and when it is analytically productive.

Writing this book, I developed the chapters with a sense of movement; into, and out of, the house. I started with ways to enter a house, then explored marital and sibling relations among people who live together, before turning the focus on the space they share and the physical structures within which they reside, and ending with relations between houses. In the remaining part of the Conclusion, my interests are broader, as I take the return of polyandry in rural Tsang as a case to illustrate a type of sociality – kinship of potentiality – that is shared, I argue, across the Tibetan ethnographic region.

A Landscape of Possibilities

Already in 1978, Aziz wrote that 'Tibet probably exhibits a greater variety of marriage types than any other society' (1978a: 134). This heterogeneity has prevailed in Tibet, albeit to different degrees. Marriage is planned and formed in relation to the state – within the frames of laws and regulations, in response to social and economic reforms and interventions, state narratives about family, love, modernity and care – but also in relation to governmentality, more broadly. Perhaps because marriage has a long history as a secular matter in Tibetan history, outside the realm of the religious authorities, the regulation of these unions has been lenient, if not non-existent. Also during the Ganden Podrang government – the Tibetan state from the seventeenth century to the Chinese invasion – which was based on the ruling principle of union between religion and state (*chösi zungdrel*), religion did not regulate marriage to any significant extent, and many different local practices coexisted. Yet, the tax obligations and land tenure system of the Ganden Podrang, including corvée taxes and monk levies, directly formed household composition, and marriage was a core element in the handling of these obligations.[4] Perhaps because the different marriage forms were potentially good responses to different state obligations, the heterogeneity that Aziz and many others have noted in the past remained. Such external factors and forces take part in the shaping of local marriage preferences and practices. At the same time, marriages are constituted, based or perhaps anchored in, ontologies and cultural values – what we might call epistemologies of kinship, resulting in local communities responding in differing ways to the same external factors.

The broad variety of potential ways for marriage to be enacted is a central and continuous part of Tibetan kin making.

A comparison between Chinese and Tibetan polyandry, and particularly the rise and fall of polyandry in China, can serve as an example. In his wonderful and comprehensive book entitled *Polyandry and Wife-Selling in Qing Dynasty China* (2015), Matthew Sommer uses legal cases from the Qing courts to investigate polyandry and other forms sexual relations between woman and several men.[5] He argues that polyandrous marriages were widespread among the poorest Chinese farmers throughout this period (1644–1912), both in number and in geographic distribution. In situations of extreme poverty and/or illness, a married man could arrange what was called 'getting a husband to support a husband' (2015: 23–54). This arrangement implied that an additional man was incorporated into the household as a husband and contributed economically with labour and income. In return, as Sommer writes, he would get sexual access to the shared wife. These incorporations were often formalised by verbal or written contracts but were only rarely planned as lifelong marriages. Although accepted as a 'marriage' in the local communities (although prohibited by Qing law), 'getting a husband to support the husband' was also associated with shame, secrecy and ridicule. As described by Sommer, Chinese polyandry during the Qing was a desperate action taken in order for the married couple and their family to survive – it was an ad hoc solution to an acute crisis. This marriage form was enabled by, on the one hand, a skewed population, where, in some rural communities, one fifth of all men remained unmarried owing to a shortage of women, and, on the other, the pervasive market for women's sexual and reproductive labour (2015: 23–85).

It seems Chinese polyandry ended with the establishment of the People's Republic of China, helped by the new 1950 Marriage Law of the PRC that prohibited polygamy and concubinage in strong language and force, one of the first legislations of the new Communist leadership. The emancipation of women was an explicit part of Mao's political project, and plural marriage (and concubinage and sex work) were at odds with the new ideology of the new People's republic. Indeed, I have not been able to find any records of a continued practice of polyandry among Han Chinese after the 1950s,[6] and this marriage form has for a long time been ridiculed in public and social media.[7] Why do we see a rapid decrease in Chinese polyandry and a persistence – and even, in some areas, increase – in Tibetan polyandry under the same state? On a macro level, Tibetans and Chinese were all part of the same newly established PRC, exposed to similar economic and social reforms and laws (although implemented in different ways) – they experienced collectivisation and decollectivisation and were exposed to the same state ideals, such as the modern family as the independent monogamous couple.[8] Yet, these external factors shaped the preferences for and practices of polyandry in very different ways. While the socio-economic context in which polyandry is found meaningful is clearly important, in addition, and this is the reason why this serves as an illustration of kinship epistemologies, the relationship between polyandry and kinship ideologies differs among Tibetans and Chinese.

During the Qing Empire, the common marriage forms were monogamy among peasants and polygyny among the gentry. Polyandry, on the other hand, was part of a larger field of practices whereby people who could not buy into the normative marriage forms would share what Sommer calls 'unorthodox households' (2015: 13). These households were unorthodox also in terms of kin formation and relations. As patrilineal descent was the normative principle for group formation, rights and obligations, the sharing of a wife between two unrelated men complicated succession of the patrilineage, as it obscured the issue of paternity. Polyandry in Tibet, as we have seen, does not challenge the kinship epistemologies but is rather part of a wide range of potential possibilities that reproduce social life in culturally, socially and morally acceptable ways. Hence, the responses to external factors, such as new Marriage laws in 1950, 1980 and the amendments in 2001, also differed among Tibetans and Chinese. Polyandry in Tibet is not a strategy to deal with one particular problem, it is not a source of shame and secrecy, and polyandrous households are not 'unorthodox households'. Chinese polyandry, on the other hand, was an ad hoc solution – a response to a desperate economic situation – rather than a practice anchored in kinship idioms and ideologies. It was associated with prostitution and other sexual relations deemed immoral and exploitative, and only to a limited degree formed long-lasting kin relations – it challenged ideas about continuity in kin relations. It is not surprising, then, that its practice easily disappeared following changes in state laws and economic reforms.

This is a marked difference from Tibet and its borderlands, where polyandry remains a valuable marriage form in certain contexts. While the preference for and practice of a particular marriage form, such as polyandry, may vary across the Tibetan ethnographic region, there is a (more or less) shared pool of acceptable and cherished possibilities from which marriage forms will emerge in certain places, at certain times, in connection with specific political, economic and social factors. These possibilities do not challenge Tibetan kinship epistemologies; on the contrary, this pool of possibilities – the availability of a broad range of socially and culturally accepted marriage forms – constitutes a potentiality of relations that is informed by a sociality with flexibility and pragmatism as core elements.

An emphasis on kinship flexibility has roots, explicit or implicit, in Bourdieu's practice theory and what he called practical kinship/kinship in practice ('parenté pratique', 1990), where he aimed to look beyond kinship as rules and rather focus on 'a set of practices that play with the rules' (Trémon 2017: 43). Such an approach is at the core of 'new' kinship studies in anthropology, post-Schneider's critique, given direction by Carsten's edited volume on relatedness, and with the speed, urgency and new theoretical vitality of reproductive technologies and their associated practices. At the same time, increase in (all levels of) mobility and migration – and, with that, dispersed families – has brought the inherent flexibility of kinship to the foreground in transnational studies.[9] The notion of flexible kinship has different connotations; it is both the activation of kin relations in flexible (and often strategic) ways in new settings, such as relocation settings (Trémon 2017), and the flexible ways in which kin relations are formed and defined at a given time and place. While both are relevant to explore also for Tibetan kinship, it is the latter meaning of flexibility that has been my concern here.[10] New kinship studies have brought the many creative ways to form families towards the centre of anthropological discourse, such as same-sex constellations and marriage relations through gamete donations and surrogacy, and friendships, work companions and other relations that matter. These studies also involved an empirical shift towards Europe and North America, as they often followed biomedical technology and queer movements. The inherent flexibility of gendered relations in the Tibetan ethnographic region – what can be seen as alterations between a broad range of socially recognised formalised relations between males and females, including marriage – brings examples of creative family and kin making from outside Europe, from a part of the world often described in opposition to 'the modern world'. The pragmatism and flexibility seen in the ways to live together, to form lives and livelihoods together in settings that are often rapidly changing, make Tibetan kinship an interesting case for anthropological explorations of social and cultural life.

Although Tibet and the broader Tibetan ethnographic region is vast and diverse, communities are interconnected in myriads of ways across this land, from the west to the east, north to south. Through centuries of direct or indirect interactions – and through (partly) shared Tibetan language and Buddhism, shared experiences of high-altitude ecologies, relations to land, and ontological orientations – these communities, despite being scattered throughout a vast landscape, share deep sociocultural commonalities. Included in these sociocultural commonalities are also, I argue, approaches to marriage, and particularly inherently flexible and pragmatic enactments of kinship. Marriage and kinship ideology and practice vary across Tibetan and borderland communities, yet shared idioms, vernaculars, sensibilities and rationalities find resonance across these variations, and practices, assemblages and patterns of relatedness are formed through a shared pragmatic sensibility and flexible approach to social organisation.

From Ladakh and southern Himalayas to the west, to Gyarong and other borderlands to the east, we see a range of socioculturally accepted marriage forms overlapping. Monogamy, polyandry, polygyny and intergenerational combinations of these, as well as post-marital neolocal, patrilocal, matrilocal residence are possibilities with different potentials at the disposal of individuals, households and communities to consider when thinking about the future generations. Throughout Tibet and its borderlands, the coexistence of marriage and residence forms has been normative, informed by the different potentials associated with the various ways to assemble people. Across these diverse areas, we see a dynamic foregrounding and backgrounding of marriage preferences and practices, of residence patterns, dialectically formed through interconnections with wider relations to social networks and to the state, and processes such as intergenerational changes, urbanisation and migration. The alternation between these socially recognised ways of living together is – only partly but significantly – shared across these communities, despite being separated by huge distances.

In a similar way, for kinship and relatedness more broadly, there are socially and culturally accepted and meaningful ways to form relations that matter that are overlapping across the Tibetan ethnographic region. The idiom of flesh/blood and bone for the constitution of a child and personhood, patrilineal ideology, bilaterality and residence, as well as the range of networks of mutual aid are all social possibilities with different potentials that in various ways form sociality in these diverse communities. I have argued for a house orientation in Central Tibet, which is also relevant in Ladakh and, although concerning larger networks, in Amdo. In the southern borderlands, however, such as Humla, Mugu, Dolpo, Mustang and Khumbu, the patrilineages play more important roles for village life, combined with the importance of residence and territory.[11] In these more patrioriented communities, or as Langelaar calls it 'dogmatically patrilineal settings', the stronger emphasis on the patrilineage come into sight, for example, in the context of *makpa* marriages, where the household might switch lineage identity and the couple's 'future offspring and heirs will belong to the father's descent group, rather than the mother's' (Langelaar 2017: 161). This is not common in Central Tibet, where the *makpa*'s patrilineage is irrelevant, particularly after marriage. Despite these differences in emphasis on descent or residence, the normative status of *makpa* marriages is shared as part of a larger landscape of marriage and residence possibilities.

Flexible practices are per definition easily adaptable to change in the form of social and political reform, land tenure systems or shifting economic policies, leading to dynamic processes within households, village tent encampments or other communal organisations. In a recent paper, Levine (2021) shows how pastoralists in eastern Tibet have adapted to decades of changing grassland organisation by adjusting decisions about residence, succession and inheritance based on practical concerns. For example, during the shared grassland system in the 1990s, both patrilocal and matrilocal residence was common along with siblings sharing camps and friends residing together. Following the household land contracts, the pastoralists chose new strategies, sometimes leading to conglomerate households (multiple generations and two or more married siblings), alternating residence patterns and again a closer cooperation between siblings. These interesting shifts of kinship practices, based on practical concerns about grassland, pastoral economy and resettlement, are based in and draw on, Levine argues, 'longstanding expectations for mutual aid between siblings' (2021: 94) but are enacted in new ways in response to changing environments. Levine's examples can also serve to illustrate the flexible approaches to kinship in Tibetans communities and show how practices and patterns alternate with time, in a dynamic process of foregrounding and backgrounding, drawn from the range of socially recognised possible lines of connections and relations, all with varying potentials for vitality, prosperity and mutuality. This is part of a broader pattern whereby, in close interconnection with external factors of social and economic change, particular Tibetan kinship and marriage forms gain more or less prominence, emerging from this plethora of possibilities that are socially and culturally available. Part of such kinship of potentiality, polyandry in Panam was not merely a reminiscence of the past but a favourable marriage form through which farmers, at that particular time, consolidated their estates as socio-symbolic, meaningful houses that served to provide individuals and groups with the relations that mattered most – to people, to nonhumans and to the wider community.

The Time Passed

The twenty years that have passed from when I first arrived in Panam have brought immense changes to the Tibet Autonomous Region, but because one of these changes is the termination of international cooperation and the persistent restriction of access for foreign researchers, journalists, diplomats and others, the details of these changes are hard to decipher. The new form of the state's presence in and surveillance of the rural areas and the changing citizen–state relations have formed new sociopolitical contexts and subjectivities with which the pragmatic and flexible kinship sensibility somehow must continue to coexist. Kinship is formed in interaction with the workings of the state, not only in totalitarian states such as PRC. Michael Lambek argues that it is 'a fact of modernity that kinship is partially encapsulated in and by the state'. Modern states, he continues, are constituted by the very making of citizens, by providing birth and death certificates, claiming taxes, registering land ownership across generations and 'producing and authorising the means by which people are related to one another as parents, offspring, siblings, spouses and the like' (2013: 257). The way such biopower has been exercised by the Chinese state on rural lives has changed many times and in many ways since 1950, in phases shifting from totalitarian interventions to more lenient approaches and to a form of governance, in the last decade, has been based on close monitoring of and potential interventions in everyday lives. The Chinese state in Tibet is fragmented and works in complex ways on different scales and dimensions in different domains of life, and the workings of the state – as exercised by state agents and local leaders – has directly influenced domestic lives in general, and the plurality of marriage forms in particular.

Despite the political restrictions in many other fields, the beginning of the 2000s was a period when the local government agents had a lenient approach towards regulating marriage in rural areas of Tsang.[12] Family issues and household constellations were of little interest to the local state in Panam. In conversations with township leaders, themselves Tibetans from the area or its vicinity, it was clear that they did not see the nature of polyandry and the illegal status of plural marriage to be important or relevant. 'We register the marriage in the household to be between the eldest brother and the wife', one leader told me, and continued 'then his brothers also live in the house'. The main concern of the township leaders at that point in time was economic development and reportable outcome, and the economic benefits of polyandrous households were obvious.[13]

A range of policies introduced after 2005 has again brought the state into the villages and into the houses, leading rural changes, including more mobility from rural to urban areas. The 11th Five-Year plan (2006–2011) introduced a major shift from previous policies in TAR as it explicitly called for 'allocation of huge financial resources for projects that reach *directly* to village households in order to improve rural quality of life' (Goldstein et al. 2010: 59, original italics). This first led to the policies to construct the New Socialist Countryside, and with the Comfortable Housing Project (CHP) starting in 2006 the state directly intervened in the domestic domain in Panam, transforming not only the houses through subsidies and loans but also, as Yeh has convincingly argued, subjectivities and citizen–state relations.[14] The CHP added another layer to the Sharlung houses – a layer of debt and loyalty, and expected gratitude to the state. How this new layer of meaning intersects with the social and ontological space and the close relations formed and enacted in these spaces is difficult to know. The more recent policy, applied in 2011 and ongoing, involves sending 'village-based cadre teams' (Ch. *zhucun gongzuodui*) to live in villages (for 2–3 months initially and later expanding to 12 months). This has the greatest potential to interfere directly in local marriage and kinship practices. A response to the protests across Tibet from 2008, the village teams' main focus is the powerful combination of political surveillance and economic assistance. But reports have also mentioned other tasks, such as 'screening and mediating social disputes', 'inculating "core socialist values" and discouraging "bad old traditions"'.[15] These are all efforts that we can imagine have consequences for polyandry, with villagers subjected to direct intervention and their sheer exposure to numerous cadre and Communist Party eyes. Both of these policies, and the totalitarian turn they represent, have challenged the lenient approach township leaders had towards local cultural practices, including marriage and kinship.

Already noted by Goldstein and colleagues through a series of articles,[16] economic development in Panam since the 2000s has had a major impact on rural lives. Their research has shown creative strategies of economic diversification, including extensive engagement in income-generating activities both on and off the farm, making entrepreneurial investments and taking up a range of roles in the booming construction industry. At the time of my fieldworks, most people in Sharlung and the neighbouring villages were still primarily engaged in subsistence farming, although 'going for income' outside the farm was not uncommon and was an aspiration for many. With time, Goldstein, Childs, Wangdui and colleagues' description of changing economic strategies has become increasingly relevant also for Sharlung. The possibility of accessing cash income, from construction work, transportation or skilled work such as carpentry or masonry, has led more people to travel out of the village for longer periods of the year. Mandatory schooling until ninth grade and the extensive use of boarding schools has also led more and young people to leave. In the early 2000s, household leaders were trying to send only an eldest son to take up work outside the farm, as they considered his sense of belonging and moral obligation to the house to be stronger. With more people leaving the village, including younger sons and daughters, the internal household dynamics also change. Both younger husbands and unmarried daughters, two positions I have described as peripheral to the order of things in a polyandrous house, are given more central roles, as their income is becoming highly valued. Yet, their willingness to remain part of the household was a collective concern. The question remains: for how long will household members continue to return to the village to bring income back home and anchor their lives in their natal households?

Close encounters with powerful nation states and economic development tend to alter marriage forms that are non-normative to the majority. Yet, the rural economic development in Tsang has so far encouraged a diversified household economy, for which polyandry is clearly valuable. But the fertility decline among Tibetans in the TAR, as documented by Childs (2008),[17] increases the vulnerability of a polyandrous household – fewer people implies less flexibility and the increased chance of a household split. Previous writings about polyandry often ends with speculations about its future. As such, the futures of polyandry have many pasts, to use Koselleck's words (2004),[18] and these past futures have often involved a notion of demise and disappearance. It is as if time works against these marriages. The narratives of a future where polyandry has disappeared are evident in Chinese reports from the 1950s and anthropological publications from the 1980s onwards, as well as journalistic pieces and accounts from Lhasa in all these periods. Because this book is set at the beginning of the 2000s, our current present is the future of that time. Then, Tibetan communities were divided in how they imagined the future of polyandry. In Lhasa, and among exiled Tibetans in India, there was the expectation that when more young people leave to study and work outside the villages they will be exposed to city life and find new partners there; filial obligations will weaken and after some time polyandry will decrease in number and perhaps even vanish. In Panam, on the other hand, although some were concerned about young people not returning from work and school outside the village, the past future of polyandry was marked by expectations of vitality and prosperity. Polyandry would continue to improve life, economically and socially, keep parents and children together, enable siblings to maintain close relations and help each other. I am reluctant to end this book with my own speculations about the future of household composition, marriage and kinship in rural Panam. From my observations in the Takrab house and among their neighbours, I learned that polyandry was not merely an adaptable socio-economic strategy in an environment with limited land resources but also a dynamic marriage form that has room for love and affection and for care within and across generations, even if these emotions and their enactments can be unevenly distributed. I hope that this book can help show the complexity involved in these marriages and the kinship they form and are formed by, and to give a glimpse of Tibetan rural lives in a period where the Chinese state was less intrusive in the everyday life of these villages than it is today. This case of Tibetan kinship and marriage, with its inherent flexibility and focus on potentiality, can also serves to illustrate the wondrous world of relatedness. When I left Sharlung in 2004, I imagined a future of revisits, of continuous relations, of long-term friendships and a way to maintain a sense of mutuality of being, as Sahlins (2013) would say. As we now know, that future did not come.

Notes

1. I was struck by the paradox of polyandrous houses and the clear association of these with the category of farmers that had been called *genbo* (*trelpa*) in the past. The *genbo* had provided work for landless labourers in the village but had been exploitive and brutal, although to different degrees. Some of the *genbo* had been 'struggled against' (*tamdzing*) during the Cultural Revolution; co-villagers participated in these public accusations and beatings and some of the *genpo*s died. More than four decades later, relations with the *genbo* were still complicated and tense, and in the process of social organisation, the association with *genbo* had not seemed to shape the cultural values attached to polyandrous houses. Despite this, it seemed that the time that had passed had perhaps backgrounded any wounds and had thus moved these events from the domestic to the political domain in the remembrance of the past.
2. Particularly in Ladakh (see Phylactou 1989; Day 2015) but also Amdo (see Langelaar 2017, 2019), as well as in the eastern borderlands (see Wellens 2010; Wang 2013).
3. Medical houses (*mendrong*) were also found at the *labrang*, or corporate property holding houses of incarnate lamas (Fjeld and Hofer 2011).
4. See the Special Section of *Inner Asia* (2021), 'Kinship and the State in Tibet and its Borderlands', edited by Bingaman, Fjeld, Levine and Samuels.
5. Including prostitution and other less formalised sexual relations.
6. Wellens was also not been able to identify polyandry among Han Chinese (personal communication, Oslo, 2005).
7. As an example, in June 2020, a heated debate arose in Chinese media after a guest professor in economy at Fudan university suggested legalising polyandry and promoting polyandry as a way to solve China's skewed population problem. See J. Feng. 2020. 'Should Chinese Women have Multiple Husbands?', SupChina, 3 June. Retrieved January 2021 from https://supchina.com/2020/06/03/should-chinese-women-have-multiple-husbands/.
8. See Yan (2003).
9. Another trajectory to flexible kinship, particularly in transnational and migration studies, comes from Ong's notion of flexible citizenship, which points to a strategic use of kin relations in transnational capital accumulation, a useful perspective when exploring dispersed families in new settings (Trémon 2017).
10. See Craig (2020) for an ethnography of flexible kinship in a migration setting among people from Mustang, Nepal.
11. Mugum village in Mugu district, a community I have worked with the last few years, can serve as an example. In Mugum, a former market place five hours' walk away from the Tibetan border, social belonging, relationality and marriageability, on the one hand, and ritual obligations and maintenance, on the other hand, are organised through social classification into ten patrilineages (*rewa gyü*). Individuals, and houses, belong either to one of these ten patrilineages, or to the thirteen private monastic estates, or the fifteen blacksmith households. The number of patrilineages and private gompas are fixed, while the number of blacksmiths (here called *gara*, without the denigrating association we know from Central Tibet) fluctuate. Each patrilineage has a defined relation to one of the private gompas, whose members perform all rituals for the household.
12. The exception was reproduction, which in some Tibetan areas in and outside TAR were regulated through measures ranging from needing permission to have two or three children and fines in the case of more (through the One-Child Policy), to outright forced sterilisation.

13. This lenient approach to domestic and marriage intervention was a stark difference to the exercise of state power in the collective period, and particularly during the Cultural Revolution. The changing phases of state workings on domestic – and sexual – lives have been shared with other minority areas in the eastern borderlands. For example, Shih describes how state efforts – particularly during the Democratic reforms in 1956, and through the 'One-Wife-One Husband' movement in 1975–76 –were launched to stop the traditional Moso *tisese* (walking back and forth) marriages and force them into formal monogamy. Shih calls this campaign 'the most brutal government assault on Moso culture' (2010: 191). The state changed approach in the 1980s, as Knödel (1995) has described, when government attempts to marry off Moso people ended. After that, processes internal to Moso communities, as well as economic development and tourism only directly associated with the state, have been drivers of the decline of *tisese* (Shih 2010).
14. As Yeh notes: 'The gift of a house is thus an exemplar of biopower as the fostering of life, and the improvement of the population associated with development' (2013: xx).
15. See Human Rights Watch. 2016. 'China: No End to Tibet Surveillance Program', 18 January. Retrieved January 2021 from https://www.hrw.org/news/2016/01/18/china-no-end-tibet-surveillance-program.
16. Goldstein et al. (2008, 2010); Childs et al. (2011, 2012, 2013).
17. Childs notes that regardless of the methodological critique, both of Chinese demographic statistics and of the relatively small sample size of his own data, in TAR 'fertility was unmistakably on a downward trend throughout the 1990s. From an estimated TFR of 6.4 births per woman in 1986, the fertility rate dropped below 3.0 in 1997 and presumably even lower since then' (2008: 201).
18. *Futures Past: On the Semantics of Historical Time* (2004).

Epilogue

Lhasa, 2016

I am sitting in a teahouse behind the Potala palace with a friend. It's been eight years since my last visit to Lhasa, so we have a lot to talk about. The city has expanded massively to the east and the west – high-rise buildings, sometimes empty, loom on the outskirts of the city. Bright colourful lights, alternating between purple, red, green, blue, and yellow, are shining on the shopping malls, and traffic seems endless. The Barkhor, the old town, looks as it did before, but the buildings are new, the cameras are everywhere, and I need to pass through checkpoints with metal detectors to enter these circular paths of commerce and pilgrimage, and now tourism. More than 30 million, mostly Chinese, tourists walked these streets in 2020, according to China Daily,[1] with the numbers having increased year by year over the last decade. Considering that the population of TAR is some 3.2 million, these numbers are astonishing. Tibet has become a destination for national travellers – a place of clean air and scenic landscapes; it is reminiscent of a romantic past.

But the sky is as bright blue as before, and the park behind the palace is still filled with families. As we sit drinking sweet tea and talking, a man at the table beside us asks me where I am from. Norway, I answer. Where are you from, I ask back. Shigatse, he says. Ah, I've been to Shigatse, but it was a long time ago, I say. Where in Shigatse are you from? Panam, he says. He is from the village next to Sharlung. I explain my relation to his village, a place I have visited many times. He remembers that he heard about a foreigner with a child who had stayed with Tashi-la, and we laugh about the coincidence of our meeting. He had not been home for some months; he lives in Lhasa with his family, but he keeps in touch. Tashi-la is healthy and active again after having had some health problems the year before, he explains, adding that 'he is such a good man', and I could not agree more. After some time, his phone rings – it's his mother calling from the village. I hear him explain about our encounter, they laugh. He asks about Tashi-la, is he still in good health? Yes. Can I ask some questions to your mother, I ask? Sure. These are

Epilogue • 183

Figure 8.1. Resting after a long day in the field. © Heidi Fjeld

the answers I got: Most of the houses have been rebuilt in their village and also in Sharlung, and most people took loans from the bank and received some support from the Comfortable Houses Project (CHP). The houses are now more beautiful than before – they look the same, but they have larger windows. Most households have a tractor, some have a truck or a minibus that they rent out to businesses in Shigatse or elsewhere. They bought these vehicles also with the help of the bank. What else has happened? The nuns have completed the residence areas (*shak*), and they now live in the nunnery. The conversation pauses, they talk about other things. I try to politely interrupt. How about marriage, I ask? For example, the marriages arranged in the previous year; were any of them polyandrous (*zasum*)? He explains – without the sense of shyness so common when people talk about polyandry in Lhasa – that his brothers, who live with his mother, are married together and that one brother works in the field, and one is a herder, 'he herds more than 80 goats and sheep', he says, smiling. I know that polyandry is common there, I confirm, and repeat my question to his mother. Of the marriages she remembers from last year, in Sharlung and the villages around, where some of them *zasum*? He answers, 'all, she says, all were *zasum*'.

Note

1. 'Tibet Makes Strong Tourism Recovery', 24 December 2020. Retrieved February 2021 from https://www.chinadaily.com.cn/a/202012/23/WS5fe32193a31024ad0ba9de08.html.

Appendix

Timeline

1949: Establishment of the People's Republic of China (PRC)
1951: PLA opens office in Gyantse
1956: The establishment of Panam Communist Party
1959: 10th of March uprising and Dalai Lama's escape to India
1959: Introduction of Democratic Reforms in Panam
1959/1960: First round of persecution of local landowners in Panam
1960: Collectivisation of land in Panam
1965: Establishment of Tibet Autonomous Region (TAR)
1965: Establishment of communes in Panam
1966: Cultural Revolution and second round of persecution in Panam
1975: Normalisation of former landowners in Panam
1978: Decollectivisation of land in the PRC
1980: Introduction of Household Responsibility System in Panam
1981: Decollectivisation: redistribution of land and animals in Panam
1989: Martial law in Lhasa
2000: Introduction of Opening of the West
2000: Construction work options opened outside Panam
2006: Introduction of New Socialist Countryside and Comfortable Housing Project
2008: Uprisings in Lhasa and across Tibetan areas of China

Glossary of Tibetan Terms

achi	a phyi	grandmother (Tsang dialect)
achung	a chung	youngest father, younger brother
ajok	a jo	second eldest father, elder brother
akhu	a khu	paternal uncle
ama	a ma	mother
ani	a ne	nun/father's sister
ashang	a shang	maternal uncle
bangsöl	bang gsol	birth celebration ritual
bar thog	bar thog	middle floor
baru		corpse-cutter, Tsang dialect
bu	bu	son
bümé	bud med	woman
butsap	bu tshab	adoption
chak zowa	lcags bzo ba	blacksmith, 'iron maker'
chang	chang	barley beer
changdrok	chang grogs	drinking buddy, 'beer friend'
changsa gyak	chang sa rgyag pa	to marry
changsa réré	chang sa re re	monogamy, 'one-to-one marriage'
chenpo	chen po	big, great
chigo	phyi sgo	gate, 'outer door'
chikhang	spyi khang	public house
chilé	spyi las	public work
chökhang	mchod khang	shrine room
chörten	mchod rten	stupa
chösi zungdrel	chos srid zung 'brel	the union of religion and politics
chuba	phyu pa	Tibetan robe, dress
chu lha	chu lha	god of the water
dadar	mda' dar	ceremonial twigs or arrows with ribbons
dak	bdag	owner

datsen	zla mtshan	female reproductive substances, menstruation
dikpa	sdig pa	moral wrongdoing
döndré	gdon 'dre	demon, negative force
dranak	sbra nag	nomad tent, 'black tent'
drangpo	drang po	fair, just, honest
dranyen	sgra snyan	Tibetan lute
drip	grib	pollution – dirt
dribtsok	grib btsog	pollution – dirt
drokpo	grogs po	friend
drong	grong	hamlet, village
drongchen	drong chen	'big house', i.e. corporate named house
drongchung	grong chung	'small house', i.e satellite unnamed household
drongpa	grong pa	household/house
dü	bdud	evil spirit
düchung	dud chung	landless farmers (small smoke)
dütsang	dud tshang	household
dzo	mdzo	cross-breed of cow and yak
gabo chewa	dga' bo bye pa	to make somebody like oneself (attract)
gang	sgang	up/above
ganyé (abbr. gabo nyebo)	dga' po nye bo	the 'near and dear'
gara	mgar ba	blacksmith (derogatory)
gen	rgan	elder
genpo	rgan po	representative of taxpayers, 'the elder'
genshö	rgan shos	the eldest (brother)
gentsang lamluk	'gan gtsang lam lugs	Household Responsibility System
gyaling	rgya gling	woodwind, oboe-like Tibetan instrument
gyelpo	rgyal po	spirit of deceased ordained relative
gyü	rgyud	lineage
Gyüzhi	rgyud bzhis	The Four Medical Treatises
imi	i mis	grandfather (Tsang dialect)
ja mar thuk	ja mar thug	tea – offerings to the *namo*
jikten	'jig rten	the (phenomenal) world
jindak	sbyin bdag	patron
ka	ka	pillar (of a house)
kak	bkag	to hinder, block
karto	dkar tho	'white books', recording the assistance received in weddings and birth cleansings

kartsi	dkar rtsi	white drawings on the wall
khambu	kham bu	apricot, offering to namo
khang	khang pa	house
khangchen	khang chen	'big house', i.e. corporate named house
khangchung	khang chung	'small house', i.e. satellite unnamed household
khangming	khang ming	house name
khatak	kha btags	white ceremonial scarfs
khathukpa	kha thug pa	'to come together', meaning couple-initiated marriage
khong	khong	he/she
khyimchen	khyim chen	large household/house
khyimtsang	khyim tshang	household/ house
kora khor	skor ra 'khor ba	'going around in circles', distribution of sexual access
khuwa	khu ba	semen/regenerative fluids
kyé lha	skyes lha	natal deity
kyéme	skye dman/ skye sman	woman, low birth/birth medicine
kyéme phala	skye dman gyi pa lags	wife's husband, father-in-law
kyen ngen	rkyen ngan	misfortune
kyiduk ngalak	skyid sdug snga lag	'happy bad', network of mutual assistance
la	bla	life force
labrang	bla brang	corporation of a lama
langchang	lang chang	bringing the bride
lé	las	karma
lérok	las rogs	work exchange
lha	lha	god, deity
lhakhang	lha khang	'house for deities', temple
lham	lham	traditional boots
lhapa	lha pa	spirit medium
longkhen	slong mkhan	beggar
loré tsok chung	lo re chogs chung	'team period'
losar	lo gsar	the New Year
lu	klu	serpentine spirit
lukhang	klu khang	'house of *lu*', shrine of *lumo*
lumo	klu mo	(female) serpentine spirit
lunglo	rlung log pa	change of sex during birth
lungta	rlung rta	'wind horse' inscribed on flags

makpa	mag pa	in-marrying husband
ma pün	ma spun	matrilateral kin
me	smad / dman pa	lower
mendrong	sman grong	medical house
menrik	smad rigs	people of low rank, 'low kind'
mépa jé	med pa byas	to disintegrate, annihilate
milak	mi lag	hired labour
mi tsokpa	mi btsog pa	people of low rank, 'unclean people'
mo	mo	divination
mopa	mo pa	diviner
mu	mu	surface measure: 0.0667 hectares
nakto	nag tho	'black book' for recording assistance received during mortuary rituals
nama	mna' ma	in-married wife
nama tang	mna' ma bthang	send a *nama* (marry off a daughter)
namo		household protector, Tsang dialect
nang	nang	inside, inner
nang-go	nang sgo	(inner) door
nangma	nang ma	female household head, nightclub
nangmi	nang mi	'insiders', family
né	nas	barley, grain
néri	gnas ri	sacred mountain ('mountain of pilgrimage')
ngakpa	sngags pa	lineage of lay tantric practitioner
ngotsa	ngo tsha	shyness, embarassment
nö chü	snod bcud	'natural world' (container-content)
nöpa	gnod pa	harm
nöpa kak (ya)	gnod pa bkag	harm stopper, talisman
nöpa yong	gnod pa yong	the arrival of harm
nor	nor	cattle, wealth, property
norkhang	nor khang	the house of the wealth
norlha	nor lha	'god of the wealth', household protector
nyebo	nye bo	near
nyelu	nyal bu	illegitimate child
ok	'og	underneath, below
ok khang	'og khang	basement
Panam	pa nams	Panam
pa pün	pha spun	patrilateral kin
pachik machik	pha gcig ma gcig	'one father one mother', siblings of same father and mother

pecha	dpe cha	religious text
pala	pa lags	father
pho lha	pho lha	protector of the patrilineage
pho yul lha	pho yul lha	the *yul lha* of Sharlung
pumba	pum ba	container used for offerings
pün	spun	relatives
pun nyebo	spun nye ba	near relatives
ralug	ra lug	goats and sheep
rik	rigs	kind, category, hereditary social status
rik ngen	rigs ngan	people of low rank, 'bad kind'
rik tsokpa	rigs btsog pa	unclean 'kind'
rokpa	rog pa	helpers/friend
rü	rus	bones
rü chikpa	rus gcig pa	'same bones', agnates
rü gyü	rus rgyud	patrilineage
rüpa	rus pa	'people of the same bones', agnates
rüpa lé	rus pa klad	bones and brain
sa	sa	earth/soil
sa chok	sa chog	site ritual
sa chü	sa bcud	fertility
sadak	sa bdag	lord of the earth
samadrok	sa ma 'brog	semi-pastoralist
sang	bsangs	incense offering
sa sum	sa gsum	three realms
sayön	sa yon	household leader
semgyü	sems rgyud	personality, stream of mind
ser sungpa	ser srung pa	hail protector
sha	sha	flesh
shar	shar	east
sha gyü	sha rgyud	'lineage of flesh', matrilateral kin
shak	shag	residence
sha khok	sha khog	slaughtered sheep brought in wedding preparations, carcass
shenba	bshan ba	butcher
sinmo	srin mo	demonness
sonam	bsod nams	merit
söndréma	gson 'dre ma	aggressive and jealous woman
Takrab	rtag rabs	group of eternity (house name)
tamdzing	'thab 'dzing	struggle sessions during the Cultural Revolution
tap	thab	stove, hearth

tapchang	thab chang	celebration marking the move of the stove to a new house
tap chik	thab gcig	one hearth
taplha	thab lha	god of the stove
tap nyi	thab gnyis	two hearths
taptsang	thab tshang	kitchen
temdrel	rten 'brel	interdependence
tenjur	bstan 'gyur	commentaries of Buddhist teachings
thang	btang ba	to send
thempa	them pa	household
tö	stod	upper
tok	thog	upper floor, roof
tokchang	thog chang	celebration marking the completion of the roof of a new house
trak	khrag	blood
trashi tendrel	bkra shis rten 'grel	to bring luck
trelpa	khral pa	taxpayer
trulku	sprul sku	reincarnate lama
tsa	rtsa	veins
tsala	tsa la	traditional stove
tsampa	rtsam pa	roasted barley flour
tsé	tshe	lifespan
tsen	bcan	spirit (of deceased non-ordained relative)
tsokpa	btsog pa	dirt, uncleanliness
uri pangden	uri spang gdan	gift to the bride's mother upon marriage
wu shing	dbu shing	twigs used for ritual purposes
xiang (Ch.)	shang	township
yang	g.yang	prosperity
yang kak	g.yang bkag	to stop prosperity
yangkhang	g.yang khang	room for prosperity, treasure
yangkhuk	g.yang khug	pouch for auspicious objects (prosperity)
yang len	g.yang len	to receive prosperity
yokpo	g.yog po	serf, landless farmer
yul chik	yul gcig	of same place
yul lha	yul lha	god of the place
zasum	bza' gsum	polyandry
zhung gyukpa	gzhung rgyugs pa	government serfs
zur khang	zur khang	'corner house', meaning adjunct house

References

Alexander, André. 2019. *The Lhasa House: Typology of an Endangered Species*. Chicago: Serindia Publications.
Allen, Nicholas. 1976. 'Sherpa Kinship Terminology in a Diachronic Perspective', *Man* 11: 569–87.
Aziz, Barbara. 1978a. *Tibetan Frontier Families*. New Delhi: Vikas.
———. 1978b. 'Social Cohesion and Reciprocation in a Tibetan Community in Nepal', in James Preston and Bhabagrahi Misra (eds), *Community, Self, Identity*. The Hague: Mouton, pp. 45–76.
Ball, Christopher. 2018. 'Language of Kin Relations and Relationlessness', *Annual Review of Anthropology* 47(1): 47–60.
Barnes, John Arundel. 1962. 'African Models in the New Guinea Highlands', *Man* 62(1): 5–9.
Bell, Charles. 1928. *The People of Tibet*. Oxford: Clarendon Press.
Berreman, Gerald D. 1962. 'Pahari Polyandry: A Comparison', *American Anthropologist* 64(1): 60–75.
———. 1975. 'Himalayan Polyandry and the Domestic Cycle', *American Ethnologist* 2: 127–38.
———. 1980. 'Polyandry: Exotic Custom vs. Analytical Concept', *Journal of Comparative Family Studies* XI(3): 377–83.
Ben Jiao. 2001. 'Socio-Economic and Cultural Factors Underlying the Contemporary Revival of Fraternal Polyandry', Ph.D. dissertation. Cleveland: Case Western Reserve University.
Benedict, Paul K. 1942. 'Tibetan and Chinese Kinship Terms', *Harvard Journal of Asiatic Studies* 6(314): 313–37.
Bingaman, Eveline, Heidi E. Fjeld, Nancy Levine and Jonathan Samuels. 2021. 'Kinship and the State in Tibet and its Borderlands', *Inner Asia*, 23 (Special Section): 2–20.
Bischoff, Jeannine. 2013. 'Right There But Still Unnoticed: Information on dga' ldan pho brang mi ser From Archival Material Published in German(y)', Charles Ramble, Peter Schwieger and Alice Travers (eds), *Tibetans Who Escaped the Historian's Net*. Kathmandu: Vajra books, pp. 9–26.
Bloch, Maurice, and Jonathan Parry. 1989. 'Introduction: Money and the Morality of Exchange', in Maurice Block and Jonathan Parry (eds), *Money and the Morality of Exchange*. Cambridge: Cambridge University Press, pp. 1–32.
Bourdieu, Pierre. 1990 [1980]. 'The Social Uses of Kinship', *The Logic of Practice*. Cambridge: Polity, pp. 162–199.
———. 1997. *Outline of a Theory of Practice*. Cambridge: Cambridge University Press.
Carrasco, Pedro. 1959. *Land and Polity in Tibet*. Seattle: University of Washington Press.
Carsten, Janet (ed.). 2000. *Cultures of Relatedness: New Approaches to the Study of Kinship*. Cambridge: Cambridge University Press.

———. 2004. *After Kinship*. Cambridge: Cambridge University Press.
———. 2018. 'House-lives as Ethnography/Biography', *Social Anthropology* 26(1): 103–16.
Carsten, Janet, and Stephen Hugh-Jones (eds). 1995. *About the House: Lévi-Strauss and Beyond*. Cambridge: Cambridge University Press.
Cassidy, Margaret L., and Gary R. Lee. 1989. 'The Study of Polyandry: A Critique and Synthesis', *Journal of Comparative Family Studies* XX: 1–11.
Chayet, Anne. 1988. 'Le Monastére de bSam-yas: Sources Architecturales', *Arts Asiatique* 43 (Tome XLIII): 19–29. Paris: L'Ecole Francaise d'Extrême-Orient.
Childs, Geoff. 2004. *Tibetan Diary: From Birth to Death and Beyond in a Himalayan Valley in Nepal*. Berkeley: California University Press.
———. 2008. *Tibetan Transitions: Historical and Contemporary Perspectives on Fertility, Family Planning, and Demographic Change*. Leiden: Brill.
Childs, Geoff, Melvyn C. Goldstein and Puchung Wangdui. 2011. 'Externally-Resident Daughters, Social Capital, and Support for the Elderly in Rural Tibet', *Journal of Cross-Cultural Gerontology* 26(1): 1–22.
———. 2012. 'What to Do with Unmarried Daughters?' *Gerontology* 26(1): 1–22.
———. 2013. 'Balancing People, Policies, and Resources in Rural Tibet', in Eduardo S. Brondízio and Emilio F. Moran (eds), *Human-Environment Interactions*. Dordrecht: Springer, pp. 53–77.
Connell, Raewyn W., and James W. Messerschmidt. 2005. 'Hegemonic Masculinity: Rethinking the Concept', *Gender and Society* 19(6): 829–59.
Corlin, Claes. 1978. 'A Tibetan Enclave in Yunnan: Land, Kinship, and Inheritance in Gyethang', in Martin Brauen and Per Kværne (eds), *Tibetan Studies, Presented at the Seminar of Young Tibetologists*. Völkerkundemuseum der Universität Zürich, pp. 75–90.
———. 1980. 'The Symbolism of the House in rGyal-thang', in Michael Aris and Aung San Suu Kyi (eds), *Tibetan Studies in Honour of Hugh Richardson*. Warminster: Aris & Phillips, pp. 87–92.
Craig, Sienna R. 2012. *Healing Elements: Efficacy and the Social Ecologies of Tibetan Medicine*. Berkeley: University of California Press.
———. 2020. *The Ends of Kinship: Connecting Himalayan Lives Between Nepal and New York*. Seattle: University of Washington Press.
Dachille-Hay, Rae Erin. 2011. 'The Case of the Disappearing Blue Woman: Understanding How Meaning is Made in Desi Sangye Gyatso's Blue Beryl Paintings', *Asian Medicine: Tradition and Modernity* 6(2): 293–320.
Da Col, Giovanni 2012a. 'The Poisoner and the Parasite: Cosmoeconomics, Fear, and Hospitality among Dechen Tibetans', *Journal of the Royal Anthropological Institute* 18(1): 175–95.
———. 2012b. 'The Elementary Economies of Dechenwa Life: Fortune, Vitality, and the Mountain in Sino-Tibetan Borderlands', *Social Analysis* 56(1): 74–98.
Das, Chandra. 1902. *Tibetan–English Dictionary*. Delhi: Book Faith.
Davidson, Ronald M. 2005. *Tibetan Renaissance: Tantric Buddhism in the Rebirth of Tibetan Culture*. New York: Columbia University Press.
Davis, Deborah, and Stevan Harrell. 1993. *Chinese Families in the Post-Mao Era*. Berkeley: University of California Press.
Day, Sophie. 2015. 'The More Things Change, the More They Stay the Same': Idioms of House Society in the Leh Area (Ladakh)', *Tibet Journal* 40: 177–98.
Desjarlais, Robert R. 1992. *Body and Emotion: The Aesthetics of Illness and Healing in the Nepal Himalayas*. Philadelphia: University of Pennsylvania Press.

Diemberger, Hildegard. 1993. 'Blood, Sperm, Soul and the Mountain: Gender Relations, Kinship and Cosmovision among the Khumbo (N.E. Nepal)', in Teresa del Valle (ed.), *Gendered Anthropology*. London: Routledge, pp. 100–39.

———. 2007. *When a Woman Becomes a Religious Dynasty: The Samding Dorje Phagmo of Tibet*. New York: Colombia University Press.

Diemberger, Hildegard, and Christian Schicklgruber. 1988. 'Preliminary Report on the Use of Architecture among the Khumbo, East Nepal', in Helga Uebach and Jampa L. Panglung (eds), *Tibetan Studies: Proceedings of the Fourth Seminar of the International Association for Tibetan Studies*. Munich: Bayrische Akademie der Wissenschaften, Kommission für Zentralasiatische Studien, pp. 99–110.

Dollfus, Pascale. 1996. 'No Sacred Mountains in Ladakh?', in Anne-Marie Blondeau and Ernst Steinkellner (eds), *Reflections on the Mountain: Essays on the History and Social Meaning of the Mountain Cult in Tibet and the Himalayas*. Wien: Verlag der Österreichischen Akademie der Wissenschaften, pp. 3–17.

Dotson, Brandon. 2012. 'At the Behest of the Mountain: Gods, Clans and Political Topography in Post-Imperial Tibet', in Christina Scherrer-Schaub (ed.), *Old Tibetan Studies: Proceedings of the Tenth Seminar of the International Association for Tibetan Studies*. Leiden: Brill, pp. 159–204.

Dumont, Louis. 1970. *Homo Hierarchicus: The Caste System and its Implications*. Chicago and London: Chicago University Press.

———. 1979. 'The Anthropological Community and Ideology', *Social Science Information* 18(6): 785–817.

Ekvall, Robert. 1968. *Fields on the Hoof*. New York: Holt, Rinehart & Winston.

Ember, Melvin, Carol R. Ember and Bobbi S. Low. 2007. 'Comparing Explanations of Polygyny', *Cross-Cultural Research* 41(4): 428–40.

Engel, John W. 1984. 'Marriage in the People's Republic of China: Analysis of a New Law', *Journal of Marriage and Family* 46(4): 955–61.

Fisher, H. Th. 1952. 'Polyandry', *International Archives of Ethnology* 46: 114.

Fisher, Andrew F. 2014. *The Disempowered Development of Tibet in China: A Study in the Economics of Marginalization*. Lanham, MD: Lexington Books.

———. 2015. 'Subsidizing Tibet: An Interprovincial Comparison of Western China up to the End of the Hu-Wen Administration', *China Quarterly* 221: 73–99.

Fjeld, Heidi. 2005. *Commoners and Nobles: Hereditary Divisions in Tibet*. Copenhagen: NIAS Press.

———. 2008a. 'When Brothers Separate: Conflict and Mediation within Polyandrous Houses in Central Tibet', in Fernanda Pirie and Toni Huber (eds), *Conflict and Social Order in Tibet and Inner Asia*. Leiden: Brill, pp. 241–61.

———. 2008b. 'Pollution and Social Networks in Contemporary Tibet', in Robert Barnett and Ronald Schwartz (eds), *Modernity in Tibet: Proceedings from the Tenth Seminar of the International Association of Tibetan Studies*. Leiden: Brill, pp. 113–37.

———. 2021. 'Relations as Potential. Pragmatism and Flexibility in Tibetan Kinship', *Inner Asia* 23(1): 103–30.

Fjeld, Heidi, and Theresia Hofer. 2011. 'Women and Gender in Tibetan Medicine', *Asian Medicine* 2: 175–216.

Fjeld, Heidi, and Benedikte V. Lindskog. 2017. 'Connectedness Through Separation: Human–Nonhuman Relations in Tibet and Mongolia', in Jon Henrik Ziegler Remme and Kenneth Silander (eds), *Human Nature and Social Life: Perspectives on Extended Sociality*. Cambridge: Cambridge University Press, pp. 68–82.

Fortes, Meyer. 1959. 'Descent, Filiation and Affinity: A Rejoinder to Dr. Leach: Part Two', *Man* 59: 206–12.

Franklin, Sarah, and Susan McKinnon (eds). 2001. *Relative Values: Reconfiguring Kinship Studies*. Durham: Duke University Press.
Frazer, James G. 1922. *The Belief in Immortality and the Worship of the Dead*. London: Macmillan.
Fürer-Haimendorf, Christoph. 1964. 'Notes on Tamang', *Eastern Anthropologist* 9(3–4): 166–77.
Gardner, Alexander. 2006. 'The sa Chog: Violence and Veneration in a Tibetan Soil Ritual', *OpenEdition Journals* 36–37: 283–323.
Goldstein, Melvyn C. 1971a. 'Stratification, Polyandry, and Family Structure in Central Tibet', *Southwestern Journal of Anthropology* 27: 64–74.
———. 1971b. 'The Balance Between Centralization and Decentralization in the Traditional Tibetan Political System', *Central Asiatic Journal* 15(3): 170–82.
———. 1976. 'Fraternal Polyandry and Fertility in a High Himalayan Valley in Northwest Nepal', *Human Ecology* 4: 223–33.
———. 1978a. 'Adjudication and Partition in the Tibetan Stem Family', in David C. Buxbaum (ed.), *Chinese Family Law and Social Change in Historical and Comparative Perspective*. Seattle: University of Washington Press, pp. 205–14.
———. 1978b. 'Pahari and Tibetan Polyandry Revisited', *Ethnology* 17(3): 325–37.
———. 1987c. 'When Brothers Share a Wife', *Natural History* 96(3): 74–78.
———. 1989. *A History of Modern Tibet. Volume I: 1913–1951. The Demise of the Lamaist State*. Berkeley: University of California Press.
———. 1990. 'Review of "The Dynamics of Polyandry: Kinship, Domesticity, and Population on the Tibetan Border", by Nancy Levine', *Anthropos* 85: 618–20.
———. 2001. *The New Tibetan-English Dictionary of Modern Tibetan*. Berkeley: University of California Press.
Goldstein, Melvin C., Ben Jiao, Cynthia M. Beall and Phuntsog Tsering. 2003. 'Development and Change in Rural Tibet: Problems and Adaptations', *Asian Survey* XLIII(5): 758–79.
Goldstein, Melvyn, Geoff Childs and Puchung Wangdui. 2008. '"Going for Income" in Village Tibet: A Longitudinal Analysis of Change and Adaptation, 1997–2007', *Asian Survey* 48(3): 514–34.
———. 2010. 'Beijing's "People First" Development Initiative for the Tibet Autonomous Region's Rural Sector – A Case Study from the Shigatse Area', *The China Journal* 63: 57–75.
Gombo, Ugen. 1983. 'Cultural Expressions of Social Stratification in Traditional Tibet: "Caste" and "Casteism" in a Non-Hindu Context', *Anthropology* 7: 43–77.
Goody, Esther. 1982. *Parenthood and Social Reproduction*. New York: Cambridge University Press.
Gough, Kathleen. 1959. 'The Nayar and the Definition of Marriage', *Journal of Royal Anthropological Institute* 89: 23–24.
Gray, John N. 1995. *The Householder's World: Purity, Power and Dominance in a Nepali Village*. Delhi: Oxford University Press.
Grent, Nellie. 2002. 'Polyandry in Dharamsala: Plural-Husband Marriage in a Tibetan Refugee Community in Northwest India', in Christian P. Klieger (ed.), *Tibet, Self, and the Tibetan Diaspora: Voices of Difference, Proceedings of the Nineth Seminar of the International Association of Tibetan Studies*. Leiden: Brill, pp. 105–38.
Gutmann, Matthew C. 1997. 'Trafficking in Men: The Anthropology of Masculinity', *Annual Review of Anthropology* 26(1): 385–409.
Gutschow, Kim. 2004. *Being a Buddhist Nun: The Struggle for Enlightenment in the Himalaya*. Harvard University Press. Cambridge, MA and London.

Gyatso, Janet. 1989. 'Down with the Demoness: Reflections on a Feminine Ground in Tibet', in Janice D. Willis (ed.), *Feminine Ground: Essays on Women and Tibet*. Ithaca, NY: Snow Lion Publications, pp. 33–51.
———. 1998. *Apparitions of the Self: The Secret Autobiographies of a Tibetan Visionary*. New Jersey: Princeton University Press.
———. 2003. 'One Plus One Makes Three: Buddhist Gender, Monasticism and the Law of the Non-Excluded Middle', *History of Religions* 43: 89–115.
Gyatso, Janet, and Hanna Havnevik. 2005. *Women in Tibet: Past and Present*. New York: Colombia University Press.
Haddix, Kimber A. 2001. 'Leaving Your Wife and Your Brothers: When Polyandrous Marriages Fall Apart', *Evolution and Human Behaviour* 22: 47–60.
Harrison, John, and Charles Ramble. 1998. 'Houses and Households in Southern Mustang', *Ancient Nepal* 140: 25–37.
Harvey, Peter. 2000. *An Introduction to Buddhist Ethics: Foundations, Values and Issues*. Cambridge: Cambridge University Press.
Havnevik, Hanna. 1989. *Tibetan Buddhist Nuns: History, Cultural Norms and Social Reality*. Oslo: The Institute of Comparative Research in Human Culture.
———. 1999. 'The Life of Jetsun Lochen Rinpoche (1865–1951) as Told in Her Autobiography', Ph.D. dissertation. Oslo: University of Oslo.
Hertz, Robert. 1973 [1909]. 'The Pre-Eminence of the Right Hand: A Study in Religious Polarity', in Rodney Needham (ed.), *Right & Left: Essays on Dual Symbolic Classification*. Chicago: Chicago University Press, pp. 3–31.
High, Casey, Ann H. Kelly and Jonathan Mair (eds). 2012. *The Anthropology of Ignorance: An Ethnographic Approach*. New York: Palgrave Macmillan.
Hildebrandt, Kristine A., Oliver Bond and Dubi N. Dhakal. 2018. 'Kinship in Three Tamangic Varieties', *Linguistics of the Tibeto-Burman Area* 41: 1–21.
Hillman, Ben, and Lee-Anne Henfry. 2006. 'Macho Minority: Masculinity and Ethnicity on the Edge of Tibet', *Modern China* 32(2): 251–72.
Hofer, Theresia. 2015. 'Gender and Medicine in Kham: An Analysis of the Medical Work and Life of Derge Phurpa Dolma', *Revue d'Etudes Tibétaines* 34: 53–77.
———. 2018. *Medicine and Memory in Tibet: Amchi Physicians in an Age of Reform*. Seattle: University of Washington Press.
Hovden, Astrid. 2016. 'Between Village and Monastery: A Historical Ethnography of a Tibetan Buddhist Community in North-Western Nepal', Ph.D. dissertation. Oslo: University of Oslo.
Howell, Signe. 1984. *Society and Cosmos: Chewong of Peninsular Malaysia*. Oxford: Oxford University Press.
———. 1989. 'Of Persons and Things: Exchange and Valuables among the Lio of Eastern Indonesia', *Man* 24(3): 419–38.
———. 1996. 'Many Contexts, Many Meanings? Gendered Values among the Northern Lio of Flores, Indonesia', *Journal of the Royal Anthropological Institute* 2(2): 253–69.
———. 2003a. 'The House as Analytic Concept: A Theoretical Overview', in Stephen Sparkes and Signe Howell (eds), *The House in Southeast Asia*. London: Routledge Curzon, pp. 16–34.
———. 2003b. 'Kinning: The Creation of Life Trajectories in Transnational Adoptive Families', *Journal of the Royal Anthropological Institute* 9(3): 465–84.
———. 2006. *The Kinning of Foreigners: Transnational Adoption in a Global Perspective*. New York and Oxford: Berghahn Books.
Hsu, Elisabeth. 1998. 'Moso and Naxi: The House', in Michael Oppitz and Elisabeth Hsu

(eds), *Naxi and Moso Ethnography: Kin, Rites, Pictographs*. Zurich: Völkerkundemuseum Zürich, pp. 67–99.
Huber, Toni (ed.). 1999. *Sacred Spaces and Powerful Places in Tibetan Culture*. Dharamsala: Tibetan Library of Works and Archives.
Humphrey, Caroline. 1988. 'No Place Like Home in Anthropology: The Neglect of Architecture', *Anthropology Today* 4(1): 16–18.
———. 1995. 'Chiefly and Shamanist Landscapes in Mongolia', in Eric Hirsch and Michael O'Hanlon (eds), *The Anthropology of Landscape: Perspectives on Place and Space*. Oxford: Clarendon Press, pp. 135–62.
Jacoby, Sarah. 2014. *Love and Liberation: Autobiographical Writings of the Tibetan Buddhist Visionary Sera Khandro*. New York: Columbia University Press.
Jansen, Berthe. 2018. *The Monastery Rules: Buddhist Monastic Organization in Pre-Modern Tibet*. Oakland: University of California Press.
Jest, Corneille. 1991. 'Settlements in Dolpo', in Gérard Toffin (ed.), *Man and His House in the Himalaya: Ecology of Nepal*. Kathmandu: Vajra Books, pp. 192–207.
Joyce, Rosemary A., and Susan D. Gillespie (eds). 2000. *Beyond Kinship: Social and Material Reproduction in the House Societies*. Philadelphia: University of Pennsylvania Press.
Kawaguchi, Ekai. 1995 [1909]. *Three Years in Tibet*. Delhi: Book Faith India.
Khosla, Romi. 1975. 'Architecture and Symbolism in Tibetan Monasteries', in Paul Oliver (ed.), *Shelter, Sign and Symbols*. London: Barrie & Jenkins, pp. 71–83.
Knödel, Susanne. 1998. 'Yongning Moso: Kinship and Chinese State Power', in Michael Oppitz and Elisabeth Hsu (eds), *Naxi and Moso Ethnography: Kin, Rites, Pictographs*. Zurich: Völkerkundemuseum Zürich, pp. 47–65.
Koselleck, Reinhart. 2004. *Futures Past: On the Semantics of Historical Time*. New York: Columbia University Press.
Lambek, Michael. 2013. 'Kinship, Modernity and the Immodern', in Susan McKinnon and Fenella Cannell (eds), *Vital Relations: Modernity and the Persistent Life of Kinship*. Santa Fe, NM: School for Advanced Research Press, pp. 252–71.
Langelaar, Reinier J. 2017. 'Descent and Houses in Reb-gong: Group Formation and Rules of Recruitment among Eastern Tibetan *tsho-ba*', in Jarmila Ptáčková and Adrian Zenz (eds), *Archiv Orientalni, Mapping Amdo: Dynamics of Change, special vol. 10*, pp. 155–83.
———. 2019. 'Historical Social Organisation on the Eastern Tibetan Plateau: The Territorial Origins and Etymology of *tsho-ba*', *Inner Asia* 21: 7–37.
Larsen, Knud, and Amund Sinding-Larsen. 2001. *The Lhasa Atlas: Traditional Tibetan Architecture and Townscape*. London: Serindia.
Leach, Edmund R. 1955. 'Polyandry, Inheritance and the Definition of Marriage', *Man* 55: 182–86.
Lévi-Strauss, Claude. 1983. 'Social Organization of Kwakiutl', in *The Way of the Masks*. London: Jonathan Cape, pp. 163–89.
———. 1983. *The Way of the Masks*. London: Jonathan Cape.
———. 1991. 'Maison', in Michel Izard and Pierre Bonte (eds), *Dictionnaire de l'Ethnologie et de l'Anthropologie*. Paris: Presses de Universitaires de France.
Levine, Nancy. 1981. 'The Theory of *rü* Kinship, Descent and Status in a Tibetan Society', in Christoph Fürer-Haimendorf (ed.), *Asian Highland Societies: Anthropological Perspective*. New Delhi: Sterling Publishers Private Limited, pp. 52–78.
———. 1987a. 'Differential Child Care in Three Tibetan Communities: Beyond Son Preference', *Population and Development Review* 13(2): 281–304.
———. 1987b. 'Father and Sons: Kinship Values and Validation in Tibetan Polyandry', *Man* 22(2): 267–86.

———. 1988. *The Dynamics of Polyandry: Kinship, Domesticity, and Population on the Tibetan Border*. Chicago: Chicago University Press.

———. 2021. 'Practical Kinship: The Centrality of Siblings in Pastoralist Life', *Inner Asia* 23(1): 79–102.

Levine, Nancy, and Walter H. Sangree. 1980. 'Conclusion: Asian and African Systems of Polyandry', *Journal of Comparative Family Studies* XI: 385–410.

Levine, Nancy, and Joan Silk. 1997. 'Why Polyandry Fails: Sources of Instability in Polyandrous Marriages', *Current Anthropology* 38(3): 375–88.

Lichter, David, and Lawrence Epstein. 1983. 'Irony in Tibetan Notions of the Good Life', in Charles F. Keyes and Valentine Daniel (eds), *Karma: An Anthropological Inquiry*. Berkeley: University of California Press, pp. 223–60.

Lindskog, Benedikte V. 2000. 'We Are All Insects on the Back of Our Motherland: Space, Place and Movement among Halh Nomads of Mongolia', MA thesis. University of Oslo.

Lopez, Donald. 1998. *Prisoners of Shangri-la: Tibetan Buddhism and the West*. Chicago: Chicago University Press.

Louie, Kam. 1992. 'Masculinities and Minorities: Alienation in "Strange Tales from Strange Lands"', *China Quarterly* 132: 1119–35.

Macartney, Jane. 1994. 'China Lashes Out at Resurgence of Tibetan Polyandry', *World Tibet News*, December 28. Retrieved November 2021 from http://old.radicali.it/search_view.php?id=109699&lang=&cms=

MacInnes, John. 1998. *The End of Masculinity: The Confusion of Sexual Genesis and Sexual Difference in Modern Society*. Buckingham: Open University Press.

Makley, Charlene E. 1997. 'The Meaning of Liberation: Representations of Tibetan Women', *The Tibet Journal* 22(2): 4–29.

———. 2003. 'Gendered Boundaries in Motion: Space and Identity on the Sino-Tibetan Frontier', *American Ethnologist* 30(4): 597–619.

———. 2007. *The Violence of Liberation: Gender and Tibetan Buddhist Revival in Post-Mao China*. Berkeley: University of California Press.

———. 2010. 'Minzu, Market, and the Mandala', in Tom Oakes and Donald S. Sutton (eds), *Faiths on Display: Religion, Tourism, and the Chinese State*. Lanham: Rowman & Littlefield Publishers, pp. 127–56.

Mandelbaum, David G. 1938. 'Polyandry in Kota Society', *American Anthropologist* 40(4): 574–83.

Manderscheid, Angela. 2001. 'The Black Tent in its Easternmost Distribution: The Case of the Tibetan Plateau', *Mountain Research and Development* 21(2): 154–60.

Maréchaux, Pascal. 1991. 'Two Houses in the Tibetan Cultural Tradition in Pisang (Nyi-Shang) and Stongde (Zanskar)', in Gérard Toffin (ed.), *Man and His House in the Himalayas*. Kathmandu: Vajra Books, pp. 209–24.

Martin, Dan. 2005. 'The Woman Illusion? Research into the Lives of Spiritually Accomplished Women Leaders in the 11th and 12th Century', in Janet Gyatso and Hanna Havnevik (eds), *Women in Tibet, Past and Present*. New York: Colombia University Press, pp. 49–82.

Mauss, Marcel. 1990 [1950]. *The Gift: The Form and Reason for Exchange in Archaic Societies*. London: Routledge.

McGranahan, Carole. 2010. 'Narrative Dispossession: Tibet and the Gendered Logics of Historical Possibility', *Comparative Studies in Society and History* 52(4): 768–97.

Meillassoux, Clause. 1984. *Maidens, Meal and Money*. Cambridge: Cambridge University Press.

Miller, Beatrice D. 1956. 'Ganye and Kidu: Two Formalized Systems of Mutual Aid among the Tibetans', *Southwestern Journal of Anthropology* 12: 157–70.

Mills, Martin A. 2000. 'Vajra Brother, Vajra Sister: Renunciation, Individualism and the Household in Tibetan Buddhist Monasticism', *The Journal of the Royal Anthropological Institute* 6(1): 17–34.
———. 2003. *Identity, Ritual and State in Tibetan Buddhism: The Foundations of Authority in Gelukpa Monasticism*. London and New York: Routledge Curzon.
Needham, Rodney. 1971. *Rethinking Kinship and Marriage*. London: Tavistock Publications.
Netting, Robert McC., Richard R. Wilk and Eric J. Arnould (eds). 1984. *Households: Comparative and Historical Studies of the Domestic Group*. Berkeley: University of California Press.
Ortner, Sherry B. 1978. *Sherpas Through their Rituals*. Cambridge: Cambridge University Press.
Otterbein, Keith F. 1963. 'Marquesan Polyandry', *American Anthropologist* 39: 366–68.
Oxford Advanced Learner's Dictionary. 1995. Oxford: Oxford University Press.
Paine, Robert. 1971. 'A Theory of Patronage and Brokerage', in Robert Paine (ed.), *Patrons and Brokers in the East Arctic*. St. John's: Institute of Social and Economic Research, Memorial University of Newfoundland, pp. 8–21.
Palmer, Michael. 1995. 'The Re-Emergence of Family Law in Post-Mao China: Marriage, Divorce and Reproduction', *China Quarterly* 141: 110–34.
Parkin, David, and Linda Stone (eds). 2004. *Kinship and Family: An Anthropological Reader*. Malden, MA: Wiley-Blackwell.
Passin, Herbert. 1955. 'Untouchability in the Far East', *Monumenta Nipponica* 11: 247–67.
Paul, Allen P. 1976. 'The Sherpa Temple as a Model of the Psyche', *American Ethnologist* 3: 131–46.
Petech, Luciano. 1973. *Aristocracy and Government in Tibet. 1728–1959*. Roma: Istituto Italiano per il Medio ed Estremo Oriente.
Phylactou, Maria. 1989. 'Household Organization and Marriage in Ladakh Indian Himalaya', Ph.D. dissertation. London: University of London.
Pommaret-Imaeda, Francoise. 1980. 'The Construction of Ladakhi Houses in the Indus Valley', Michael Aris and Aung San Suu Kyi (eds), *Tibetan Studies in Honour of Sir Hugh Richardson*. Warminster: Aris & Phillips, pp. 249–255.
Prince Peter of Greece and Denmark. 1963. *A Study of Polyandry*. The Hague: Mouton & Co.
Radcliffe-Brown, Alfred R. 1941. 'The Study of Kinship Systems', *Journal of Royal Anthropological Institute of Great Britain and Ireland* 71: 1–18.
Rajan, Hamsa. 2014. 'The Impact of Household Form and Material Residence on the Economic Dimensions of Women's Vulnerability to Domestic Violence: The Case of Tibetan Communities', *Genus* 70(2–3): 139–62.
———. 2018a. 'When Wife-Beating is Not Necessarily Abuse: A Feminist and Cross-cultural Analysis of the Concept of Abuse as Expressed by Tibetan Survivors of Domestic Violence', *Violence Against Women* 24(1): 3–27.
———. 2018b. 'The Ethics of Transnational Feminist Research and Activism: An Argument for a More Comprehensive View', *Signs: Journal of Women in Culture and Society* 43(2): 269–300.
Ramble, Charles. 1996. 'Patterns of Places', in Anne-Marie Blondeau and Ernst Steinkellner (eds), *Reflections on the Mountain*. Wien: Verlag der Österreichischen Akademie der Wissenschaften, pp. 141–53.
———. 1999. 'The Politics of Sacred Space in Bon and Tibetan Popular Tradition', in Toni Huber (ed.), *Sacred Spaces and Powerful Places in Tibetan Culture*. Dharamsala: Library of Tibetan Works and Archives, pp. 3–33.
———. 2008. *The Navel of the Demoness: Tibetan Buddhism and Civil Religion in Highland Nepal*. New York: Oxford University Press.

———. 2019. 'The Tibetan Novel as Social History: Reflections on Trashi Palden's *Phal pa'i khyim tshang gi skyid sdug*', *Revue d'Etudes Tibétaines* 49: 149–91.
Robbins, Joel. 1994. 'Equality as a Value: Ideology in Dumont, Melanesia and the West', *Social Analysis* 36: 21–70.
Robin, Francoise. 2009. 'The "Socialist New Villages" in the Tibetan Autonomous Region: Reshaping the Rural Landscape and Controlling its Inhabitants', *China Perspectives* 3: 56–64.
Rozario, Santi, and Geoffrey Samuel. 2002. 'Tibetan and Indian Ideas of Birth Pollution: Similarities and Contrasts', in Santi Rozario and Geoffrey Samuel (eds), *Daughters of Hariti: Childbirth and Female Healers in South and Southeast Asia*. London and New York: Routledge, pp. 182–208.
Samuel, Geoffrey. 1993. *Civilized Shamans: Buddhism in Tibetan Societies*. Washington and London: Smithsonian Institution Press.
———. 2003. 'Spirit Causation and Illness in Tibetan Medicine', in Mona Schrempf (ed.), *Soundings in Tibetan Medicine. Anthropological and Historical Perspectives: Proceedings of the Tenth Seminar of the International Association of Tibetan Studies*. Leiden: Brill, pp. 213–24.
Samuels, Jonathan. 2016. 'Are We Legend? Reconsidering Clan in Tibet', *Revue d'Etudes Tibétaines* 37: 293–314.
———. 2021. 'Incest Classified: A Seventeenth-Century Tibetan Ruler's Perspective on Sexual Proscriptions and Boundaries of Kinship', *Inner Asia* 23(1): 21–50.
Sangree, Walter H. 1972. 'Secondary Marriage and Tribal Solidarity in Irigwe, Nigeria', *American Anthropologist* 74(5): 1234–43.
Schicklgruber, Christian. 1992. 'Grib: On the Significance of the Term in a Socio-Religious Context', in Ihara Shōren and Yamaguchi Zuihō (eds), *Proceedings of the Fifth Seminar of the International Association of Tibetan Studies*. Narita-shi: Naritasan Shinshoji, pp. 723–34.
Schneider, David M. 1980 [1968]. *American Kinship: A Cultural Account*. Chicago: University of Chicago Press.
———. 1984. *A Critique of the Study of Kinship*. Ann Arbor: University of Michigan Press.
Schneider, Nicola. 2011. 'The Third Dragkar Lama: An Important Figure for Female Monasticism in the Beginning of Twentieth Century Kham', *Revue d'Etudes Tibétaines* 21: 45–60.
———. 2013. *Le Renoncement au Féminin: Couvents et Nonnes Dans le Bouddhisme Tibétain*. Nanterre: Presses Universitaires de Paris Ouest.
Schrempf, Mona, and Nicola Schneider. 2015. 'Female Specialists Between Autonomy and Ambivalence', *Revue d'Etudes Tibétaines* 34: i–viii.
Schuler, Sidney Ruth. 1987. *The Other Side of Polyandry: Property, Stratification, and Non-Marriage in the Nepal Himalayas*. Boulder and London: Westview Press.
Seddon, David (ed.). 1978. *Relations of Production: Marxist Approaches to Economic Anthropology*. Oxford and New York: Frank Cass and Company.
Shih, Chuan-kang. 2010. *Quest for Harmony: The Moso Traditions of Sexual Union and Family Life*. Stanford: Stanford University Press.
Sillander, Kenneth, and Jon Henrik Z. Remme. 2018. 'Introduction: Extended Sociality and the Social Life of Humans', in Jon Henrik Z. Remme and Kenneth Sillander (eds), *Human Nature and Social Life: Perspectives on Extended Sociality*. Cambridge: Cambridge University Press, pp. 1–25.
Sneath, David. 2006. 'Transacting and Enacting: Corruption, Obligation and the Use of Monies in Mongolia', *Ethnos* 71(1): 89–112.
Sommer, Matthew H. 2015. *Polyandry and Wife-Selling in Qing Dynasty China: Survival Strategies and Judicial Interventions*. Oakland: University of California Press.

Sparkes, Stephen, and Signe Howell. 2003. *The House in South- East Asia: A Changing Social, Economic and Political Domain*. London: Routledge Curzon.
Stein, Rolf. 1972. *Tibetan Civilization*. Stanford: Stanford University Press.
Steward, Julian H. 1936. 'Shoshoni Polyandry', *American Anthropologist* 38: 561–64.
Strathern, Marilyn. 1992. *After Nature: English Kinship in the Late Twentieth Century*. Cambridge: Cambridge University Press.
Swank, Heidi. 2014. *Rewriting Shangri-la: Tibetan Youth, Migration and Literacies in McLeod Ganj, India*. Leiden: Brill.
Sykes, Karen. 2005. *Arguing with Anthropology: An Introduction to Critical Theories of the Gift*. London: Routledge.
Tambiah, Stanley J. 1966. 'Polyandry in Ceylon: With a Special Reference to the Laggala Region', in Christoph von Fürer-Haimendorf (ed.), *Caste and Kin in Nepal, India and Ceylon: Anthropological Studies in Hindu-Buddhist Contact Zones*. London: Asia Publishing House, pp. 264–358.
Taring, Rinchen Dolma. 1970. *Daughter of Tibet: The Autobiography of Rinchen Dolma Taring*. Delhi: Rupa & Co.
Tashi Tsering. 2005. 'Outstanding Women in Tibetan Medicine', in Janet Gyatso and Hanna Havnevik (eds), *Women in Tibet: Past and Present*. New York: Colombia University Press, pp. 169–194.
Tidwell, Tawni, Nianggajia, and Heidi E. Fjeld. Forthcoming. 'Chasing *dön* Spirits in Tibetan Medical Encounters: Transcultural Affordances and Embodied Psychiatry in Amdo, Qinghai', *Transcultural Psychiatry*.
Toffin, Gérard (ed.). 2016 [1991]. *Man and His House in the Himalayas: Ecology in Nepal*. Kathmandu: Vajra Books.
Travers, Alice. 2008. 'Exclusiveness and Openness: A Study of Matrimonial Strategies in the Ganden Phodrang Aristocracy (1880–1959)', *Journal of the International Association of Tibetan Studies* 4: 1–27.
Trémon, Anne-Christine. 2017. 'Flexible Kinship: Shaping Transnational Families among the Chinese in Tahiti', *The Journal of the Royal Anthropological Institute* 23(1): 42–60.
Tucci, Giuseppe. 1961. *The Theory and Practice of the Mandala*. London: Rider.
Van Schaik, Sam. 2011. *Tibet: A History*. London and New York: Yale University Press.
Vinding, Michael. 1998. *The Thakali: A Himalayan Ethnography*. London: Serindia Publications.
Wang Ting-yu. 2013. 'The House, the State and Change: The Modernity of Sichuan Rgyalrong Tibetans', in James Wilkerson and Robert Parkin (eds), *Modalities of Change: The Interface of Tradition and Modernity in East Asia*. New York and Oxford: Berghahn Books, pp. 21–36.
Waterson, Roxana. 1990. *The Living House: An Anthropology of Architecture in South-East Asia*. London: Thames and Hudson.
Watkins, Joanne C. 1996. *Spirited Women: Gender, Religion & Cultural Identity in the Nepal Himalaya*. New York: Columbia University Press.
Wellens, Koen. 2010. *Religious Revival in the Tibetan Borderlands: The Premi of Southwest China*. Seattle: University of Washington Press.
Whitehead, Stephen M. 2002. *Men and Masculinities*. Cambridge: Polity Press.
Yan, Yunxiang. 2003. *Private Life Under Socialism: Love, Intimacy, and Family Change in a Chinese Village, 1949–1999*. Stanford: Stanford University Press.
Yanagisako, Sylvia J. 1979. 'Family and Household: The Analysis of Domestic Groups', *Annual Review of Anthropology* 8: 161–205.

Yeh, Emily T. 2004. 'Property Relations in Tibet Since Decollectivization and the Question of Fuzziness', *Conservation and Society* 2(1): 108–31.
———. 2013. *Taming Tibet: Landscape Transformation and the Gift of Chinese Development.* Ithaca and London: Cornell University Press.
Yuthok, Dorje Y. 1990. *House of the Turquoise Roof.* Ithaca: Snow Lion.
Zenz, Adrian. 2020. 'Xinjiang's System of Militarized Vocational Training Comes to Tibet', *China Brief* 20(19): 7–17.

INDEX

About the House (Carsten and Hugh-Jones), 9–10, 117
achung (youngest husband), xiii–xiv, 2, 70, 99
adjunct house (*zur khang*), 44
adopted groom (makpa butsap), 63n9
adoptee, 56, 58–61
adoption (*butsap*) and house membership, 57–58
  exchanges between houses, 60
  kinship idioms and, 61
affection, distribution of, 65, 67–79
age gap, between youngest husband and *nama*, 76, 82–83
agnates, 49, 51–52, 103–04, 155
agrarian areas, 5, 151
agricultural areas, xi, 4, 13, 19, 36, 62
ajok (middle husband), 2, 70, 99, 102–103
androcentric tropes, 91
architecture, of house, 19, 23, 117–20
associations (*kyiduk*), 147–50
authoritative position
  of eldest brother/husband, 67–73
  of spinster in natal house, 54
authority, of *nama* in household, 90, 103–4
Aziz, Barbara, 13, 14–15, 144–46, 147, 171

bangsöl (birth celebrating ritual), 162
baru (funeral workers), xiv, 18, 143, 155–63, 165n21, 166n29
Ben Jiao, xix, 4, 12, 16, 27, 36, 53–54, 167–68
bilateral filiation, 54–55, 62n5, 169, 174
birth as woman, as misfortune, 91
birth celebrating ritual (*bangsöl*), 150, 162

blacksmiths, xii–xiii, 3, 19–20, 139, 143, 155–66, 180n11
black tent (*dranak*), 118, 121–22
Bloch, Maurice, 161–62
bones (*rü*), 49–51, 61, 70
bones as idiom for social strata, 158–159
boot-making, 108, 109, 115n18
bounded efficacious space, 133–40
Bourdieu, Pierre, 73, 117–18, 173–74
butchers, xii, xiv, 3, 138, 143, 155–66, 165n14, 165n21, 166n29
butsap (adopted child), 57

cardinal directions, 122
caring masculinity, 76, 102
Carsten, Janet, 6–7, 9, 174
caste, 115n19, 143, 155, 164n3
caste-like dynamics, 143, 163
CCP. *See* China's Communist Party
centripetal orientations, 40, 62, 118, 142–43
change, in sex of baby (*lunglok*), 110–11, 115n24
changes, in marriage practices, xiv
changsa (parent-initiated weddings), 12, 31–32, 46n5
Chen, Quanguo, xvi
Chewong people, 131–32
chigo (gate), 119, 134
chikhang (public house), xi, xii, 35
Childs, Geoff, 44, 53, 98, 107, 113n3, 165n10, 178
China, polyandry in, 172–73
China's Communist Party (CCP), 25
Chinese invasion, 1, 12, 23n1
Chinese polyandry, as ad-hoc solution, 173

Chinese rule, xiv, 3–4, 167, 176–77
chökhang (shrine room), 116, 122, 127
CHP. *See* Comfortable Housing Project
clan, concept of, 14–15, 48
classificatory and descriptive system, of Morgan, 7
clustering *kora khor*, 69
collaborative masculinity, 75–76
Comfortable Housing Project (CHP), xv–xvi, 117, 177
common division, of polyandrous households, 82
configuration of marriages, change in, 46n9
conjugal relations, with husbands, 99–100
conversion myth, 130
cooperation, between houses, 142–44
corporate household, 11, 41–42, 90, 111, 151, 168
cosmological collapse, 133
cosmological space, interior house as, 120–25, 168, 180n1
couple initiated marriages (*khathukpa*), 12, 93, 95, 98
courtyards, 19, 119–20
cross-dressing, 109–10, 115n23
Cultural Revolution, 30–31
Cultures of Relatedness (Carsten), 9
cumulative patrifiliation, 54–55, 104

Day, Sophie, 11, 43, 45
deceased lay relative (*tsen*), 121, 128
deceased ordained relative (*gyelpo*), 121, 128
decollectivisation, 27–33, 35, 168, 172
Democratic Reforms, 12, 35, 58, 145, 181n13
demographic aspect, of polyandry, 39–40, 104, 181n17
demoness (*sinmo*), 130
dependency between households, 150–53, 163
descent, alliance contrasted with, 8
descent, as kinship principle, 6–7, 49, 52, 169, 173
descent, contrasted with residence, 13–15, 55, 175
development, economic, xv
devotional architecture, 130
dikpa (moral wrongdoing), 109
Dingri, Tibet, 14

disclosure, of genitor of child, 70–71
disconnection, between polyandry and kinship theory, 6
diversification, economic, 5, 168
diversity, of marriage forms, 25, 175
dojung (mortar), 135
domestic violence, 91–92
döndré (ghosts), 111, 121
doxic, age hierarchy sensibility as, 73
dranak (black tent), 121–22
drip (pollution), 138–39, 155, 157–58
dü (spirit), 131
düchung (landless farmers), 12
Dumont, Louis, 66–67
Dynamics of Polyandry (Levine), 41

economic
  contribution, lack of, 79
  development, xv, 178
  diversification, 5, 168
  reasons for polyandry, 39, 98
economic re-engineering, 45
economic success, *menrik* and, 156
eldest brother (*genshö*), 65, 86
  as dominant value, 66
  as father (*pala*), 69
  as household leader, 72–73
electricity, in rural Tsang, 17
embarrassment, when talking about sex, 101, 114n12
English corner (language initiative), 37–38
epistemologies, of kinship, 171–72
ethnography, doing in Tibet, 19–20
evolutionary drive, to spread genes, 10
Explanatory Tantra, 50
extended socialities, 118, 131, 139
extra-marital relations, 65, 87n2

father (*pala*), 69–70, 89–90
father-child relations, 71–72
fatherhood, 70–72
father of children, ignorance about biological, 71
female body, as polluted, 92–93
female doctors, 169–70
female household head (*nangma*), 72, 104–5
female roles, in polyandrous marriages, 89–90

female serpentine spirit (*lumo*), 123–24, 134, 138, 141n15
fertility decline, in TAR, 178–79
field distribution, in Sharlung, 183
filiation, 53–54, 62
first floor, 124–25
Fisher, Andrew, xv
Fisher, H., 24n10, 66
flesh (*sha*), 49, 50, 51–52, 64, 175
flexibility, pragmatism and, 6, 173
flexibility of kinship, 6, 173–74, 179
flexibility of marriage, 16, 34
former monks and nuns, 58, 63n11
Fortes, Meyer, 54
fostering, 56, 57
fraternal polyandry (*zazum*), 3, 5, 13, 35–36, 38, 61, 64–65, 87n1, 168
fraternal solidarity, 42, 65, 84, 87
freedom, of unmarried women, 112
friendship, 157–62
functionalist turn, in social sciences, 7
funeral workers (*baru*), 155–56, 162, 166n29
future, of polyandry, 179

Ganden Podrang, 41, 171
ganyé network, 80, 81, 144–47, 164n6, 165n9
gara, blacksmiths, , xii, 155, 165n15, 180n11
gate (*chigo*), 119, 134
gender hierarchies, 111–12
gender inequality, 95–96
gender manipulation, 110, 112
genpo (government representatives), 19, 40, 180n1
genpo (taxpayer houses, Panam vernacular), 12–13, 35
genpo and polyandry, 40, 45
genshö (eldest brother), 65, 86
ghosts (*döndré*), 111, 121
The Gift (Mauss), 148
god of stove (*taplha*), 125
going for income, 100–101, 178
Goldstein, Melvyn C., xviin4, xvii, 4, 17, 35, 41–42, 164n1, 178
  on corporate households, 41–42
  Levine on, 46n10
  on monomarital principle, 5, 34, 41
  on standard of living in Panam, 151
  on stem families, 41
government representatives (*genpo*), 19, 40, 180n1
government serfs (*zhung gyukpa*), 17–18
ground floor, 123–24, 140n9
ground floor shrine (*lukhang*), 123, 124, 130
Guo, Jinlong, xiv–xv
gyaling (instrument), 96
Gyatso, Janet, 91, 93, 110, 130
gyelpo (deceased ordained relative), 121, 128

Han Chinese, in-migration of, xv
hardship, of moving to new village, 93, 98
harm stopper (*nöpa kak*), 134–35, 138
Havnevik, Hanna, 91, 92
hegemonic masculinity, 74
Henfry, Lee-Anne, 74–75
heroic masculinity, 74
Hertz, Robert, 66
heterogeneity, in social organisations, 15, 171
hierarchical gender models, 90, 169–70
hierarchy, within marriage, 64–65, 72–73, 78
hierarchy, within village, 143, 164n3
High, Casey, 71
Hillman, Ben, 74–75
historical ethnography, xiv, 167
Hofer, Theresia, xvii, 114n4, 169–70
house
  building (*khang*), 116–17, 135
  cooperation between, 142
  as heuristic device, 43, 169
  as locus for kinship studies, 9
  as microcosmos, 118, 121–135
  as moral person, 6, 170–71
  names (*khangming*), 12, 34, 43, 54n3, 61
  naming practices, 34–35
  as ritually efficacious space, 135
house for deities (*lha khang*), 128, 129
household (*khyimtsang*), 5, 11, 38, 39, 42–45
  animals in Sharlung, 85, 123
  as central unit in Tibetan studies, 11
  futures, 33

household (*khyimtsang*) (*cont.*)
  membership of unmarried sisters, 53
  other terms contrasted with, 47n12
Household Responsibility System reform, 4, 28–29, 32, 35, 45, 80
  ganyé and, 145, 150–51
  social status and, 156
house members (*nangmi*), 52
house protector (namo), 116, 126, 135–36, 141n14
Howell, Signe, 14, 57–58, 113, 131, 163
Hsu, Elisabeth, 9–10
human body, as impure, 122, 140n7
human realms, nonhuman realms and, 133

ideal age, of wife, 82–83
ideal division of labour, in polyandrous house, 84
ideal number, of co-husbands, 36–37
ignorance, cultural production of, 71
illegal status, of polyandry, 177, 180n7
incense (*sang*), xii, 116, 128, 136, 139
independence, of Tibetan women, 91
individual friendships, 157–62
inheritance, of land, 5, 32, 40, 81, 83
in-married husband (*makpa*), 33, 52–53, 56–57, 83, 93–94
  patrilineage and, 175
in-married wife (*nama*), xiii–xiv, 20, 33, 65, 67–68
  conflicts with husbands of, 76–81
  negotiation for transfer of, 87n8
in-migration, of Han Chinese, xv, 23nn4–5
inner door (*nang-go*), 123, 134
interdependence (*temdrel*), 131, 133
interdependence, between houses, 143
interior architecture, of houses, 120–30
internal power relations, in sibling group, 77
interpersonal relations, 40
inter-*rik* relations, 159–63

jikten (phenomenal world), 118, 131
jindak (patron), 152, 154

karto (list of wedding exchanges), 147
'keeping prescribed things apart', 134, 164n7
khang (house building), 116–17, 135

khangchen (large house), 11, 43–44
khangchung (small house, adjunct house), 11–12, 43–44, 58
khathukpa (couple initiated marriages), 12, 93, 95, 98
khyimtsang. *See* household
kin (*pün*), 149
kinning, 57–58
kinship flexibility, 174–76
kinship of potentiality, 6, 14–16, 171, 173, 176
kinship studies, polyandry in, 10, 168–69
kinship theory, 49–50, 173–74
kitchen, placement of, 121
kitchen-living room (*taptsang*), 27, 122, 125
kyiduk (associations), 147–50
kyiduk ngalak (mutual assistance networks), 147–50
Kyiling Township, xii–xiii, 16–17, 36, 157

labourers (*yokpo*), 12, 32
labour exchange (*lérok*), 161
Ladakhi studies, 14, 175
Lambek, Michael, 176–77
landless farmers (*düchung*), 12
large house (*khangchen*), 11, 43–44
Leach, Edmund R., 10
lenience, of local government, toward polyandry, 177, 180nn12–13
lérok (labour exchange), 161
Levine, Nancy, 41, 46n10, 50, 65, 70
  on adaptation to changing organisation, 175–76
  on bones (*rü*), 49–51, 158
  on corporate households, 107
  on differential childcare , 107
  on fraternal solidarity, 42, 65
  on gender preference, 90
Lévi-Strauss, Claude, 6, 7–8, 13, 24n14, 43
  on house as moral person, 170–71
lhapa (spirit medium), 134, 136, 141n15
Lhasa, xi, 15, 37–38, 182
lineage disruption, 169
list of funeral exchanges (*nakto*), 147
list of wedding exchanges (*karto*), 147
local explanations, of polyandry, 37–39
local procreation theory, 71, 84
longkhen (beggars), 156, 165n18
lord of the earth (*sadak*), 139

loss, of labour, 81
low ranked skill workers (*menrik*), xi, 40, 143, 155–63, 166n15, 166n28
lu disease *(luné)*, 124
lumo (female serpentine spirit), 123, 141n15
luné (*lu* disease), 124
lunglok (change in sex of baby), 111, 115n24

Makley, Charlene E., 74, 75, 84, 91
makpa (in-married husband), 33, 52–53, 56–57, 83, 93–94
    patrilineage and, 175
male household leader (*sayön*), 72, 89–90
management, of poverty, 58–59
Manderscheid, Angela, 121
maning (third sex category), 110
'manly man' (*pho khyokha*), 74–75
ma pün (matrilateral kin), 49, 148
marriage definitions, 65–66
Marriage Law, of 1950, 4, 25, 172
marriage practices, changes in, xiv
Martin, Dan, 93
masculinities, 73–74
material resources, 33
material transfers, 148–49
matrifiliation, 53–54
matrilateral kin (*sha gyü*), 15, 48–49, 50–52, 56
matrilineal, 163
matrilocal residence, 36
Mauss, Marcel, 148, 160, 162–63
McGranahan, Carole, 92–93, 109, 112
medical lineages, 169–70
membership in household, 22, 48–49
    by adoption, 57–61
    by filiation, 52–55
    by marriage, 55–57
mendrong (medical house), 170, 180n3
menrik (people of low rank), 143, 155–59
middle husband (*ajok*), 2, 70, 103
milak (wage/hired labour), 144, 149, 160–61
Miller, Beatrice, 147
Mills, Martin, 121
misogyny, 91
Mongolia, 131, 148
monkhood, 74–75
monks and nuns, former, 58

monogamy (*réré*), 25, 38
monomarital principle, 5, 34, 41, 44, 60
morality, 59, 143–44, 161–64
moral person, house as, 6, 13–14, 43
moral wrongdoing (*dikpa*), 109
mortar (*dojung*), 135
motherhood, marriage and, 21
Mugum village, 180n11
mutual assistance (*kyiduk ngalak*), 147–50
mutual networks, of care, 143–44

nakto (list of funeral exchanges), 147
Nalang Dorje Denshong, 16
nama (in-married wife), xiii–xiv, 20, 33, 65, 67–68
    conflicts with husbands of, 76–81
    negotiation for transfer of, 87n8
nangma (female household head), 72, 104–5
National Inheritance Law, 80
natural world (*nö chü*), 131
negative marriage rules, 49
network, of village, 140, 142
New Socialist Countryside, xv–xvi
nö chü (natural world), 131
nomads, 75, 91, 117, 121
non-marriage, 33–34
normative masculinity, 73–74
notable Tibetan women, 91
nunnery, in Sharlung, 30
nuns, motivation for becoming, 112
nuns, workload of, 95, 96

obligation, concept of, 149
organic symmetry, 66
organisational principles, of residence, 14–15

pachik machik (siblings, of same mother and father), 70
paid labourer *(milak)*, 161
Paine, Robert, 152–53
pala (father), 69–70, 89–90
Panam County, Tibet, xi, xvi, 3, 14–17, 168
Panam Integrated Rural Development Project, xviin3
pa pün (patrilateral kin), 49, 51, 55, 148
parent-initiated weddings (*changsa*), 12, 31–32

Parry, Jonathan, 161
passing, of *Achi*, 146
pastoral communities, xvi, 15, 122, 175–176
paternity, 69–72
patri-dominated kinship categories, 52
patrifiliation, 55
patrifocal organisation, 89–90
patri-ideology, 15
patrilineage (*rü gyü*), 48–51, 169
patrilineal descent, 14–15, 49
patronage, dependency and, 151–54, 163–64
performative aspects of kin-making, 9
perspective, of wife, 23, 89–90
phenomenal world *(jikten)*, 118, 131
pho khyokha ('manly man'), 74–75
placement, of kitchen, 121
plural mating, 24n10
politico-economic setting, 156
politico-jural obligations, 42
pollution *(drip)*, 139, 155, 157–58
polyandry. See *specific topics*
polyandry-specific conflicts, 76–77
polygamy, 26
polygyny, 10–11, 15, 25
polygyny and polyandry, lack of comparison in social sciences, 73
poor households, 148, 151–53
Potala palace, 182
poverty, 31, 46n10, 112, 154
poverty alleviation policies, xvi
poverty as explanation of polyandry, 171
pragmatic approach, to polyandry, 26
'The Pre-eminence of the Right Hand' (Hertz), 66
preference for polyandry, of women, 95–96
primary schools, xv
privacy, of sex, 69
prosperity *(yang)*, 39, 116, 125, 127, 142n12
prosperity room *(yangkhang)*, 116
protectors, of house, 135–39
proverbs, on women as lower-born, 92
public house *(chikhang)*, xi, xii, 35
pün (kin), 149

Qing Empire, 172–73

Rajan, Hamsa, 91–92
Ramble, Charles, 46n25, 63n12, 155, 165n17, 166nn24–25
rear of tent, as sacred space, 122
reciprocation *(ngalak)*, 147
refusal to marry multiple husbands, acceptability of, 95–96
relationality, 22
relationship
  between daughter-in-law and mother-in-law, 98–99
  between nama and eldest husband, 69, 99
relative age, of husbands, 64–67
remarriage, 83
réré (monogamy), 25, 38
research methods, 19–22
research routine, 20–21
residence, and descent, 13–15, 55, 175
residence, formation of close relations by, 53
residence for the elderly *(gentsang)*, 44
residence principle, of Aziz, 13
responsibilities, of *nama*, 103–4
return, of *nama* to parents, 100, 114n10
rik (social status), 157–59, 166n25
Robbins, Joel, 66
roof, 128–30
rü (bone), 49–50. 158–159
rü gyü (patrilineage), 48–51, 169
rural surplus labourers, xvi

Sachung monastery, xiii, 30–31, 34
sacred space, rear of tent as, 122
sadak (lord of the earth), 139
Samdrup (co-researcher), xiii, 20–22, 146
*sayön (*male household leader*)*, 72, 89–90
Schneider, David, 8, 174
Schneider, Nicola, 112
Schuler, Sidney Ruth, 107
security, of multiple husbands, 100
serfs *(yokpo)*, 19
serpentine spirit *(lu)*, 123–24, 132
sex, privacy of, 69
sex of baby, change in *(lunglok)*, 110–11, 115n24
sexual distribution *(kora khor)*, 2, 67–68, 101–3, 114n12
sha (flesh), 49, 50

sha gyü (matrilateral kin), 48–49, 50–52
shared values, of Tibetans, 174
sharing of food, with *menrik* households, 159–60
Sharlung, Tibet. *See specific topics*
short-term relations, 162
shrine room (*chökhang*), 116, 122, 127
siblings, of same mother and father (*pachik machik*), 70
sibling unity, 77
sinmo (demoness), 130
site rituals (*sa chok*), 133–34
size of networks, house social standing and, 150
small house (*khangchung*), 11
Sneath, David, 148–49, 161–62
social exclusions, 143, 155–57
social fatherhood, 70–72
social hierarchy, 14
socially validated paternity, 70
social obligations, 163
social status (*rik*), 157–59, 166n25
Sommer, Matthew, 172
space, three-tiered, 121
spinster, authoritative position in natal house of, 54
spirit (*dü*), 131
spirit medium (*lhapa*), 134, 136, 141n15
stone stove (*tsala*), 125
style of dress, of Tibetan women, 108–9
subsistence farming, 178
superiority, of eldest son, 65, 66–67, 72–73
symmetry, organic, 66

taboo, of talking about recently deceased person, 146
taking house name, upon marrying, 55–56
taplha (god of stove), 125
TAR. *See* Tibet Autonomous Region
Tashi-la (household lead in Takrab house), 21, 27–33, 80, 111, 122
 on new house rituals, 135–37
 on Sobnub house, 152–53
 update on in 2016, 184
tax obligations and polyandry, 41, 42
taxpayer houses (*genpo*, Panam vernacular), 12–13
taxpayers (*trelpa*), 3, 12, 19, 36, 45

Team Period, 28
temdrel (interdependence), 131
third gender, 110, 115n20
three-tiered organisation of space, 121, 130
Tibetan masculinities, 75
Tibet Autonomous Region (TAR), xii, 21, 176–77, 182
Toffin, Gérard, 118–19
training, of daughters, 169–70
transfer
 of household to new house, 135
 of leadership, 72–73, 105
 of *namo*, 136–37, 139
Travers, Alice, 170
trelpa (taxpayers), 3, 12, 19, 36, 45
tsala (stone stove), 125
Tsang, xi, 16, 46, 62, 117–18
tsen (deceased lay relative), 121, 128
twigs (*wu shing*), 128

Ugen Gombo, 156
unmarried women, number of, 53–54, 62n6, 112
unorthodox households, 173

vertical axis, 122, 127
vertical tripartite ordering (*sa sum*), 120
village-based cadre teams, 177–78
vulnerability, of women to conflict, 90, 113, 114n9

Watkins, Joanne C., 109
wealth, accumulation of, 42
white ceremonial scarf (*khatak*), 146
women
 independence of in Tibet, 91
 as inferior, 113n3
 as a low birth, 92
 notable, 91
 proverbs on, 92
 style of dress of, 108–9
 unmarried, 53–54, 62n6, 63n7, 112
 vulnerability to conflict of, 90, 113, 114n9
 workload of, 93, 94, 115n19
women's issues, discussion of, 21, 95–102
words, for 'woman' in Tibetan, 92, 114n4
workload, of women, 93, 94, 115n19
wu shing (twigs), 128

Xi, Jinping, xvi
Xibu da kaifa (Opening of the West), xiv, 5

yang (prosperity), 133, 141n12
yangkhang (prosperity room), 116
Yeh, Emily, xvi, xvii, 177
yokpo (labourers, serfs), 12, 19, 32
younger sons, options for, 81, 83–84

youngest husband (*achung*), xiii–xiv, 70

zazum (polyandry), 1, 30, 35–36, 38–39, 94, 97, 100, 104, 184
zhung gyukpa (government serfs), 17–18
Zurkarwa Lodro Gyalbo, 110
zur khang (adjunct house), 44

www.ingramcontent.com/pod-product-compliance
Lightning Source LLC
Chambersburg PA
CBHW051539020426
42333CB00016B/2012